CONTENTS

INTRODUCTION

Once a upon a time we went on vacation to treat ourselves – to indulge in food and drink, tour sights and maybe partake in a little retail therapy. But recently there has been a shift in the reasons many of us go away. More and more of us are seeking a new kind of break – one far from the stresses and chaos of modern-day life, where we can focus on our health and wellbeing. Wellness tourism has become a booming industry, with retreats opening faster than a high-intensity yoga vinyasa.

For this book we asked wellness experts and travel writers from around the globe to tell us about their favourite wellness holiday spots. We soon discovered that 'wellness' means different things to different people – while some want to slow down and concentrate on sleep and nutrition, others want to be energised by creative endeavours. Our book covers the full array of wellness escape, from yoga retreats in India and hot spring resorts in Australia to Buddhist meditation temples in Korea and writers' retreats in Paris.

Don't know where to start? Our five chapters will help you navigate the vast choice of retreat out there. Each corresponds to how you may want to feel: Active, Calm, Healthy, Indulged or Inspired. Within each chapter, the profiles are labelled with the main wellness features you can enjoy while at the retreat – be they outdoor adventure, spa treatments, nutrition or others. The practicalities panel gives you an indication of the price and type of food served at the retreat, while the On Your Doorstep feature lets you know what there is to explore in the region beyond the retreat itself.

We hope that this book will inspire you to start planning the 'new you'. To book a trip that will help improve your health and wellbeing, and make changes that should last long after your holiday is over.

FITNESS ON THE ROCKS

USA // Some 10,000 people fill Colorado's famed Red Rocks Amphitheatre for this day-long, mountain-surrounded fitness fest. Participants stretch in yoga classes, dance in Zumba classes and kick in martial arts classes, while DJs stoke the sweat and tears. Cool-down is via an epic water gun fight. // WWW.FITNESSONTHEROCKSCOLORADO.COM

WANDERLUST

VARIOUS LOCATIONS // Wanderlust holds mindful triathlons that feature yoga, meditation and a 3-mile (5km) run in 25 city parks from Santiago, Chile to Calgary, Canada. Need more? It adds mountain biking, paddle boarding and DJs to the mix at its multi-day fests in adventure towns. // WWW.WANDERLUST.COM

BHAKTI FEST

USA // The otherworldly landscape of Joshua Tree, California, sets the scene for six days of hardcore yoga, meditation and devotional music. Workshops cover tantric practices, the contemplation of existence and personal growth. World-renowned teachers pack the schedule. // WWW.BHAKTIFEST.COM

WELLNESS FESTIVALS A

ENVISION FESTIVAL

COSTA RICA // Set in a humble Costa Rican village where the rainforest meets the beach, Envision is all about consciousness-raising and transformation. It's a four-day extravaganza of fire dancers, performance artists, yoga classes, astrologers, environmental workshops and dreamy beats from international musicians. // WWW.ENVISIONFESTIVAL.COM

INTERNATIONAL YOGA FESTIVAL

INDIA // Held in Rishikesh, India – the birthplace of yoga – this week-long festival draws yogis from around the globe. They come for lectures and training, to flow in enormous group classes, to bliss out to chanting and tabla drums, and to meet yoga's spiritual masters. // WWW.INTERNATIONALYOGAFESTIVAL.ORG

BALI SPIRIT FESTIVAL

INDONESIA // Over 6000 wellness seekers descend on Ubud for a week of health and wellbeing workshops. There are yoga classes across all traditions, sitar-led meditations, dharma talks and trippy concerts featuring everything from gamelan music to bamboo flutes and tribal rock. **// WWW.BALISPIRITFESTIVAL.COM**

SOUL CIRCUS

UK // Buzzy wellness trends meet hip music fest at this three-day bash in England's Cotswolds region. By day festival goers join in blindfolded yoga, aerial classes, gong baths and reggae meditation. By night they dance to funky bands and DJ-fuelled after-parties in the woods. **// WWW.SOULCIRCUS.YOGA**

LoveFit

UK // LoveFit materialises for three days at a genteel estate in Kent, England. Think of it as a gym in the forest, offering yoga, spin classes, trail runs and dodgeball games amid the trees. It morphs into a glowy electronic dance music festival in the evenings. **// WWW.LOVEFITFESTIVAL.COM**

ROUND THE WORLD

GROOVE FESTIVAL

VARIOUS LOCATIONS // Groove puts on intimate, weekend-long gatherings that offer plenty of yoga, ambient music, creative play, sound baths and community-building workshops. Events take place in Canada and Germany, but also pop up in other countries, such as Croatia and India. **// WWW.THEGROOVEFESTIVAL.COM**

SpiritFest

SOUTH AFRICA // A bucolic farm in South Africa's Western Cape welcomes all who want to nourish the self. This alcohol- and smoking-free five-day event features lots of yoga, camping and even shamanic dance if you so desire it. **// WWW.SPIRITFEST.CO.ZA**

Active

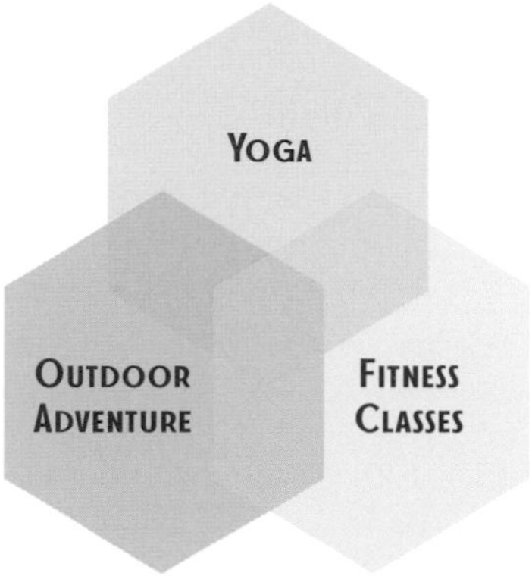

YOGA

OUTDOOR
ADVENTURE

FITNESS
CLASSES

● **Outdoor Adventure** ● **Fitness Classes**

AUSTRALIA
GOLDEN DOOR

● *Restorative yoga and mindfulness classes*
● *A range of fitness classes for all levels in scenic surrounds*

If you are looking for the perfect all-inclusive health retreat package, book into one of the 74 luxury villas at Golden Door's Elysia Health Retreat and Spa in the stunning Hunter Valley. Enjoy sweeping views across neighbouring mountain ranges and vineyards as you work towards your wellness goals.

While Elysia offers indulgent and pampering treatments, the retreat is about far more than a good massage. Visitors can enjoy a range of activities, from qigong, t'ai chi and yoga to Pilates and even high-intensity cardio activities, such as boxing and water polo. If you like your exercise outdoors, embark on one of the many guided walks, a hike through the Hunter Valley or an outdoor military-style boot camp.

The retreat hopes to inspire a lifetime of healthy living and also offers a daily workshop or seminar on topics ranging from work-life balance to nutrition. For those wanting to learn more about anything from kung fu to swimming-stroke correction, book in for a private session at the Elysia Wellness Centre. Let an expert in nutrition, movement or restoration provide tailored tutoring to help you reach your goals.

ON YOUR DOORSTEP

Just 2½ hours from Sydney, Elysia is nestled in the scenic Hunter Valley, one of Australia's oldest wine regions. Visit a farmers market, float above it all in a hot-air balloon or enjoy the scenery on a hike.

$ *1-week program in a one-bedroom villa single AU$4395*
|◉| *Delicious healthy vegetarian meals*

☛ **Pokolbin, Hunter Valley, NSW**
+61 2 4993 8500
www.goldendoor.com.au

COOK ISLANDS

WORKOUT ON WATER SUPYOGA RETREAT

● *Mastering yoga poses on a stand-up paddleboard while tropical fish dart through colourful coral beneath you* ● *Cross-island hikes*

Real-life *Moana* Charlotte Piho is known for singing tunes from the movie as she paddles out on to the lagoon with guests. And she knows all the words.

This former Sydney-sider has a background firmly planted in the Cooks – you'll meet her dad Tuhe on the retreat – but her previous city existence gives her an insight into what her clients are looking for when they arrive, and what they are escaping from.

Rarotonga is a magical place and during the week-long retreats Piho showcases the best of the island. She takes guests out to the prettiest parts of the lagoon where she teaches yoga classes that challenge just a little bit. If you've never done a headstand while floating over a coral reef, now is your chance. Piho has also incorporated into her retreats a hand-picked selection of adventures from around Rarotonga including cross-island hikes and local dance lessons.

The accommodation – in a beachside house – is basic but the food is abundant; the volcanic soil produces the delicious organic fruits and vegetables that you'll feast on and the waters provide fresh fish dinners. Enjoy rehydration from coconut water (direct from coconuts you might have husked yourself). As well as soaking up the rays, you'll soak up a bit of the *Moana* feel just by hanging with Piho.

ON YOUR DOORSTEP
Climb the island's mountain, hop on a bicycle or scooter and do a loop around the island (approx 18 miles; 30km), or catch the round-island bus. Enjoy the bustle of the Saturday morning market in Avarua.

$ *6-night retreat AU$1450*
|◉| *Chia, quinoa, fresh fish, fruits and coconuts are all on the menu*

☛ *Rarotonga, Cook Islands*
www.workouton water.com

SUPYOGA

"No SUPYoga class is the same: you might be joined by a school of birds, butterflies, flying fish or a stunning rainbow. The water beneath you, the fresh air, sky and nature surrounding you…it provides a spiritual enlightenment which I really can't put into words."
Charlotte Piho, master SUPYoga teacher and internationally certified yoga teacher

COSTA RICA

Samasati Retreat & Rainforest Sanctuary

● *Week-long retreats with stand-up paddleboard yoga, acro yoga and qigong*
● *Rainforest enclave with waterfall bathing, guided hikes and bird watching*

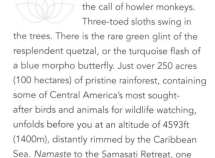

The canopy resonates with the call of howler monkeys. Three-toed sloths swing in the trees. There is the rare green glint of the resplendent quetzal, or the turquoise flash of a blue morpho butterfly. Just over 250 acres (100 hectares) of pristine rainforest, containing some of Central America's most sought-after birds and animals for wildlife watching, unfolds before you at an altitude of 4593ft (1400m), distantly rimmed by the Caribbean Sea. *Namaste* to the Samasati Retreat, one of Costa Rica's foremost yoga getaways.

In two beautiful hexagon-shaped buildings – one for yoga and one for meditation – surrounded by thick jungle, guests can take part in courses ranging from acro yoga to t'ai chi and qigong (the Chinese system of breathing, meditation and coordinated movement).

Yoga retreats, among the continent's best and quite possibly conducted within the continent's most spectacular setting, typically embrace the stunning nature that begins within stretching distance of your mat. Visits to the Caribbean coast, and trips into the jungle, hiking and wildlife watching, are included in most packages. Amongst the more singular yoga experiences is stand-up paddleboard yoga, carried out on a nearby stretch of photogenic shoreline. It is all good, peaceful fun. You can also try unwinding in the resort's outdoor

jacuzzi, soaking up the sights and sounds of the jungle, or swinging from a hammock outside your ecologically friendly *casita*.

ON YOUR DOORSTEP
Puerto Viejo, with its top-rated surfing, is 4 miles (7km) away. Also close is a tempting swath of coastline containing many of Costa Rica's best beaches. The Parque Nacional Cahuita, an important sea turtle nesting ground with superb coral reefs, is just north.

$ *Week-long yoga retreat from US$1040*
🍽 *Caribbean/ Central American/ Mediterranean fusion*

☛ *By Puerto Viejo de Talamanca, Limon*
+506 8428 3918
www.samasati.com

COSTA RICA, GREECE, SPAIN, ZANZIBAR

WILDFITNESS

- *Back-to-basics outdoor workouts*
- *Multiple locations, with sessions tailored to each environment*

The brainchild of Kenya-born Tara Wood, Wildfitness is a back-to-basics bootcamp that teaches movement, intra-personal skills and nutrition all in the context of the great outdoors. Wood takes inspiration from our hunter-gatherer ancestors in her belief that nature is our best teacher, and that our bodies are our most useful tool. Each Wildfitness retreat focuses on teaching attendees to move with purpose, to interact with their surroundings creatively and collaborate with each other playfully and joyfully.

Retreats are held in locations with wildly different climates and environments, from the jungles of Costa Rica to the beaches of Zanzibar and the mountains of Crete. Immersed in each landscape you will learn to climb mountain peaks, explore gorges, surf, canoe and swim across glorious coral gardens. Just as each retreat is completely different so, too, is each day, with physical activities broken up with bite-sized lectures on the Wildfitness philosophy. Coaches are dedicated and great fun, specialising in fields as varied as dance, free diving and bushcraft.

While the physical activities are challenging, the group bonding and bonhomie are inspiring and the variety keeps you pushing through. Dirty, hungry and tired at day's end, guests are rewarded with an on-site sauna, stretching yoga sessions, massages and a fireside dinner.

ON YOUR DOORSTEP

Each retreat allows time for off-site eco-adventures and cultural experiences. Cookery lessons are also a constant feature and allow you to get to grips with local recipes.

$ *7-night retreats from £1300pp*
🍽 *Menus feature lean meat, fish and vegetables*

☛ **+7415 884 312**
www.wildfitness.com

FIJI

MATANIVUSI

● *Surf the world-famous Frigates*
● *Daily yoga classes held overlooking the lush rainforest*

Swaying coconut palms, colourful tropical flowers, pawpaw trees, a soundtrack of calming rainforest sounds and a pristine coastline – it's hard to imagine anyone can be bothered doing any physical activity in surrounds like this. But this boutique eco-resort, situated on Fiji's Coral Coast, is one of the best places to combine relaxation with some hardcore surfing. There is surf year-round but two distinct seasons: from April to October surfers can expect consistent ground swells up to around 8–10ft (2.5–3m), while December to April brings more tropical conditions with shorter duration swells of one to three days. The big draw is the world-famous Frigates, a long peeling left-hander 12 miles (20 km) offshore. The surf breaks are all over coral reef and conditions are best for experienced and confident surfers. Matanivusi offers two-hour surf lessons to get you up on your feet.

Designed by an Australian architect and surfer, the resort features accommodation *bures* (traditional straw-and-wood huts) with large decks that are perfect for taking in views of the ocean and rainforest. There is also a cocktail bar and heated spa. Everything has been designed to have minimal interruption with the natural environment.

If you need to stretch out your muscles after pounding the waves, daily yoga classes are held in a stunning studio built on an elevated wooden deck overlooking the lush rainforest.

ON YOUR DOORSTEP
Surrounded by the turquoise waters of the Coral Coast, there are endless water activities to keep you going here: snorkel among clown fish and sea turtles, dive with schools of barracuda or jump in a kayak for an evening paddle.

$ *All-inclusive per night for a couple FJ$1075*
🍴 *Fijian and Indian cuisine*

☛ ***Coral Coast,***
+679 992 3230
http://surfingfiji.com

INDONESIA
NIHI

● *Stretch it out in a cliffside pavilion* ● *Legendary surf breaks and world-class instructors* ● *Horse riding along miles of sandy beaches*

This beautiful tropical island, 248 miles (400km) east of Bali in the Lesser Sundra Islands, is busy redefining what wellness means. Instead of seeing a trip to Sumba Island as a temporary escape, Nihi owner Chris Burch sees it as an opportunity for guests to reconnect with a natural way of life that we were all once familiar with and that the 650,000 islanders still enjoy today.

Thus, all the activities at Nihi are driven by a passion for the rugged beauty of the place. Rise at dawn and hike up the lushly forested hillside to the yoga platform to greet the morning with the waking birds. Then launch yourself into activities aimed at reconnection with the earth and your fellow human beings.

Activities can include anything from surf safaris with world-class instructors to spear fishing, trekking through wild valleys and rice paddies, or horse riding with the resort's sweet Sumbanese horses. Everything has been conceived to take advantage of the natural playground that the island offers, whilst always being mindful of the local community.

ON YOUR DOORSTEP
Beyond the resort, the island is undeveloped. That said, the resort has a a full roster of activities that enable you to explore every corner of the island – from hiking, surfing and riding to visiting the new resort-sponsored chocolate factory and foundation.

$ *Surfing Nihi's premier wave, 'God's Left', US$100 (only 10 passes per day; book in advance)*
🍽 *Grilled fish and Indonesian curries*

☛ *Sumba Island, Bali*
+62 361 757 149
http://nihi.com

INDONESIA

SEVENTH SEAL

● *A wellness retreat to re-establish balance, mindfulness and joy in your life*
● *Exciting outdoor exercise and adventures with a Fitness Kickstart package*

If you're in need of a little nurturing and some time to de-stress, book a week-long wellness retreat at Seventh Seal in Bali and start packing. Seventh Seal is a private paradise where visitors can focus on their mental and physical health in idyllic surrounds.

The luxurious Journey to Wellness package is perfect for those looking to feel re-energised and inspired. You can attend classes on stress management, nutrition, yoga and meditation. Imagine waking up in the resort's luxury accommodation and greeting the day with a morning yoga class. It doesn't matter if you're a novice or an experienced yogi, the expert team at Seventh Seal will tailor the practice to suit.

Perhaps you'd rather skip straight to the organic breakfast and a relaxing spa treatment. Seventh Seal offers a wide selection of treatments, from ayurvedic massage to manicures and facials.

If you're after something a little more vigorous, try the Fitness Kickstart package. Over five days you'll climb a volcano, cycle among rice paddies and learn about the effects of certain foodstuffs as you work your way towards a healthier body and mind.

If that's not enough to get you packing, Seventh Seal also contributes 10% of its profits towards helping the local community through various initiatives.

ON YOUR DOORSTEP
Discover Balinese culture and find great restaurants and streets of shops in Ubud, or head to Jimbaran Bay for the white-sand beach and string of sea-front *warungs* (food stalls) serving seafood.

$ *1-week retreats start at AU$1850 for twin-share*
🍽 *Organic vegetarian and pescetarian gourmet menus*

☛ *Seminyak, Bali*
+61 4 1551 6569
www.theseventh
sealretreat.com

INDONESIA

Surf Goddess Retreats

● *Expert surfing or SUP instruction* ● *Daily yoga and meditation sessions*
● *Optional snorkelling, cycling and white-water rafting*

In a departure from traditional surf camps, Surf Goddess Retreats are designed by women, for women, with daily surf or SUP (stand-up paddleboard) lessons tailored to your individual skill level. Lessons in Bali's warm, tropical waters are complemented by daily yoga and meditation sessions, spa treatments, healthy meals and luxury villa accommodation.

In the hands of highly qualified coaches, you may even be riding your first wave by the end of the day. If you can drag yourself away from the Goddess Sanctuary pool between spa sessions, you can customise your seven-day retreat with all manner of additional activities, from outdoor adventures to cooking classes, silver jewellery making and batik printing. Access to boards throughout the day is a bonus for those who prefer to spend extra time in the water perfecting their surfing technique.

ON YOUR DOORSTEP
The Goddess Sanctuary is tucked away from the centre of Seminyak, which is home to some of Bali's best restaurants, shopping and nightlife. Wandering north along the beach, you'll hit more laid-back Canggu with its beach bars, good waves and hip cafes.

$ *US$1995 for all-inclusive 7-day retreat*
|●| *Raw and simply prepared local ingredients*

☛ *Ubud, Bali*
+61 8 9467 9887
http://surfgoddess retreats.com

Surfing for the soul

"Something wonderful happens when women surf. We grow more confident in ourselves, find new places in our soul, wash away the cares of the world and see the big picture of our lives and our place within it. Surfing is more than simply a sport; it's a state of mind and way of being that stays with you long after you step out of the ocean."
Chelsea Ross, Founder, Surf Goddess Retreats

ITALY

Vigilius Mountain Resort

● *Nordic walking, hiking, snow-shoeing and skiing* ● *Daily supervised exercise sessions and personal training programs* ● *Aqua Pilates, watsu and qigong*

The only way to reach this mountain eyrie in the pink-hued Dolomites is via a magical, private gondola ride that whisks you 5000ft (1524m) up Vigiljoch where the air is crisp, clean and scented by the surrounding pine forest. There you'll find Matteo Thun's startlingly modern Tyrolean eco-resort with two decks of rooms housed in a low glass cube clad in a gently silvering larch-wood skin.

Sustainability and wellness go hand-in-hand here. Not only is the area entirely car-free, but the hotel is an A-class ClimateHouse and has won a cabinet-full of awards from the WWF, Legambiente (the Italian environmental association) and EarthCheck. Protecting the paradisal mountain environment makes sense as it is at the root of the healing magic of the place.

Take an invigorating hike through the mountain forest, meditate on the rose-tipped peaks through the floor-to-ceiling windows, transition to the spring-water infinity pool that extends outdoors into a small larch wood or plunge into a warm hay bath and appreciate the myriad ways nature helps us relax.

An energising program of yoga, qigong, watsu (pool-based shiatsu), barefoot hiking and daily supervised exercise sessions (you'll find a list in your room) are also offered. There is an extensive menu of spa treatments that make use of natural oils infused with mountain herbs. The mountain pine peel, a scrub of dried pine cones, is a particularly fragrant way to slough off dead skin cells.

ON YOUR DOORSTEP

Hop on the chairlift and glide up the mountain for woodland walks and exhilarating views, or head back down the valley in the cable car to Lana where you'll find cafes, restaurants and good shopping.

$ *Mountain pine peel €72*
⭐ *Contemporary Tyrolean cuisine*

....

☛ **Via Villa 3, Lana**
+39 0473 556600
www.vigilius.it

● **Yoga**   ● **Outdoor Adventure**

MOROCCO
SURF MAROC

● *Morning and evening yoga classes looking out over the waves*
● *Daily surf lessons tailored to individual skills*

Think of it as a yoga retreat with a side of surfing. Or maybe it's a surfing retreat with a side of yoga. Both activities require concentration, flexibility and balance. At Surf Maroc you also get to hang out on the butterscotch beaches of bohemian Taghazout.

Each day begins with a two-hour vinyasa class on the rooftop overlooking the Atlantic Ocean. The sound of crashing waves enters the flow, which is good inspiration for the afternoon's activity: a two-hour surf lesson. Afterwards it's time to free surf and use those new skills. Then it's back to the villa for 1½ hours of restorative yoga. Soon the bed in your tidy, whitewashed room beckons. And when the sun rises, the routine begins anew.

By week's end you'll be striking warrior poses on the sand and eyeballing frothy swells like a pro.

ON YOUR DOORSTEP
The port city of Agadir lies 15 miles (25km) to the south. It has an intriguing hilltop kasbah and a bustling souk where vendors sell saffron, argan oil, carpets and other Moroccan goods.

$ *Week-long stay from US$1010*
!◉! *Moroccan and internationally inspired vegetarian food*

☞ **Centre Ville, Tagahzout**
+44 (0) 208 123 0319
https://surfmaroc.com

● **Yoga**   ● **Outdoor Adventure**   ● **Fitness Classes**

NEW ZEALAND
Aro Hā

● *Sub-alpine hiking in a pristine environment* ● *Yoga with mesmerising lake views*
● *Functional strength training for a lean, strong and flexible body*

Commanding a sub-alpine terrace overlooking the cobalt expanse of Lake Wakatipu, Aro Hā's philosophy is less about pampering and more about jump-starting a healthy lifestyle.

Beginning with morning yoga, a typical day at Aro Hā – meaning 'love' in the Māori language – is packed with activities including a 6–9-mile (10–15km) hike in the mountains, strength training, mindfulness practice and nutrition demonstrations. Alcohol, meat, caffeine, dairy, gluten and sugar are all off the menu and replaced with nutrient-packed meals.

It might sound strict, but it's all part of the Aro Hā way of life. Built on the principles of permaculture, the stunning property runs completely off-grid using its own solar and hydro systems, New Zealand's first renewable heating system and a composting septic system. Yet luxury has not been compromised in the retreat's state-of-the-art design. Furnished with recycled timber and organic linen, the guest rooms all have great views. And if you thought the view from the yoga studio was special, just wait until you see the vista from the Finnish sauna.

ON YOUR DOORSTEP

Just a 10-minute drive away, the ultra-picturesque village of Glenorchy is a popular base for hiking, jetboating and other activities. Queenstown, New Zealand's adventure capital, is just 45 minutes away.

$ *NZ$5200 for a 5-night Wellness Adventure*
🍽 *Gluten-free and vegetarian cuisine*

☛ *Glenorchy, Otago*
+64 3 442 7011
http://aro-ha.com

NEW ZEALAND

SOLSCAPE

- *Grab a board and take to Raglan's famous surf break*
- *Strike a pose in the yoga studio overlooking the ocean*

Solscape has a reputation for leaving its visitors spellbound, and plans for short stays often lead to the reshuffling of itineraries to allow just a little more time in this serene space.

The sleepy surfer town of Raglan is a two-hour drive south of Auckland – the journey itself is a soothing road trip through rolling hills and past expansive beaches. On arrival at Solscape you'll find a community of families, backpackers, surfers and yogis all living together atop a hill, overlooking an ocean. An abundance of eco-friendly accommodation is on offer, from cool train-carriage dorms to self-contained cabins and secluded tipis set inside the rainforest. The feeling is communal and laid-back, with people from all walks of life bustling about, and no shortage of engaging conversations on offer.

Yoga and meditation classes are taught up to three times daily, and the upstairs studio overlooks the ocean. Guests can also take a surf lesson or hire a board and experience Raglan's world-famous break.

Solscape abides by the ethics and practices of permaculture, and offers workshops and intensive courses on topics such as organic food production, composting, energy efficiency and local food resilience, among many others.

For true immersion in nature, stay in the tipi forest, and make sure you take an evening stroll to see the glow worms – a truly enchanting experience.

ON YOUR DOORSTEP

Raglan is a surfing hotspot and boasts a dramatic scenery of black sand coastline. Locals brag that Manu Bay (also known as The Point) has the longest, most accessible and consistent left-hand break in the world.

$ *Double tipi, NZ$87 per night*
🍽 *Organic, plant-based meals, or bring your own food to prepare in the communal kitchen*

☞ *Raglan*
+64 7 825 8268
www.solscape.co.nz

NICARAGUA

Buena Vista Surf Club

● *Attend yoga classes on the 'infinity deck'*
● *Take a surf lesson or rent a board* ● *Try a canopy tour or horseback riding*

A Dutch couple – a pair of surf enthusiasts who wanted to get away from it all – built this cosy six-cabin surf retreat in a remote beach village near San Juan del Sur, Nicaragua. As the name suggests, Buena Vista does indeed have a 'good view', located as it is high up in the treetops, on a cliff over the water. It's not a camp but a do-it-yourself getaway: there's no pressure to join in any one activity, though most come here for surfing as well as yoga, which is taught on an open-air deck by in-house yoga teachers.

The lodge mostly runs on solar power and is an ideal place in which to reconnect with nature. Buena Vista has a digital detox ethos: the owners encourage guests to leave their smartphones turned off, and they have an iPad at the bar, should you need to check your email or send a message. Meals are served communally, encouraging a social atmosphere: it's fun at breakfast, when most guests rise early to feast on fresh fruit, yogurt, granola and locally sourced coffee before hitting the waves, and at night, when there's a convivial environment and plenty of beer and rum to go around. There's lots to do in the immediate surroundings, including sailing, horseback riding and canopy tours, but you can't leave without trying a surf lesson or renting a board for a few hours.

ON YOUR DOORSTEP
Playa Maderas is one of several gorgeous white sandy beaches located near the coastal village of San Juan del Sur. Head into town for a lively dining and drinking scene, or stay out in the wild and enjoy the peace and quiet.

$ *Surf lesson US$35*
🍽 *Locally sourced seafood, fresh fruit and Nicaraguan coffee*

☞ *San Juan Del Sur*
+505 8863 4180
http://buenavista
surfclub.com

SPAIN
KALIYOGA

- ⬤ *Four hours of yoga and meditation classes daily*
- ⬤ *Hiking amid a backdrop of mountains, gorges and waterfalls*

Located in a farmhouse in a valley of olive groves, surrounded by mountains and Andalusia's renowned painterly light, Kaliyoga was designed for peace. The soft chime of Tibetan bells wakes guests in the morning, when it's time to gather for a half-hour guided meditation, followed by a two-hour yoga class. Instructors teach the discipline as 'meditation in motion', so sessions are gentle rather than strenuous. There's another meditation/yoga class in the late afternoon. Otherwise, it's free time to swim in the pool, enjoy a reflexology session or relax in your room, either in the sunny farmhouse, one of the standalone *casitas* or a glamping tipi.

Kaliyoga's most interesting retreats add hill walking to the mix, so that a couple of days during your stay you hike to a Buddhist monastery and to a mountaintop picnic hideaway.

ON YOUR DOORSTEP
Islamic architecture and Arab-flavoured street life set the mood in Granada, but it's the Alhambra – the city's exquisite medieval palace, rich with fountains, gardens and Moorish decorative art – that really pops the eyeballs.

$ *6-night stay £895–1300*
🍴 *Vegan and gluten-free dishes*

☛ *Órgiva, Granada*
+44 (0) 208 123 6946
www.kaliyoga.com/ yoga-retreat-spain

⬤ **Yoga** ⬢ **Outdoor Adventure**

SRI LANKA
TRI

- ⬤ *Owner Lara Baumann's own-brand Quantum Yoga* ⬤ *Follow a holistic parkour circuit around the lake* ⬤ *Learn to stilt fish or climb a coconut tree*

As well as taking care of your mind and body, Tri owners Robert Drummond and Lara Baumann are thoughtful custodians of their patch of paradise on Lake Koggala. Award-winning Shanghai AOO Architects were enlisted to create the cinnamon-clad structures, living roofs, water features and edible gardens. The highlights are the cantilevered infinity pool, which juts out over the lake, and the treetop *shala* (yoga studio) where Lara instructs guests in her unique brand of Quantum Yoga.

An ayurvedic expert, Lara develops bespoke wellness programs for guests that target diet, balance and structural realignment. Beyond the spa, more creative experiences await, including stilt fishing, kayaking, learning to climb a coconut tree (tremendously difficult) and even tuk-tuk driving. Likewise, the food at Tri is fun and fabulous, a celebration of the bright, flavourful ingredients that abound in and around the lake.

ON YOUR DOORSTEP
Kayaking and boating are possible and it's worth visiting Cinnamon Island to see how the spice is harvested. Otherwise, there are dozens of fantastic nearby beaches and the heritage town of Galle Fort is a 25-minute drive away.

$ *Quantum Yoga 90-min group class £9.50*
🍴 *Sensational, contemporary Sri Lankan cuisine using local ingredients*

☛ *Koggala Lake*
+94 77 770 8177
https://trilanka.com

Tri, Sri Lanka (see p25)

TANZANIA

DIVINE DIVING, YOGA & DIVE CENTER

● *Classes in yogic breathing techniques to aid diving*
● *Countless dive sites in colourful coral gardens*

Ringed by some of Africa's best coral and blessed with fine beaches, Zanzibar is an idyllic island to retreat to. Taking advantage of the island's pristine coral gardens and naturally laid-back tropical vibe, Divine Diving combines yoga and diving instruction. Their five-star PADI courses run alongside yoga classes and instruction in pranayama breathing techniques. The meditative effects of Marisa van Vuuren's sivananda yoga practice, combined with the increased breath control of pranayama, make for more relaxed diving. Dive classes take place in an open-sided, thatched beach shack while yoga sessions are performed on the rooftop of the main bungalow at Flame Tree Cottages, where guests are accommodated. Don't miss the dive at Mnemba Atoll, which is considered one of the best dive spots in the world.

ON YOUR DOORSTEP
Divine Diving is located in the large fishing village of Nungwi. Other than diving, snorkelling, fishing and *dhow* (traditional boat) trips, you can go exploring with Nungwi Cycling Adventures. The culture-rich capital of the island, Stone Town, is a 1½-hour drive south.

$ *Mnemba Atoll dive US$30*
🍽 *Restaurants in the village serve grilled fish and Swahili curries*

☛ **Nungwi, Zanzibar**
+255 777 771914
www.divine-diving.com

THAILAND

AMANPURI

● *Individually tailored wellness programs*
● *Boat trips and scuba diving to nearby reefs. And beaches – lots of them*

You might not come to Phuket just to laze about in a resort. After all, the island is famous for its gorgeous coastline and beach parties. But with its villas set in the shade of a coconut plantation, its ocean-fronting infinity pool and first-class spa, Amanpuri can easily become a place to spend some serious downtime at – if you can afford the hefty price tag that is. The wellness programs here come in the form of personally tailored 3- to 14-night packages and are based around four main wellness goals: fitness, weight-loss, detox and awareness. Classes and treatments could include anything from Muay Thai, kickboxing or movement classes to raw-food diet and reiki. The choice (with guidance on hand) is yours. In the spa, partake of Thai massage or an Andaman sea salt and roasted coconut scrub.

ON YOUR DOORSTEP
There many beaches to choose from on Thailand's largest island, and each has a different vibe. Try upmarket Surin, for example, or low-key, family-friendly Rawai. For culture, seek out Phuket's fascinating Buddhist temples. The resort also hosts cruises around the island.

$ *3-night Wellness Immersion with accommodation and dinner US$7050*
🍽 *Washoku (Japanese), Thai and Italian; strong on seafood*

☛ **Pansea Beach, Phuket**
+66 76 324 333
www.aman.com/ resorts/amanpuri

UNITED KINGDOM

GLENEAGLES HOTEL

● *Daily schedule of gym-based fitness classes* ● *Outdoor fitness regimes with a personal trainer* ● *Broad range of country pursuits*

The resort of choice for G8 summits and professional golf tournaments, Gleneagles is a hotel with bags of history. The impressive baroque pile offers five-star accommodation amid 850 acres (344 hectares) of prime Scottish countryside where guests can be found indulging in every conceivable country pursuit, including golf, clay target shooting, riding, cycling, fishing, off-road driving, archery and falconry.

Expert instructors are on hand to tutor guests on the finer points of trout fishing and dressage, and days can be spent exploring the estate on miles of jogging and cycling trails, or in the company of professional wildlife photographer Mike Clifford.

There's a state-of-the-art gym and a daily roster of fitness classes offering Aquafit, yoga and cardio workouts, but why confine yourself here when you can get the same aerobic workout canoeing on Laich Loch or climbing trees to zipline back down to earth again. Personal trainers are available for fitness assessments and can tailor individual programs to meet personal goals.

To ease aching muscles at the end of the day, there's a relaxing thermal suite with bubble pool and onsen, or you can retire to Scotland's pre-eminent spa for an ayurvedic, bamboo or hot-stone massage.

For the ultimate pampering session, book a Gleneagles Time Ritual where you can place yourself in the hands of the ESPA team for four hours of personally tailored treatments.

ON YOUR DOORSTEP

Set in the beautiful Perthshire countryside, the Gleneagles estate offers dozens of outdoor sports and activities, a leisure complex and even a mini Burlington arcade. If this fails to satisfy you, both Edinburgh and Glasgow are an hour's drive away.

$ *Clay target shooting lesson £75* **|◎|** *Fine Scottish and French cuisine served in elegant surroundings*

☛ *Perthshire*
+44 (0) 1764 662 231
www.gleneagles.com

UNITED KINGDOM

YEOTOWN RETREAT

● *Vigorous daily activities including boxing workouts* ● *Varied program of morning yoga classes*
● *Hours of hikes and cycling across the picturesque North Devon coast*

'I've switched off my mobile phone and left it in the car for five days. I hope I'll be okay,' says another first-time Yeotox retreater nervously. She's right to be nervous. Because here among the luxurious eco-lodges, the massages (try the shiatsu massage from Amanda), the super-friendly staff cooking up nutritious meals and vegan hot chocolates, is...a certain fear of the unknown. At Yeotown, they don't always tell you what's on the program for the day – mystery activities are all part of the mental and physical challenge. There is definitely a schedule each day but it's not uncommon to hear 'After yoga and breakfast, there'll be a surprise' and the only clue given is what to wear. It certainly keeps participants on their toes and encouraged to go with the flow. While no-one is ever forced to do anything they don't want to do (there is nothing 'bootcamp' about Yeotown), it's this kind of boundary-pushing that is integral to the retreat's philosophy of personal growth. It's clear the mysteries also create camaraderie among the small groups (many are repeat visitors) who share hopes and fears with increasingly open hearts. There are occasionally special events and collaborations, but the main retreat here is the Yeotox program.

ON YOUR DOORSTEP

Top and tail your Yeotox retreat with some beach time on the North Devon coast. A 20-minute drive west from Yeotown, Saunton Sands is popular with surfers and swimmers because it's a particularly long beach: 3.5 miles (5.6km) of golden sand.

$ *5-day Yeotox retreat from £1870pp*
○ *Free from caffeine, refined sugar, gluten, dairy, alcohol and meat*

☛ **Snapper, Devon**
+44 (0) 1271 343 803
www.yeotown.com

PHILOSOPHY OF THE YEOTOWN RETREAT

"The invigorating coastal hiking on our Yeotox retreat is one of the best activities to help cultivate optimum wellbeing in both body and mind. Physically, it gets the blood flowing, heart pumping and muscles stronger while you can enjoy big breaths of fresh ocean air. Mentally, being out in nature helps calm a busy mind, de-stress and gain better perspective around life and one's place in it."
Mercedes & Simon Sieff, Founders, Yeotown Retreat

UNITED STATES

CANYON RANCH

● *Attempt the high ropes challenge course and zipline, blindfolded!*
● *Customised fitness programs using battle ropes, kettle bells and advanced Pilates techniques*

Located in the Santa Catalina Mountains, surrounded by Arizona's iconic saguaro cacti, Canyon Ranch offers respite from hectic city living. Mel Zuckerman co-founded the flagship Tucson property as the first in an expanding collection of life-improvement spas that began in the Sonoran Desert in 1979. After realising a personal health overhaul was necessary and experiencing a short disastrous stay at a weight-loss ranch, Mel was inspired to launch a multi-disciplinary approach to health and wellness.

Canyon Ranch attempts to address all kinds of wellness concerns and offers a structured counselling service, as well as luxury facilities and indulgent spa experiences. There is certainly no shortage of variety on offer at this 80,000-sq-ft (7432-sq-metre) complex – choose to swim in one of the four pools or select from hundreds of fitness and wellness classes, including the innovative aerial Pilates class featuring a hammock suspended from the ceiling.

Each day starts with a group walk in nature or sunrise yoga before a nutritious breakfast. The kitchen leads daily classes teaching healthy cooking techniques that you can try at home, or reserve your spot on the 7 Days to Change program, which promises a dynamic approach to improving your life.

There is a no tipping policy here and the rate includes all classes, activities and meals. Additional spa services, including massages, are also available.

ON YOUR DOORSTEP
Once the sun sets the desert provides the ideal conditions for exploring the night sky free from light pollution. Visit nearby Kitt Peak National Observatory, which houses the largest collection of telescopes and other astronomical instruments in the northern hemisphere.

$ *All-inclusive experience from US$1217 per night*
|◉| *Fresh, Mediterranean-influenced, plant-based meals*

☛ *Tuscon, Arizona*
+1 877 756 3678
www.canyonranch.com/tucson

UNITED STATES
FEATHERED PIPE RANCH

● *Stretch out the stress with a week-long yoga retreat*
● *Swim or canoe on the lake and strike out on hiking trails*

Feathered Pipe comes from an era before yoga went luxury. The Feathered Pipe Foundation is a registered non-profit organisation with heartfelt service and a vision for a better future at the core of its mission. Welcome home to the ranch: a country utopia that prides itself on good people, good food and all-round good vibes, sleepily nestled in the dense forest of the Rocky Mountains.

The epitome of big-hearted, simple American living, the retreat instantly welcomes with its spacious forestland, elegantly designed country cabins and warm staff, leaving guests feeling completely at ease. To stay at the ranch, visitors can choose from a variety of week-long retreats offered by visiting teachers who share their wisdom of yoga, self-development and wholesome living.

Accommodation ranges from chalet style or humble luxury to tipis and tents tucked in the forest, all reminiscent of a simpler time, free from the chaos of modern life. Choose from a range of massage and bodywork treatments at the wellness cabin, browse through the on-site boutique or enjoy a lazy afternoon swim or canoe on the spring-fed lake at the centre of the ranch. Adventurous travellers can take advantage of the pristine surrounds and enjoy a hike through Helena National Forest, which boasts almost a million

acres (4500 ha) of mountainous wilderness – your hosts can point you in the direction of trails and equip you with a map.

ON YOUR DOORSTEP
Montana's capital city, Helena, is a perfect change of scenery and features 19th-century architecture, including a Gothic cathedral and domed Capitol Building (below). Health and wellness enthusiasts will delight in the Real Food Market & Deli, Helena's certified organic supermarket.

$ *1-week retreats start at US$1795 with basic accommodation*
🍽 *Organic, home-cooked meals*

....

☛ **Helena, Montana**
+1 406 443 0430
www.featheredpipe.com

UNITED STATES
L'AUBERGE DE SEDONA

● *Vinyasa yoga and customised yoga sessions*
● *Captivating canyon and creek country that begs to be explored*

Out of the broccoli-green woods swoop the glowing red-rock formations that make the Sedona area so alluring. And besides a lush creek amidst surrounds that rival the nearby Grand Canyon for beauty you can find L'Auberge de Sedona, one of the foremost retreats and wellness centres in the southern US.

Understandably in such a serene spot, reconnection with nature is a predominant theme. The woodsy creek veritably presses in through the windows of the restaurant and tranquil views of trees or sheering rocky pinnacles greet guests' eyes from their rooms. Many of the accommodation options have outdoor showers and wood fires, allowing for further affinity with the craggy countryside outside.

The on-site spa specialises in forest bathing, the Japanese technique of *shinrin-yoku*, which is said to have a positive impact on health. In-depth vinyasa yoga sessions are offered too, along with individually tailored yoga programs. There is a fun 'feet in the creek' treatment, involving a paddle in the creek that tumbles through the extensive grounds, and ending with a foot-washing and reflexology session. Sound healing, using crystal bowls, is also practised.

So breathe in the essence of those trees, go dunk your toes in the creek and roam the

surrounding canyons, and you may well end up leaving L'Auberge feeling a lot better.

ON YOUR DOORSTEP
Jeep tours, hiking, mountain biking, a wine trail and hot-air balloon rides are all options in Sedona. The Grand Canyon is a two-hour drive away.

$ *Forest bathing US$150*
|●| *3- to 6-course tasting menus enlivened by local plants*

☛ *Sedona, Arizona*
+1 855 905 5745
www.lauberge.com

UNITED STATES
NEMACOLIN WOODLANDS RESORT

● *Wildlife watching, golfing, cross-country skiing and plenty more*
● *Adult gymnastics and a fully equipped gym*

How many spa resorts boast a Wildlife Academy that offers a safe home for rescued animals including black bears, buffalo and hyenas? Located just outside Pittsburgh, Pennsylvania, on 2000 acres (809 hectares), Nemacolin Woodlands is a family-friendly vacation spot offering wildlife watching, a variety of accommodation options, spa packages, wellness retreats and a holistic 'healing centre', so you can combine all your mind–body desires and even entertain your kids!

The Holistic Healing Center spa, in a private and serene setting at Nemacolin's Horizon Point, focuses on integrative methods of wellness. It offers ayurveda, Thai massage, fitness classes such as adult gymnastics, yoga and meditation, as well as specialists who will do one-on-one work with guests. And if you still have any energy left, there's a fully equipped gym to keep the workout going.

Once you've had your fill of massages and indoor activities, the resort has an abundance of outdoor activities on offer – from golfing and tennis to clay shooting and fly fishing. In winter, there is cross-country skiing, as well as snowshoeing and even dogsledding. Kids are well catered for, too, with bowling, arcade games, visiting wild animals and mini golf.

No matter what type of weekend or longer retreat you choose, you have the choice of many lodging themes, including Falling Rock (inspired by Frank Lloyd Wright), Chateau Lafayette (in the style of a French château) or the Lodge (English Tudor style).

ON YOUR DOORSTEP
The resort is located in a rural area of coal country, not far from Pittsburgh and close to West Virginia. Pittsburgh has beautiful parks and universities (Carnegie Mellon, among others), as well as the Andy Warhol Museum.

$ *3-day family stay with spa services approx US$3500*
I◉I *Dine on local seasonal cuisine at Lautrec restaurant*

....

☛ **Farmington, Pennsylvania**
+1 866 344 6957
www.nemacolin.com

UNITED STATES

THE ASHRAM

● *Hike the dramatic Santa Monicas' Backbone Trail* ● *Twice-daily yoga practice in a groovy redwood dome* ● *Get toned at the barre or in a hula hoop*

Since 1974, The Ashram has been teaching people to chill out through an intense week-long program of hiking, yoga, nutrition and mindful meditation. Given the elite guest roster (there's a strict code of no name-dropping), the place is surprisingly down-to-earth and non-glitzy, just a little two-storey stucco house tucked in a canyon north of Los Angeles. Some bedrooms are shared, all bathrooms are common and the pool is a postage stamp. What makes it special is its tiny scale, with no more than a dozen guests each week, and its genuine, family vibe.

Many of the staff have been working at the place for decades, and the same guests return year after year. Swedish co-founder Cat Hedberg plays the mother-hen role, fully committed to leading her clutch towards mental and physical wellbeing.

Early mornings start with four-hour hikes to dramatic sandstone mountaintops and awesome views of the Pacific Ocean. Afternoons are for massages, meditation, yoga and barre classes – and super-energetic (and silly) pool volleyball. Hedberg was partly inspired by ashrams in India, and by the end of the week, you're empowered to choose your own hike and devise your own yoga flow. 'We teach you to be your own guru,' she says.

The Ashram is a single six-night, seven-day program, run year-round. Hiking and other activities are adapted to your fitness level.

ON YOUR DOORSTEP
Malibu's gorgeous beach beckons, just 20 minutes from The Ashram. For an almost guaranteed star sighting, grab coffee in Malibu's town centre. Or head further south to Hollywood proper, and all the arts and culture that Los Angeles offers.

$ *1-week retreat US$5000*
|●| *Organic salads, green drinks and the occasional egg*

....

☛ *Los Angeles, California*
+ 1 818 222 6900
http://theashram.com

UNITED STATES

THE LODGE AT WOODLOCH

● *A resort and spa that incorporates yoga, dance and indoor cycling classes*
● *500 private acres (200 hectares) of trails for hiking*

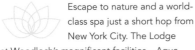

Escape to nature and a world-class spa just a short hop from New York City. The Lodge at Woodloch's magnificent facilities – Aqua Garden, soaking pools, indoor activity pools, fitness amenities, as well as 27 spa treatment rooms – are surrounded by both paved and unpaved hiking trails. Each guest room features a private verandah and overlooks either the lake or the rock garden waterfall. Despite the luxurious accommodation, you will be wanting to leave your room because the great outdoors provides a spectacular background to this beautifully designed location. The resort offers fly fishing, bird watching, kayaking, tennis and hiking, among other activities.

If you want to stay indoors for your exercise, the Lodge offers indoor cycling, rowing, dance, yoga and meditation among its fitness classes. Themed weekends include art programs, cooking demonstrations and seasonal fitness and spa classes, so you might golf in summer and snowshoe in winter. No matter the weather, though, the lake and surrounding nature will bring a sense of calm to even the most harried visitor from the city. In fact, staff members at The Lodge at Woodloch are certified in forest bathing, a practice founded in Japan, which helps visitors reap the benefits of being in such a serene natural setting.

ON YOUR DOORSTEP

Driving from New York City to the Lodge you will cross northern New Jersey, passing through industrialisation to the beauty of the Delaware Water Gap Recreational Area and the mountains (and shopping outlets) of the Poconos.

$ *2-night weekend getaway including treatments, meals and activities approx US$2200 per couple*
🍽 *Local farm-to-table cuisine, from casual to elegant*

➤ **Hawley, Pennsylvania**
www.thelodgeat woodloch.com

FOREST BATHING

"Forest bathing is a beneficial activity for everyone. Trees, plants and shrubs produce compounds called phytoncides that help protect them from insects, fungus and disease. These compounds are also found in the air of the forest and are said to lower blood pressure and cortisol levels in humans. Additionally, fresh air gives a great boost to your energy levels."
Joshua Heath, Outdoor Adventure Manager, The Lodge at Woodloch

Calm

YOGA

NATURE   MEDITATION

ARGENTINA

Lahuen Co Eco Lodge & Spa Termal

● *Ample quiet space both inside and out* ● *Outdoor yoga classes with experienced instructors* ● *Guided trek to a petrified lava river*

You'll need a good map (and a 4WD vehicle) to get to this state-of-the-art eco-spa in Parque Nacional Lanín, Argentina – the largest protected area of Patagonia. But the journey is worth it, especially since most visitors stop here after hiking, horseback riding, glacier-trekking, rafting or rock climbing in the pristine natural playground that surrounds the spa.

Lahuen Co mixes elements of Japanese onsen (natural hot spring bath) and traditional Greco-Roman spas, featuring a bathing circuit that starts with the tepidarium (a lukewarm immersion pool) and ends with the caladarium (a pool so hot you'll need several minutes to get used to the temperature). Since the spa is encased in glass, bathers can feast their eyes on the gorgeous landscape while soaking in the water, no matter the weather – and that's saying something, since this is a part of the world that's notorious for seeing all four seasons in one day.

Since the gourmet restaurant on site provides floating menus and waterproof wine lists, you can choose your lunch without leaving the pools. Restaurant attire is simple: bathrobes and plush slippers. When you're sufficiently relaxed, take a yoga class in the studio upstairs, follow one of the guides on a hike to a petrified lava river nearby, or just linger over a cup of tea and a gorgeous view of the great outdoors: they're just a few of the relaxing activities included in Lahuen Co's day spa experience.

ON YOUR DOORSTEP

Lahuen Co is located within Parque Nacional Lanín, a national park graced with a snow-capped volcano and glacial lakes. It's within easy reach of the postcard-pretty lakeside town of San Martín de los Andes, not to mention the Chilean border.

$ *Day spa US$100*
⦿❙ *Fresh seafood and produce, teas, local wines*

....

☛ **Parque Nacional Lanín, Patagonia**
+54 2972 424709
www.lahuenco.com

AUSTRALIA

BILLABONG RETREAT

● Twice-daily yoga sessions looking out at the treetops ● Learn a variety of meditation techniques ● Wandering wildlife and the chirp of birds among bushland

Only one hour northwest from the frenetic pace of Sydney lies the Billabong Retreat, a peaceful fully certified eco yoga retreat set amidst Australian bushland and birdsong. Husband-and-wife team Paul and Tory von Bergen opened the retreat in 2010, aiming to create a space where people could reconnect with nature and themselves. And it's not hard to do at Billabong, where relaxation spaces range from the magnesium aqua therapy swimming pool to the hammock hideaway overlooking the large waterhole the retreat is centred on.

As you'd expect, yoga is the main focus here, and classes are held in an airy room with floor-to-ceiling windows offering uninterrupted views out to the treetops. The pace is relaxed and classes are welcoming to all levels.

There is a range of programs on offer; in the mid-week Wellness Essentials package guests can take two daily yoga classes, practice mindfulness in evening meditation, and learn about gut health and diet in a number of workshops. There are similar programs centred around meditation and mindfulness, and even a 'lucky dip' program offering daily surprise workshops. You can opt in or out of anything on the schedule or just kick back in your room – particularly inviting if you score one of the deluxe treetop cabins complete with balcony bathtub.

The on-site spa offers hot stone massages, reiki, and facials using ingredients derived from native Australian plants.

ON YOUR DOORSTEP
There's not much in the immediate vicinity but there are plenty of walking trails around the retreat grounds or you can take a dip in the waterhole. Sydney's sightseeing, shopping and dining are a one-hour train ride away.

$ 2-night Wellness Essentials AU$600 in a private room
|●| Tasty and creative vegetarian cuisine

☛ Maraylya, NSW
+61 2 4573 6080
www.billabongretreat. com.au

● Yoga ● Meditation

AUSTRALIA
Byron Yoga Retreat Centre

● *Practise yoga in Australia's boho capital*
● *Learn some take-home strategies that may help transform your life*

Byron Yoga Centre was established in 1988 and is one of the longest-running yoga schools in Australia, offering retreats, teacher training and studio classes. The retreat centre is designed along the lines of a traditional ashram rather than a resort, and despite being less than half an hour's walk (or an enjoyable ten minutes by bike) from yoga and wellness hotspot Byron Bay and its beaches, it feels miles away from everything, set in a quiet spot where the focus is on eco issues rather than luxury – right down to composting toilets.

The feeling of the centre is communal and expansive, with opportunities to interact with other guests at mealtimes. The accommodation is simple, with a variety of options to suit different budgets, and the schedule is flexible, allowing time to relax in or around the saltwater pool or explore the town's offerings.

ON YOUR DOORSTEP
The picturesque little town of Byron Bay has a good mix of activities suited to its laid-back, boho vibe; take a walk around the lighthouse, which boasts gorgeous views from Australia's most easterly point, or visit the weekly farmers, crafts and artisan markets.

$ *3-day yoga retreat (twin-share accommodation) AU$725 (single, en-suite rooms also available)*
⑩ *Vegetarian local fare*

☛ **Byron Bay, New South Wales**
+61 2 6685 8327
www.byronyoga.com

● **Yoga** ● **Nature** ● **Meditation**

AUSTRALIA

Griffins Hill Iyengar Yoga Retreat

● *Iyengar yoga retreats for all levels*
● *Take a hike in the stunning Grampians National Park*

The sleepy town of Dunkeld sits at the southern end of Grampians National Park – not a bad spot for a yoga retreat. Situated just outside the town, Griffins Hill Iyengar Yoga Retreat is run by Frank Jesse and Jane Gibb.

All classes are taught by Frank, who has spent over 25 years practising yoga, including attending classes run by the iyengar founding master himself, BKS Iyengar, in India. His skill and experience have been at the heart of Griffins Hill since 1995, when he and Jane, a landscape gardener, set up their first yoga studio.

Set in 6 acres (2.4 ha) of landscaped gardens, the retreat offers a choice of three-, five- and seven-day retreats, where the day's yoga classes are broken up with delicious meals prepared by Jane and walks through the nearby Grampians, where you can spot kangaroos.

ON YOUR DOORSTEP

The Grampians is made for hiking, with stunning views to be had from the summit of Mt Abrupt and Mt Sturgeon (both a three-hour return walk), and shorter river walks close to the retreat. Be sure to book in a meal at one of Victoria's best restaurants, The Royal Mail in Dunkeld.

$ *3-day retreat in a deluxe room AU$990*
|◉| *Homegrown organic vegetarian fare*

☞ **Dunkeld, Victoria**
+61 3 5577 2499
**www.griffinshill.
com.au**

AUSTRALIA

Krishna Village

● *Learn about yoga's deeper philosophies on an organic farm*
● *Be inspired and energised by a walk to nearby Mt Warning*

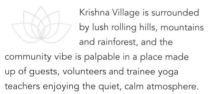

Krishna Village is surrounded by lush rolling hills, mountains and rainforest, and the community vibe is palpable in a place made up of guests, volunteers and trainee yoga teachers enjoying the quiet, calm atmosphere.

Guests can stay for a few days or up to many months, and volunteer programs are available for those who really want to immerse themselves in the yogic way of life. Yoga classes run twice a day and there are regular yogic living lectures that cover topics such as philosophy, meditation and health.

Beyond yoga, the retreat offers a wealth of other activities associated with wellness, from life coaching and a Balinese massage course to designing and creating a permaculture space and 'super soul' seminars on a range of inspirational themes. And should you need to retreat from all that learning, the Wellness Centre offers massages and reiki.

ON YOUR DOORSTEP
Serious trekkers can hike to the top of Mt Warning and be the first in Australia to see the sun rise over breathtaking 360-degree coastal views stretching from the Gold Coast to Byron Bay.

$ *AU$120 per night for a double room*
🍽 *Vegetarian whole foods*

☞ **Eungella, New South Wales**
+61 2 6672 7876
**www.krishnavillage
-retreat.com**

Hare Krishna

The Hare Krishna movement dates back to the 15th century, when its founder advocated a devotional method of faith in which followers entered into a relationship with the Hindu God Krishna, expressing their adoration through dance and chanting. Residents at the Krishna Village take part in devotion through song, dance and service.

AUSTRALIA

PREMA SHANTI

● *Evening yoga in the heart of the Daintree's World Heritage rainforest*
● *Immerse yourself in some of Australia's richest nature*

Set amidst lush grounds in a rustic wooden eco-lodge, the Prema Shanti yoga and meditation retreat is the real deal for soaking up not only some incredible nature but also some seriously inspiring yogic philosophy.

Owned by knowledgeable and experienced couple Mara Staffieri and Janardhan McInosh, the retreat is communal and friendly, with guest rooms that are simple and Zen-inspired, and a schedule that allows plenty of time for exploring the area. Activities include morning meditation and evening yoga, and in between there's plenty of time for indulging in a massage or simply enjoying the serenity while you take in the beautiful rainforest around you from one of the cosy couches perched on the wraparound veranda.

Classes are catered to all levels, and hosts Mara and Janardhan encourage and embrace folks from all walks of life and all abilities, while gently inviting their guests to slow down and feel the spiritual energy of the natural surroundings. Ask them and they'll happily give you directions to secret rainforest walks, spiritual attractions and sacred swimming holes.

ON YOUR DOORSTEP
Endless forests surround you in this secluded and serene space. You can explore local nature trails, wander along peaceful beaches, go searching for endangered cassowaries and even take a trip to the local bio-dynamic ice-cream parlour during your downtime.

$ AU$120pp per night for a boutique private room (inclusive of 2 x meals per day, yoga, meditation)
🍽 Ayurveda-inspired vegetarian home-cooked meals

☛ **Cape Tribulation, Daintree Rainforest**
+61 7 4098 9006
www.premashanti. com.au

IN THE WORDS
of the founder

"There is an emphasis here on awakening to what serves you, and letting go of that which does not. We share with our guests the Eastern tradition of self-enquiry balanced with Western insights and wisdoms. We allow our guests the opportunity to explore their own innate spiritual nature in an environment specifically designed for self-empowerment and awakening self-awareness."
Janardhan McInosh, Founder of Prema Shanti

AUSTRALIA

Samadhi Health & Wellness Retreat & Spa

● *Feel the stress melt away amid the bushland surrounds* ● *Indulge in a three-hour Himalayan Rejuvenation Treatment including massage, facial, mud wrap and scalp massage*

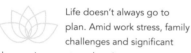

Life doesn't always go to plan. Amid work stress, family challenges and significant changes in our external environment we sometimes need or want to find an internal strength or resolve, or just a different, better way of coping and shaping our lives. Enter husband-and-wife team Wayne and Annah Mirananda, who, with more than four decades of meditation, counselling and therapy experience, have built an award-winning retreat that helps people cope with, and learn skills and practices to manage, life change.

Set in the lush surroundings of Daylesford and on the doorstep of Wombat State Forest, Samadhi consists of two private retreat centres in which guests' privacy is 'policed', meaning you'll never bump into another guest at reception, outside or while awaiting treatment.

In addition to a variety of meditation, magnetic therapy and spa treatments, Wayne and Annah try to help people looking to make a large shift in their life through a variety of therapies and personal growth work. Their signature therapy program LifeShaping™ is centred around working with guests to understand their individual beliefs, values, cultural influencers and internal stories, and helping them come to their 'whole self' again.

In addition to individual growth work, the retreat also offers spa treatments (including the signature Himalayan Rejuvenation Treatment – three hours of massage, exfoliation, saunas, facials and healing), meditation, forest walks and, on request, customised yoga sessions.

ON YOUR DOORSTEP

Just 10 minutes from the centre of Daylesford, guests often spend part of their days exploring the sights, or going for long walks in Wombat State Forest, which sits adjacent to Samadhi Retreat.

$ *Getaways for individuals start from AU$995 per night. Fully customised retreats (including 10 to 15 hours of treatments and customised therapy sessions) from AU$3500 for 3 nights* ⚬ *Healthy, organic, whole foods that are sourced locally. Food can be customised to suit guests (gluten-free, vegan etc)*

....

☞ **Daylesford, Victoria**
+61 3 5348 7926
**http://samadhiretreat.
com.au**

BENEFITS OF LIFESHAPING™

"LifeShaping™ is really personal growth times 10! Our LifeShaping™ approach offers a powerfully compelling invitation to you to become a living expression of your limitless, untapped full potential. It supports the recognition of the inherent power of each individual to access abundant skills and knowledge, thereby assisting you to make those long-awaited, lasting changes, to transform your life!"
Wayne Mirananda, Samadhi Health & Wellness Retreat & Spa

AUSTRALIA

SANCTUARY RETREAT

● *Discover secluded beaches and endangered species where the rainforest meets the reef*
● *Choose from a wide range of yoga retreats at one of Australia's biggest yoga centres*

Sanctuary is one of Australia's biggest yoga retreat centres, where guests can sign up for one of the many yoga retreats on offer or simply enjoy a stay in a unique eco-hut set in 50 acres (20 hectares) of rainforest – so long as you don't mind sharing your space with a critter or two. In the rainforest huts, screens are all that protect you from the elements – so expect a cacophony of forest sounds throughout the night as you experience a nature lover's dream. The huts are simple, power-free and inviting, with the choice of shared bathrooms or ensuites. Guests can also opt for a more upmarket deluxe option with all the creature comforts of home. Outside the huts, there are shared kitchen facilities and beautiful viewing decks where guests can mingle and get to know fellow travellers – from serious yogis to youthful backpackers.

The Sanctuary's owners are dedicated to protecting the ecosystem of the area, and clearly hope to inspire guests to feel the same way – wellness programs build in plenty of time for swimming in the rainforest pool, or birdwatching and wildlife watching along the walking tracks. Too strenuous? The open-air restaurant and bar is a perfect spot from which to soak up the sounds and sights of the natural world – keep your eyes peeled for the resident endangered cassowary and the frogs that like to pretend they're fridge magnets.

ON YOUR DOORSTEP
Mission Beach is the closest mainland access point to the Great Barrier Reef. Explore offshore deserted islands or simply stroll along the long local beaches. The area is quiet and the nature abundant, so visitors can take advantage of serene sunrises, peaceful picnics and forest action galore.

$ *Rainforest hut with ensuite, AU$100 per night*
|©| *On-site simple cafe, or BYO food to prepare in the communal kitchen*

☛ **Mission Beach, QLD**
+61 7 4088 6064
www.sanctuary
retreat.com.au

BAHAMAS

SIVANANDA ASHRAM YOGA RETREAT

● *An authentic experience of a true yogic lifestyle*
● *Deepen your practice of meditation in paradise*

Drawing from the philosophies of the Sivananda yoga lineage, this retreat is for anyone who wants to experience and practise the tenets of this classic yoga. Guests range from serious yoga students to volunteers and curious practitioners seeking a glimpse into an authentic, yogic lifestyle – all in the tropical surrounds of Paradise Island.

The simple rooms take advantage of the natural surrounds, with the ocean-view accommodation just a step away from the sand. For the more adventurous (and budget-conscious) traveller, camping is also available among the palm trees. The ashram welcomes new and experienced yogis alike, its aim being to promote peace in the world through the education of yoga's philosophies and practices. Expect a truly authentic experience whilst immersing yourself in yoga and meditation, and happily taking in the white-sand beaches, clear blue waters and lush tropical gardens.

ON YOUR DOORSTEP
Nassau (Paradise Island) is a magnet for holidaymakers and the little slice of tropical heaven is packed with resorts and water sports. So after dedicating some time to yoga, meditation and prayer in the ashram, you can enjoy some of the island's more worldly offerings – from luxurious spa treatments to fine dining.

$ *US$159 per night for a deluxe ocean-view room for 2 (includes meals and all classes)*
🍽 *Buffet-style, hearty vegetarian meals inspired by ayurveda*

☛ *Paradise Island,* **Nassau**
+1 416 479 0199
www.sivananda bahamas.org

SIVANANDA *yoga practice*

There are a number of Sivananda ashrams around the world, all following an authentic lineage of classical yoga inspired by yoga master Swami Sivananda, whose teachings can be summarised in six words: Serve, Love, Give, Purify, Meditate, Realise. The Sivananda yoga practice is an authentic hatha style that focuses not only on the physical postures but also on pranayama (breathing exercises), meditation and yogic living.

BELIZE

AK'BOL YOGA RETREAT

● *Daily yoga classes in a breezy studio surrounded by the Caribbean Sea*
● *Tropical beachfront digs and a fish-filled reef nearby*

At breezy Ak'bol, the idea is to slow down and live the island life. It's not difficult. The resort sits on jungly seaside grounds, the Caribbean kissing its beach. Hammocks sway between palm trees. Iguanas skitter through the bushes. Cold drinks flow at the beach bar.

And if you're still feeling uptight, there's yoga – not just any yoga, but yoga in what surely is the world's most serene studio. It beckons at the end of a long dock, in a palm-thatched *palapa*, surrounded by true-blue water. Classes take place every morning, plus in the afternoon during weeks when retreats are in session. Styles vary depending on the teacher, maybe dharma yoga or vinyasa flow.

Ak'bol's comfy, Mayan-inspired design is another sweet distinction. Lodgings are in colourful *cabanas* that have delightful details, such as handcrafted hardwood furniture and mosaic sinks with conch shell faucets. Plantation-style shutters open to the sea, and mosaic-tiled showers are open to the sky. Rustic barracks with shared bathrooms provide a lower-cost option.

Wherever you stay, just make sure to attend the morning yoga class. Rolling out your mat in the *palapa*, feeling the ocean breeze and hearing the waves while you tree pose is sublime. Afterwards, it's perfectly fine – encouraged, even – to jump off the dock and into the surrounding blue.

ON YOUR DOORSTEP
The second largest barrier reef in the world unfurls a short distance offshore, prime for diving and snorkelling. Operators in San Pedro, a skip away from Ak'bol, can set you up. The town also has creative restaurants and beach bars aplenty.

$ *Week-long stay US$1225–2500*
|◉| *Mostly vegetarian dishes, with freshly caught seafood options available*

☛ *San Pedro Town, Ambergris Caye*
+501 626 6296
www.akbol.com

● **Yoga**　● **Meditation**

CAMBODIA

Hariharalaya Yoga & Meditation Retreat Centre

● *Two-hour morning, and one-hour afternoon and evening yoga classes each day*
● *Sitting silent meditation twice daily and digital detox*

Leave your digital devices at home and surrender to silence, nature and self-absorption at Hariharalaya, situated among farming villages just a 30-minute drive from Siem Reap. Jungle gardens, coconut and mango trees, and huts made in the traditional Cambodian thatch-and-wood style, set the scene for relaxation.

Six-day retreat programs at Hariharalaya include digital detoxing and start with silence every morning, while morning and evening yoga and sitting meditation sessions build on this and teach the importance of mindfulness in an increasingly stressful modern world.

Activities are available throughout the day, ranging from insightful dharma talks to ecstatic dance, a workshop exploring ancient yogic tools, and even rock-climbing. Or you can indulge in a traditional Khmer Massage, take a dip in the pool or simply kick back in your open-air bungalow and listen to the birdsong.

ON YOUR DOORSTEP
The stunning temples of Angkor Wat (above) – Cambodia's national symbol and the epicentre of Khmer civilisation – are a 30-minute drive away in Siem Reap. If you get templed out, Siem Reap has plenty of dining, shopping and culture.

$ 6-day retreats
US$290–360 per night
|◉| *Homemade vegan and seasonal Cambodian cuisine; no alcohol or coffee*

☞ *Siem Reap*
+855 31 222 6570
www.hariharalaya.com

CAMBODIA
Navutu Dreams Resort & Wellness Retreat

● *Daily hatha, vinyasa and ashtanga yoga* ● *Private meditation and pranayama (breath control) practice* ● *Tropical gardens a stone's throw from Angkor's temples*

The temples of Angkor are astounding, for sure, but all that traipsing from wat to wat in the jungle heat can leave you weary. Enter Navutu Dreams: a sublime resort set in tropical gardens on the edges of Siem Reap. With breezy blue-and-white tones, cabana beds and a pool rimmed by loungers, the mellow mood has a definite beside-the-sea feel, with an all-pervading atmosphere of calm, but there's lots more to it than that. The Navatu offers daily hatha, vinyasa and ashtanga yoga sessions, as well as private meditation and pranayama (breath control) classes.

If you fancy some pampering, take your pick of such treatments as knot-loosening, joint-stretching Khmer massage, luscious coconut and papaya scrubs, and 'Queen Bee' facials with rice exfoliation and wild honey. Utter bliss.

ON YOUR DOORSTEP
Marvel at the spirituality and symmetry of the mind-blowing temples of Angkor, the heart and soul of Khmer civilisation. Beyond moat-rimmed Angkor Wat lie many lesser-known temples and ruins tucked away in the jungle to explore by tuk-tuk or bike.

$ *60-minute Khmer massage US$32*
|●| *Italian, international and Khmer cuisine*

☛ *Siem Reap,*
Cambodia
+855 63 964 864
http://navutu
dreams.com

● Yoga ● Nature

COSTA RICA
Blue Spirit

● *Choose from a range of retreats, including yoga, in the Costa Rican tropics*
● *Relax and unwind in an eco-cottage surrounded by rainforest*

Perched on a hilltop overlooking white-sand beaches and the Pacific Ocean, Blue Spirit is a beautiful space for a rejuvenating wellness holiday. There's an abundance of week-long retreats on offer, with programs held each week by visiting teachers. Guests can choose from a variety of focused programs, from yoga and mindfulness to tantra and beyond.

The simple rooms take advantage of ocean or nature views, and real nature enthusiasts can choose to stay in an eco-cottage or glamping-style tent pitched in the lush rainforest. There are spa treatments aplenty, a saltwater infinity

pool and an inviting ocean (that's accessed via a lush walk through coconut palms) to enhance your relaxation. You can also add a 'longevity' program to your visit, taking advantage of the opportunity to thoroughly cleanse and detox during your stay.

ON YOUR DOORSTEP
Guiones Beach beneath Blue Spirit is home to a turtle refuge, and early risers may be lucky enough to spot a sea turtle during an early-morning walk. If you're not so fortunate, you can still enjoy the untouched beach protected by the refuge.

$ *All-inclusive retreats start at AU$1500*
|●| *Local, organic, gourmet, mostly vegetarian food (with some fresh fish)*

☛ *Guiones sur, Playa*
Guiones, Nosara
+506 2656 8300
www.bluespirit
costarica.com

COSTA RICA
RYTHMIA LIFE ADVANCEMENT CENTRE

● *Herbal medicine journeys to the sounds of bird song* ● *Stimulating yoga workshops designed by a yoga master*

Famous for its herbal medicine journeys, life coaching and spa treatments, Rythmia is situated in one of the world's Blue Zones, known for the longevity of its inhabitants. The retreat gives guests access to trained practitioners in plant medicine, psychologists and spiritual teachers, creating a combination of East-meets-West wellness programs.

The accommodation is comfortable, stylish and surrounded by the sounds and sights of the forest. The daily schedule consists of workshops, ceremonies, meditation and, of course, twice-daily yoga that has been designed by Shiva Rea – founder of the Prana vinyasa style (think feminine, intuitive movement combined with traditional poses).

ON YOUR DOORSTEP
Guanacaste is not only famous for being one of only five Blue Zones in the world, but also for its stunning shorelines, mountainous views, volcanoes, waterfall hikes and surfing.

$ All-inclusive retreats (7 or 14 nights) *from US$381pp per night.* |◉| *Locally sourced, organic food*

☛ *Playa Avellana*
+1 844 236 5674
www.rythmia.com

CROATIA
SUPERSOUL

● *Transformative yoga sessions in a beachfront villa on Brač island*
● *Coastal walks through olive groves and pine forests*

When Supersoul founder Dejana Koprivc moved to Croatia, her 13th home country, after a dedicated humanitarian career campaigning for children's rights in Asia, she decided to blend her two big passions: yoga and travel. Supersoul retreats now happen in places as diverse as Bali, Goa, Nepal, Italy and Ibiza, but the big draw is the annual summer gathering in Supersoul's flagship destination: Croatia.

Held in a beachfront villa in the seaside village of Mirca on Brač island, the retreat is led by Croatia's pioneer yogini Nina Vukas, one of Europe's most innovative teachers of vinyasa flow. Nina's two daily classes, on a shaded terrace overlooking the Adriatic and the spectacular Mt Dinara on the mainland, focus on using the breath to align mind and spirit. Sessions are interlaced with traditional yoga tools, such as chanting, focused breathing and meditation, and delivered through beautifully sequenced asanas.

Though yoga is the glue, Supersoul sets you off on a larger experience, sparked by delightful scenery, dips in the villa's infinity pool, soothing massage treatments and garden-to-table meals around a huge communal table. Prepared by a leading vegetarian chef who pioneered the healthy food movement in Croatia, the macrobiotic-inspired dishes showcase seasonal veggies, fruit and herbs picked from the villa's organic garden and hearty whole grains, all doused in handcrafted local olive oil. The sunset yoga session is a daily treat – it's a gorgeously woven sequence enacted to the sound of waves, the scent of pine trees and sea salt, and with music and mantras drifting on the wind.

ON YOUR DOORSTEP
Take gentle walks through olive groves, fragrant pine forests and along the island's seaside; get some thrills on with boat rides and SUP (stand-up paddbleboard) jaunts; or roam through the narrow stone alleyways of low-key Mirca village.

$ *€1430/1760 double/single*
🍽 *Garden-to-table vegetarian meals by pioneering chef, served communal-style*

☛ **www.supersoul.yoga**

INDIA

HIMALAYAN IYENGAR YOGA CENTRE

● *Five-day yoga programs to suit a variety of levels* ● *Yoga therapy courses*
● *Meditation and yoga retreats on offer*

Based from April to October in the Himalayan foothill village of Dharamkot, near Dharamsala, the highly regarded HIYC (established in 1985) follows the teachings of immensely influential 20th-century yoga guru BKS Iyengar. Between November and March, it relocates to Arambol (Harmal) on northern Goa's shores.

After sun-saluting through the signature Five-Day Introductory Course (three hours daily), you'll be thoroughly equipped for independent practice, though many yogis can't resist staying on. As a first-time student here, you'll need to take the beginners' course before advancing. There's also yoga tailored to kids and women. Arambol students sleep in bathroom-equipped hut-tents; Dharamkot's accommodation offers more variety.

Rigorous six-week teacher-training courses (at Himalaya Shanti Ashram, just west of Dharamsala) and 26-day yoga therapy courses (at Dharamkot) are led by HIYC founder Sharat Arora, a long-time student of Iyengar himself.

ON YOUR DOORSTEP
Beautifully scenic hikes from Dharamkot include a three-hour climb to the panoramic 9514ft-high (2900m) mountain meadow Triund.

$ *5-day yoga course ₹5500 (excl accommodation)*
¶●¶ *Dharamkot has some self-catering; no food at Arambol*

☞ **Dharamkot, Himachal Pradesh www.hiyogacentre. com**

INDIA

INDEAYOGA

● *Sign up for intensive back-bending yoga courses, or just drop in to perfect your form*
● *Set aside time for mindfulness sessions in between yoga*

While Mysuru (formerly Mysore) has always been synonymous with its world-famous palace, these days a whole new set of travellers are descending upon the town; and they're here for one thing – yoga. As the birthplace of asthanga yoga, the last decade has seen Mysuru experience a boom that's transformed it into one of India's most thriving yoga hubs.

Though Mysuru has only recently exploded into the mainstream consciousness for aspiring yogis, the town has a long lineage of esteemed yoga masters. For those in the know, names such as Krishnamacharya, Jois and Iyengar are all revered gurus of 20th-century Mysuru yoga. While they've all passed on in recent years, their legacy and teachings remain intact, with a whole new generation of world-class yogis taking over to keep the torch burning.

Bharath Shett, who studied under the late BKS Iyengar, is one current guru who's in demand. Together he and his wife Archana – both youthful, accessible and well-respected teachers – have opened IndeaYoga, one of the big players in the town's current-day yoga renaissance. As with all yoga centres in Mysuru, ashtanga yoga is a big drawcard, but the hatha yoga and philosophy classes offer a good point of difference. Indea teaches the more traditional form of yoga, hatha, using a 'Mysore-style' practice in an atmospheric space enlivened by its bright Om symbol backdrop. Whether you're seeking a casual drop-in class or back-bending intensive month-long yoga retreats, IndeaYoga makes a great choice for study in Mysuru.

ON YOUR DOORSTEP
In between classes, take the time to explore Mysuru itself, a town famous for its regal history. Mysore Palace (below) is undoubtedly its crowning jewel, but there's a whole string of other palaces to visit, along with galleries and tasty South Indian restaurants.

$ *4 weeks*
₹14,160–₹21,240
🍽 *Indian vegetarian food served three times a day*

....

☛ **Mysuru (formerly Mysore), Karnataka**
+91 988 6091 291
http://indeayoga.com

INDIA

Krishnamacharya Yoga Mandiram

● *Renowned, intensive, long-term yoga and teacher-training courses, plus yoga therapy*
● *Meditation classes and two-week courses*

Join a carefully selected group of dedicated yoga lovers at the rigorous, serious-study Krishnamacharya Yoga Mandiram (KYM) in the far south of India's fourth-largest city. Founded in 1976 by TKV Desikachar, son of the great Tirumalai Krishnamacharya ('the father of modern yoga'), KYM is highly respected for its demanding, in-depth yoga courses. Practice here is rooted in Desikachar's idea of vinihatha yoga tailored to individual needs and as part of everyday life. Chanting and the study of yoga philosophy and Indian culture are essential course elements, as is yoga therapy, an integral part of the KYM ethos.

KYM's most popular program is the very established Heart of Yoga – a four-week, 200-hour immersion in all aspects of yoga (both physical and spiritual). It's open to yoga students and teachers alike, but you'll have to apply. Heart of Yoga courses run Monday to Friday in February and September, and include South Indian breakfasts starring such beloved specialities as *dosas*, *idlis* and *idiyappams*, pepped up with zingy chutneys.

Committed yoga teacher-students might continue with a two-year International Yoga Teacher Training (IYTT), which involves a challenging, extremely selective application process for 560+ hours of small-group training spread across three modules of four to five weeks.

The school itself is a suitably practical, simply styled space, and also offers general fitness group yoga classes as well as two-week meditation courses. You'll need to find your own accommodation (fear not, southern Chennai has some good options).

ON YOUR DOORSTEP
Chennai's Mylapore neighbourhood entices with its street-food delights, rainbow-painted Kapaleeshwarar Temple and flower-fringed Sri Ramakrishna Math. Further afield, explore neo-Gothic San Thome Cathedral and Marina Beach.

$ *4-week Heart of Yoga course US$1200*
○● *Chennai breakfast favourites:* dosas, vadas, idlis, idiyappams

☛ *Chennai,*
Tamil Nadu
+91 442 4937 998
www.kym.org

Tirumalai Krishnamacharya

One of 20th-century yoga's major leaders, Tirumalai Krishnamacharya is considered the reviver of hatha yoga for the contemporary world. Born in Karnataka in 1888, he was a prolific scholar who lived to 100. His teachings centre on adapting yoga to individuals and fusing yoga and ayurveda. Krishnamacharya's disciples include world-renowned yogis Indra Devi, BKS Iyengar and TKV Desikachar (his son).

● **Yoga** ● **Meditation**

INDIA
MARARI BEACH RESORT

● *Yoga classes for all levels*
● *Early-morning meditation sessions*

True to CGH Earth's eco-cultural values, the expansive resort at Marari Beach is a serene sanctuary for body and mind, designed in harmony with the local environment and community. Rise with the sun and enjoy birdsong from the outdoor shower of your thatched-roof, fisherfolk-inspired cottage. Centre yourself with an early-morning yoga and meditation session or stimulate your senses with a dip in the sea before dining on locally sourced seafood and organic eats, produced at the on-site farm.

Whether you spend your time strolling through the butterfly garden, lounging in a hammock hung in the coconut grove, taking in your surroundings on a guided nature walk, cooking with a local chef, or indulging in an ayurvedic treatment, you'll find your mind and body aligning effortlessly with the slow pace of this seaside village.

ON YOUR DOORSTEP
With the sea in front and the backwaters behind, visitors to Marari Beach have an opportunity to experience coastal culture and cruise the backwaters by houseboat. This South India escape is also a quick flight to Sri Lanka or the Maldives from Cochin Airport.

$ *US$200–600 per room per night (includes meals and some activities, such as yoga, butterfly garden and nature walk)*
🍽 *Coastal cuisine of organic produce and locally sourced seafood*

....

☛ *Marari Beach, Kerala*
+91 484 3011 711
http://cghearth.com/ marari-beach

INDIA

PARMARTH NIKETAN ASHRAM

● *Complete 'vinyasa yoga as living' experiences* ● *Kriya and naada yoga with vedic chanting*
● *Havan and aarti rituals; satsang, kirtan and darshan*

Rishikesh gets dubbed the yoga capital of the world, quite rightly, and, as many pilgrimage centres can be, is a profoundly spiritual but rather overwhelming place – abuzz with the frenetic commerce involved in tending to the needs of the devout. Of the dozens of yoga retreats in town, Parmarth Niketan Ashram is the biggest: a 1000-room, Ganges-fronting colossus set amidst beautiful gardens that will almost surely meet all of your yoga and meditation needs.

As you'd expect, a huge variety of courses is on offer, from beginners to intensive yoga-instructor programs, and even a series of environmentally focused 'Clean, Green & Serene' programs. The yoga practised is holistic and faithful to the ancient yoga as practised by the rishis – sages whose meditation is thought to have granted them access to supreme truth. Among the eminent figures who have attended a course or ceremony at the retreat are heir to the British throne Prince Charles and his wife Camilla, who participated in a havan ritual for world peace in 2013.

According to the ashram, guests should plan on spending at least three weeks here in order to feel a real benefit from the way of life and style of yoga observed. Do not miss the moving highlight of the day's spiritual activities, the sunset Ganga aarti, where hundreds of visitors gather besides the Ganges to give thanks for the light the day has given them in a Divine Light ceremony full of prayer and song.

ON YOUR DOORSTEP
Rishikesh is primarily devoted to the needs of its thousands of pilgrims. But the city is also known as the gateway to the Garhwal Himalayas, a sublime tract of the mountain range including verdant hill stations such as Mussoorie, and the wildlife-rich Valley of Flowers National Park.

$ *7-day retreat from US$250*
|O| *Vegetarian/non-alcoholic; on-site dining hall and nearby restaurants*

....

☛ **Rishikesh, Uttarakhand**
+91 135 2434 301
www.parmarth.org

INDIA

RAAS DEVIGARH

● *Om chanting sessions* ● *Bespoke Ila Only yoga focused on breath and energy*
● *Set in an 18th-century palace in the Aravalli Hills*

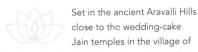

Set in the ancient Aravalli Hills close to the wedding-cake Jain temples in the village of Delwara, the Ila Only Spa at Raas Devigarh is rooted deep in the heritage of this landscape. Days start with a pot of masala chai and a sticky energy ball before a session of soft, stretching dawn yoga where you watch the sun rise over a surreal and beautiful scene of plodding cows and soaring birds.

Then, if you've signed up for one of the three-, five- or nine-night Devi Blessing Journeys, you'll embark on an extraordinary journey through the chakras, combining ancient ayurvedic techniques with treatments incorporating wild-harvested ingredients aimed to relax the average urbanite's hyperactive central nervous system.

Ila Only founder, Denise Leicester, personally hand-picked all the ingredients, from the Rajasthani damascene rose otto oil to the Tamil Nadu jasmine and the Mysore sandalwood. Burning amber is used to ground the root chakra; purifying palo santo incense is wafted around with a giant feather and bodies are scrubbed head-to-toe with 200-million-year-old Himalayan salt.

Tibetan and Bhutanese therapists lull you with crystal sound bowls and deliver treatments with such a devotional air that you feel as nurtured as a newborn. Treatments are enhanced by Om and ram chanting sessions in a room graffitied by a long-departed sadhu, Vedic astrology readings, kite flying and candlelit dinners heavy with the scent of jasmine.

ON YOUR DOORSTEP
Borrow one of the hotel's bikes and explore the Jain temples of nearby Delwara. Excursions to the Kumbhalgarh and Chittorgarh Forts or the temples at Nathdwara and Eklingji can also be arranged. Udaipur is a 40-minute drive south.

$ *3-night Devi Blessing Retreat (double room)* ₹198,600
🍽 *Wellness menus of mooq lentils and homegrown salads*

....

☛ *Udaipur, Rajasthan*
+91 291 2636 455
http://raasdevigarh.com

YOGA A

01

DOWNWARD-FACING DOG
(ADHO MUKHA ŚVĀNĀSANA)

- Begin on all fours with hands slightly forwards of shoulders, knees in line with hips.
- Spread fingers wide and press palms into the mat. Curl toes under.
- Breathe in and on the exhale lift body into an inverted V, keeping knees slightly bent and feet hip-width apart.
- Make sure shoulders are pressing away from ears and lift bottom towards the ceiling.
- Hold for 30 seconds to one minute.

02

CHAIR POSE
(UTKAṬĀSANA)

- Stand straight and tall, rooting from your feet firmly pressed to the mat.
- Inhale and raise arms perpendicular to the floor and join the palms.
- Exhale, bend your knees, trying to keep thighs parallel to the floor. Press thighs down towards heels.
- Press shoulders towards back and hold for 30 seconds to one minute.
- To release, straighten knees on an inhalation and lift through your arms, exhale back to standing position.

03

CHILD'S POSE
(BĀLĀSANA)

This is a restful pose that can be used when you need to take a break in between more challenging ones.

- Sit on your heels and separate knees hip-width.
- Exhale, roll your torso forwards and lie between your thighs, resting your head in front of you.
- Stretch your arms forward in front of you, in line with your knees, hands palms down. Relax your body and hold for 30 seconds to a few minutes.

T HOME

04

BRIDGE POSE (SETUBANDHĀSANA)

- Lie on your back with arms by side, knees bent and heels as close to the bottom as possible.
- Exhale, press feet into the floor and lift hips and buttocks off the floor.
- Clasp hands below pelvis and press arms down, keeping thighs and inner feet parallel.
- Lift chin slightly away from sternum and press sternum towards chin.
- Hold for 30 seconds to one minute. Gently release arms and lower to the floor.

05

WARRIOR II POSE (VĪRABHADRĀSANA II)

- Stand with legs apart. Raise arms parallel to the floor and reach out to the side, palms down.
- Turn right foot 90° to the right and left foot in slightly. Align left heel with right heel.
- Exhale, bend right knee so that the knee is over the ankle. Press outer left heel firmly into the mat. Tuck your tailbone in.
- Turn your head to look out over right knee and hold for 30 seconds to one minute. Repeat on the other side.

06

TREE POSE (VṚKṢĀSANA)

- Stand tall, rooting from the feet pressed firmly on the mat, with arms by your side.
- Shift your weight to left leg and bend your right knee to place the sole of your right foot on the inner left thigh.
- Lengthen tailbone towards the floor.
- Once balanced, bring hands together in a prayer position with palms together, gaze softly at a point in front of you to retain balance.
- When ready, raise your hands above your head and hold for several breaths.

INDIA

Sattva Retreat Resort

● *Enjoy the most authentic experience of yoga traditions in its birthplace*
● *A spiritual wonderland at the foothills of the Himalayas*

The yoga offered at Sattva is aimed at giving visitors an authentic insight into the heart of the practice. Located on the outskirts of Rishikesh, a city revered as the 'capital of yoga', there's no place to delve more deeply into its traditions than at the foot of the Himalayas, alongside the holy river Ganges. Rooms are quirky and humble, with some cottages taking in vast views of the peaceful, natural surroundings.

Retreats range from three days to 21, and whichever one they opt for, guests can expect a schedule of authentic yoga teachings, cleansing rituals and magical meditations. There are six special healing packages to choose from, each one offering elements targeted to its core aims. Signing up for the special yoga retreat ensures daily practice sessions with your own private yoga teacher. The Ayur cleanse incorporates guided nature walks and two ayurvedic treatments a day, or you can choose a sacred silent retreat for deep self-enquiry and connection with nature.

The retreat's ethos is to create a space in which guests can transform though immersing themselves in ancient yoga traditions and healing their bodies through nourishment and relaxation. Treatments are based on traditional ayurvedic practices as well as popular Western indulgences, and no one should leave without experiencing shirodhara

– the blissfully relaxing Indian practice of pouring warm herbal oils over the forehead.

ON YOUR DOORSTEP

Every evening, as dusk descends in Rishikesh, it's time for the Ganga Aarti – a devotional ritual using fire as an offering. Unlike anything you've experienced before, it's an absolute joy to watch the hundreds of thousands of Indians ecstatically engage in this awe-inspiring ceremony.

$ *3-day retreats from ₹28,500 (inclusive of accommodation, food, yoga, meditation and more)*
❑ *Organic vegetarian Indian and Western cuisine*

☞ *Rishikesh, Uttarakhand*
+91 819 1055 551
www.thesattva.com

● **Yoga** ● **Nature** ● **Meditation**

INDIA
Soukya

● *From ashtanga asanas to yoga nidri* ● *The sound of silence but for birdsong in coconut and fruit orchards* ● *Chakra, om and transformation meditation*

In naturopathic circles, Dr Issac Mathai has a reputation as a bit of a miracle worker. The guru runs this holistic haven in the countryside east of Bengaluru (formerly Bangalore) – a world apart from its crowds and chaos. Set aside at least a week to enjoy the holistic therapy programs on offer here. Whether it's Om meditation, yoga asanas (postures), acupuncture, hard-core detoxes, mudpacks, touch therapy, or ayurvedic treatments like the flowing-oil-on-forehead shirodhara, the practitioners here are second to none.

And although the estate isn't flash, word has slipped out about its wonders – to the likes of Sting, Tina Turner and Prince Charles, no less. It's strictly digital- and alcohol-free, but you'll soon forget about the stimulus of the modern world when you have the birds, bees and coconut trees for company?

ON YOUR DOORSTEP
Throw yourself into the chaos of modern-day Bengaluru, 15.5 miles (25km) west, with its botanical gardens, markets and cafe scene offering a progressive slice of Indian life. Whimsical Bangalore Palace (above), residence of the current maharaja, evokes bygone royal splendour.

$ 7-day Ayurvedic Special (including 22 treatments) US$200
🍽 Organic, vegetarian and largely homegrown

☞ **Whitefield, Bengaluru (formerly Bangalore)**
+91 802 8017 000
www.soukya.com

INDIA

Sri K Pattabhi Jois Ashtanga Yoga Institute

● *Learn and practise ashtanga yoga in its birthplace* ● *Teaching focuses on breathing, strengthening and purifying the mind and body*

When it comes to ashtanga yoga, there's no better place in the world to practise than Mysuru (formerly Mysore). Home to the late Sri K Pattabhi Jois, the founder and guru of ashtanga yoga, it's also where this hugely popular form of modern-day yoga was developed. Today, it's a booming industry that attracts tourists in their thousands, from newbies to those looking to get certified.

Despite the passing of Sri K Pattabhi Jois in 2009, aged 93, the popularity of his yoga school Sri K Pattabhi Jois Ashtanga Yoga Institute (KPJAYI) hasn't skipped a beat since his grandson Sharath took over the reins. In fact, such is the demand that you'll need to apply to book into a class two to three months in advance of your arrival date. Once accepted, you'll find the school located in the affluent residential suburb of Gokulam, where a thriving (yet relaxed) scene features meditation ashrams, restaurants with yogi-oriented menus, ayurveda treatments and organic stores opening by the week.

KPJAYI's courses – which have attracted celebrity guests from Madonna to Mike D of the Beastie Boys – last from a minimum of one month to a maximum of three. Sharath will expertly guide you through all the techniques based on ancient Indian yoga scripts. Incorporating elements of vinyasa and tristhana, teaching focuses on breathing, strengthening and purifying the mind and body.

ON YOUR DOORSTEP

Given its touristy make-up, Gokulam can feel removed from everyday Mysuru, so be sure to explore the town proper to experience its intoxicating energy. The town's also close to the cosmopolitan city of Bengaluru (formerly Bangalore), and Bandipur National Park, where you can spot tigers and elephants.

$ *2 weeks from* ₹*18,000*
🍽 *Rates exclude food, though tasty, healthy ingredients abound*

☛ **Mysuru (formerly Mysore), Karnataka**
+91 988 0185 500
www.sharathjois.com

INDONESIA

Bliss Sanctuary for Women

● *Restorative yoga, meditation and so much more, for women only*
● *Reconnect and recharge – or make new connections – in beautiful Bali*

There are few things better than hanging out with a bunch of great new friends in a wonderful new location. Bliss Sanctuary in Bali takes that to the next level. No kids, no couples. This is a women-only retreat for those who are looking to relax and connect with friends, old or new, while enjoying a wide range of activities and packages.

Retreats and packages on offer here are mind-boggling in their scope. If your idea of unlimited yoga classes is heaven, opt for the yoga package and enjoy a blissful week of saluting the stunning Bali sun, as well as three one-to-one lessons. If you've always wanted to learn to surf try one of the surfing retreats. If you want to burn some calories, get active with the CrossFit retreat, or for those less interested in lunges, try the self-empowerment or humanitarian packages. Other activities on offer include a cycle around the island, snorkelling, hiking, horse riding and venturing out on an eco-walk.

Whatever activities you choose, make sure you don't miss the organic meals. Bliss prides itself on the quality and abundance of food on offer for visitors, from tropical fruit platters to delicious Balinese curries – and it's unlimited. Also unlimited are the massages and spa treatments included in each package.

ON YOUR DOORSTEP

Canggu and Seminyak are the perfect locations for exploring Bali, and Bliss offers unlimited access to personal drivers to help you explore the stunning scenery or visit the many nearby attractions.

$ *1-week retreat AU$2935 for a single room*
|⊙| *Delicious meals with a focus on Balinese cuisine*

☛ *Canggu & Seminyak, Bali*
+61 4 1213 1040
www.blisssanctuary forwomen.com

INDONESIA
BLOOMING LOTUS

● *Daily yoga classes at sunrise and sunset in the jungle-facing studio*
● *Daily meditation classes that teach silence is golden*

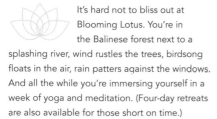

It's hard not to bliss out at Blooming Lotus. You're in the Balinese forest next to a splashing river, wind rustles the trees, birdsong floats in the air, rain patters against the windows. And all the while you're immersing yourself in a week of yoga and meditation. (Four-day retreats are also available for those short on time.)

Here's how a typical day goes down: staff ring a singing bowl to wake the crowd, and everyone meets for a complete asana flow sequence at sunrise. Then there's breakfast, with fresh coconut milk, fruit and granola. Workshops take place in the late morning, when you might learn about opening chakras or healthy eating patterns. Afternoons are free – a good time to check out artisan shops in Ubud. It's yoga and meditation time again in the late afternoon, and then dinner, a vegetarian affair that skews Thai, Indian, Mexican or whatever else the chef cooks up that night. After the meal, Blooming Lotus arranges cultural outings. So you might see a Balinese fire dance or take a trip to a water temple.

The retreat caters to beginners and advanced students alike, and promises to teach two complete asana flow sequences each day. Accommodation runs the gamut from small rooms with shared bathroom to private villas with your own plunge pool.

Whatever your level, be sure to attend the evening sessions. There's nothing like doing yoga in the open-air studio as the sun sets and the jungle chirps in surround sound.

ON YOUR DOORSTEP
Ubud has terrific shops and restaurants. The Neka Art Museum is a good place to learn about Balinese painting. The Sacred Monkey Forest Sanctuary is a must-see, complete with 600 greedy macaques and three holy temples.

$ *4-day retreats US$397–597; 7-day retreats US$795–1197*
🍽 *Healthy, international vegetarian dishes*

📍 ***Ubud, Bali***
+62 021 2955 3600
www.blooming-lotus-yoga.com

INDONESIA

Desa Seni

● *An eco-village surrounded by verdant gardens with tropical beaches close by*
● *Escape in true yogic style with an abundant yoga schedule*

Desa Seni is a quirky eco-village whose owners have a goal: to create a luxurious, utopian community of conscious travellers. Anyone who practises yoga and has travelled to Bali has probably heard of this magical little resort reminiscent of a children's fairy tale. By day stroll the perfectly manicured gardens and laze by the sparkling pool surrounded by Balinese huts; by night discover an inviting sanctuary lit up with colourful lanterns and fairy lights.

The accommodation, from the one-person 'village cabin' to two-bedroom 'village homes', is inviting and unique, with luxuriously eccentric wooden homes imported from Indonesian islands used as cabins and filled with pieces of antique local furniture that tell a story. The outdoor yoga spaces are equally well-thought-out and enticing, and best of all they boast a wealth of daily yoga classes taught by world-class teachers who invite students to explore yoga's philosophies on both a physical and spiritual level. The sunrise classes are a perfectly peaceful and easy start to your Balinese day.

There's something for everyone, and all guests are welcomed to enjoy the vibrant space and indulge in whatever tickles their fancy – including a glass of wine in the tropical-garden restaurant. The spa treatments range from Balinese massages and chakra readings to sunburn relief and ear candling.

Try the Javanese Lulur Body Scrub to give your senses some serious indulgence.

ON YOUR DOORSTEP

Canggu is Bali's up-and-coming yoga paradise, with more and more on offer each year. The beachside town is not short of expats, and has a range of yoga studios and nutritious cafes attracting tourists who flock to soak up the town's good vibes.

$ *Village House (double) 2200Rp per night*
🍽 *Organic Asian and Western cuisine, made with 80% on-site garden ingredients*

☛ *Canggu, Bali*
+62 361 844 6394
www.desaseni.com

INDONESIA

SUKHAVATI

● *Morning yoga overlooking the rainforest surrounds of the estate*
● *Guided meditation sessions to calm the mind before lunch*

Situated 15 minutes from Canggu in idyllic rainforest surrounds, Sukhavati is the ultimate luxurious destination for yogis. The retreat is based on the philosophies of yoga's sister science, ayurveda, and each guest receives a personalised program during their stay. After a consultation with an ayurveda practitioner, a schedule is tailored to suit your individual needs, including traditional ayurvedic treatments, nutritious meals, yoga sessions, and advice on how to continue a health-centred lifestyle back in the 'real world'. Morning yoga classes are held with local Balinese guides in a pavilion that overlooks the estate and guests are invited to join staff in a group meditation before lunch each day.

For the ultimate luxury you can opt for a majestic villa with your own private pool and outdoor bathroom set amid lush gardens. Programs offered are as short as one day (a taste of ayurveda) and up to 21 (complete rejuvenation and wellness program). The treatments range from a massage overlooking the lush surroundings to more unique offerings to complement your personal detox regime. And dining options are equally varied, ranging from the communal dining experience in the River Dining Pavilion to a private meal on your villa balcony with full butler service.

It's essentially all about indulging in your own personalised health retreat whilst being treated like royalty by the meticulous staff. There's nowhere to be, nothing to do and no one to please – it's all about you.

ON YOUR DOORSTEP

The bustling health and yoga beachside town of Canggu is a short drive from the retreat. However, Sukhavati is designed with the idea of guests taking a break from busy, modern life, so you could easily spend the whole time at the retreat; just sink into a daybed whilst enjoying tropical rainforest views.

$ *3-day recharge program from $1355 (inclusive of all meals and treatments in a 1-bedroom luxury room)*
🍽 *Personalised ayurvedic cuisine created by on-site gourmet chefs*

....

☞ *Br Bebengan Tangeb Abianbase Mengwi Badung, Bali*
+62 361 900 6128
www.sukhavatibali. com

AYURVEDA DOSHAS

Ayurveda – meaning 'science of life'– is a traditional Indian system of medicine. Practitioners use sanskrit terms to describe each individual's body type (dosha) and prescribe treatments accordingly. In the system, 'vata' types are typically thin with restless minds, 'pittas' have a moderate physique and alert mind, and 'kapha' constitutions are broad and patient.

INDONESIA
Yoga Barn

● *Yoga, dance, treatments and more in a hip, vibrant yoga community*
● *Learn more about breathwork and meditation in daily classes*

A yoga mecca within a yoga mecca, anyone who knows the practice will have heard of this vibrant wonderland in Bali's cultural capital, Ubud. The space is filled with hip yogis laughing and socialising – it's true, this is the place to be and be seen. But it's not all fancy leggings and green smoothies, and any visitor will delight in the overflowing yoga schedule, inspiring teachings and community vibe.

The space consists of six yoga studios, a 10-room guest house and newer boutique 'Nest' rooms, centre for wellness, ayurvedic treatment centre, gift shop, outdoor amphitheatre, juice bar, swimming pool and restaurant. And with more than 100 classes per week ranging from yoga and community astrology to breathwork and meditation, there's something for the least and most experienced yogis. Don't miss the Sunday Dance for an ecstatic, fun and friendly addition to your ultimate yoga holiday.

ON YOUR DOORSTEP
Ubud has so much to see and do – especially around health and wellness. Yoga lovers can easily stay for a month (and often do) exploring the many deliciously healthy cafes and amazing range and number of yoga studios in the area.

$ *Deluxe rooms from 1,220,000Rp per night; yoga classes from 115,000Rp*
🍽 *Healthy, colourful plant-based treats at the on-site Kafe*

☛ *Ubud, Bali*
+62 361 971 236
www.theyogabarn.com

ITALY

EREMITO

● *Monastic contemplation in 7000 acres (2833 hectares) of woodland* ● *Silent, communal dining and Gregorian chant workshops* ● *Ashtanga and hatha yoga, fasting and Sthira and Sukha practice*

This sturdy Umbria *eremo* (hermitage) is set in arboreal seclusion up a mountain in the heart of Umbria. Accessible only by 4WD it is a 30-minute drive from the nearest road, an hour from the nearest village and a million miles away from the chaotic, digitally dependent buzz of modern life. For those seeking a secluded place to physically, mentally and spiritually detox, this is it. Within its thick-walled confines are monastic *celluzze* (monks' cells) stripped of modern fripperies and distractions – TVs, fridges, phones and wi-fi – with long views down the wooded valleys to aid contemplation. Sensual pleasures come in the form of a rock-hewn steam bath, a mesmerising soundtrack of Gregorian chanting, warming wood fires and a thick cloak of velvety darkness come night-time when guests make their way to the refectory by candlelight and dine on deliciously simple Umbrian fare in the kind of silence that lets you appreciate your meal.

Upstairs there's a tiny chapel where voluntary, daily psalm-reading sessions are held in Italian. They're curiously meditative and precede morning sessions of ashtanga or hatha yoga. Afterwards days are filled with long, contemplative walks in the woods, horse riding and even icon painting, as well as specialist retreats focusing on the art of Sthira (steadiness) and Sukha (ease). Although

there are no doubt immense benefits to be derived from the monastery's thoughtful program of practice, the real revelation here is reconnecting with your innermost self amid the luxurious silence of the forest.

ON YOUR DOORSTEP
Fabro Ficulle is the nearest town and Orvieto is a 1½-hour drive south. That said, it's best to make the most of what is on offer at Eremito: long woodland walks, horse riding and lazy afternoons spent dozing on the terrace overlooking the valley.

$ *€196 per night, all inclusive*
|◉| *Rustic vegetarian dishes inspired by monastic traditions*

☞ *Terni, Umbria*
+39 0763 891010
www.eremito.com

ITALY

Lefay Resort & Spa

● *Movement meditation through t'ai chi, qigong, walking and outdoor fitness*
● *Surrounded by olive and lemon groves above Lake Garda*

Lake Garda is the largest of the Italian lakes and is ringed by Alpine mountains that create a balmy Mediterranean microclimate. High above its surface, near the town of Gargnano, the Lefay Resort sits amid lemon and olive groves that have been farmed here since Roman times.

As impressive as the views is the resort's award-winning eco-spa, which takes its cue from the landscape. There's a saltwater lake, five different saunas, a natural turquoise-tinted grotto and an outdoor infinity pool that merges seamlessly with the horizon. Outside, a fitness path winds around the glorious gardens, while five meditation areas look out on such artfully framed views that you feel like nirvana might actually be within arm's reach.

World-class therapists such as Teddy Trevisan devise bespoke holistic programs – focused on detox, sports/posture, rejuvenation and weight management – framed within the context of classical Chinese medicine. Within them you can expect sessions of qigong, tuina massage and stretching of the Meridians combined with moxibustion, postural gymnastics and personalised phytotherapy.

The whole place is blissfully relaxing as is evidenced in the Grande Limonaia restaurant, where leafy interiors recall the area's traditional lemon houses and menus focus on sustainable, locally sourced ingredients.

ON YOUR DOORSTEP
Set high above Lake Garda, there are a host of things you can do. Hike trails once walked by DH Lawrence; visit Salò where Mussolini made his last stand; or, tour Il Vittoriale degli Italiani, the madcap home of Italian poet Gabriele d'Annunzio.

$ *Lightness & Plasticity 5-day sports/posture program €2250 excl accommodation*
|○| *Gourmet Italian health food*

☞ *Via Angelo Feltrinelli 136, Gargnano*
+39 0365 241800
www.lefayresorts.com

ITALY

LOCANDA DEL GALLO

● *Relax in a luxurious environment immersed in nature*
● *Try to take your eyes off the rolling hills as you enter the downward-facing dog pose*

Locanda de Gallo oozes the kind of romance that could see you relocate to the hills of Umbria permanently. Situated in the heart of the Italian countryside, this bed-and-breakfast is set in a corner of the hills in a 12th-century mansion. With lawns bordered by rosemary and lavender, a saltwater infinity pool, an organic garden that inspires much of the cuisine served on site, and a beautiful yoga space overlooking the hills, there's a good chance you'll never want to leave.

Each guest room is unique, with hand-picked furnishings brought back from the owners' travels and deliberately designed with deep rest in mind. The friendly hosts go the extra mile to facilitate this relaxation.

One interesting feature that's uncommon for this kind of luxury is the family friendliness of the space – visitors are welcome to bring their children along for the ride (although many understandably opt for a romantic getaway).

Guests can explore the many nearby nature walks, book a massage at the retreat's spa, enjoy a self-guided yoga practice in the peaceful *shala* (yoga studio) or simply relax and enjoy the expansive views of gardens and woodland by day and a star-filled sky by night.

ON YOUR DOORSTEP
The Umbria region of Italy is a nature lovers' paradise featuring untouched landscapes and winding green valleys. The medieval towns of the area boast rich history, art and boutique shopping, all of it linked by roads and walking trails offering stunning views. One, a ten-minute stroll from the B&B, takes you to a hand weaving workshop where you learn to hand loom and dye fabric with vegetable dyes in courses ranging from a half day to a full week.

$ *Rooms from €160 per night (includes breakfast and access to wellness space)*
|●| *Organic, healthy Mediterranean cuisine*

☛ **Frazione S. Cristina, 06020 Gubbio PG**
+39 0759 229912
www.locandadelgallo.it

JAPAN

Kōya-san

● *Dawn meditation with Buddhist monks*
● *Lamp-lit walk through a sacred forest resting place*

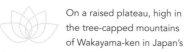

On a raised plateau, high in the tree-capped mountains of Wakayama-ken in Japan's Kansai region stands Kōya-san, an ancient settlement of the enlightened. Founded in the 9th century by the monk Kōbō Daishi, it is the active headquarters of the Shingon school of Esoteric Buddhism, and attracts visitors from all over the world who seek peace, serenity and space for reflection.

Of the 117 Buddhist temples scattered across Kōya-san, some 50 of them cater to visitors, offering guests the chance to don *yukata* (light summer kimono), sleep on simple futons laid on *tatami* (straw mat) floors and rise at dawn to meditate with the monks. *Shukubō* (temple lodgings) hold ceremonies every morning, usually at 6am, with some also offering afternoon sessions. During these services, the chief priest and monks chant sutras in rhythmic unity in the main temple hall, where guests sit in silent observation and take part in the extraordinary tradition.

Travellers interested in wellness will also be enthralled by the unique cuisine served at the temples. Called *shōjin-ryōri*, each of the several dishes is made exclusively from vegetables, cereals, seaweed, bean curds and edible wild plants, with a focus on balance, seasonality and harmony with nature.

A late-night guided stroll through the nearby Oku-no-in cemetery is essential, with the snaking, lamp-lit pathway leading through a forest plot of more than 200,000 graves to the sacred mausoleum of the town's founder.

ON YOUR DOORSTEP

The top of Kōya-san is reached via a breathtaking cable-car ride that soars above forests, hills and valleys. Once there, explore Danjo Garan, the settlement's original complex made of up temples, halls, pagodas and Buddhist statuary.

$ *3-day retreat*
¥42,000
◎| *Locally sourced vegetables, seaweed and wild plants*

☛ *Mt Kōya,*
Wakayama Prefecture
eng.shukubo.net

JORDAN

PINK SPIRIT JORDAN

● *Mindfulness retreat with the assistance of horses, yoga and meditation* ● *Sunrise or sunset yoga on the ancient pink sandstone of Little Petra or in the otherworldly desert-scape of Wadi Rum*

Embark on an inner journey with Sandra Jelly and her troupe of Arabian horses as your guides. Start your day with sunrise yoga on the sandstone rocks of Little Petra or in the epic desert landscape of Wadi Rum. Here you'll have a chance to connect to your breath and become fully present in preparation for the 'soul sessions' that are conducted in the company of the horses. Self-exploration and growth are the goal, so step into the paddock with an open heart and mind. As prey animals, horses need to sense whether or not a situation is safe and are highly intuitive. Through group sessions (individual sessions are also available) they're used to giving participants a chance to observe and learn from them.

While you'll spend much of your time inspecting your inner world through multiple yoga, meditation and equine sessions, Sandra's approach is holistic. Retreats include hearty, locally prepared meals and can be customised to incorporate rejuvenating massages, guided hikes and horseback riding. When you gather around the crackling campfire at night to reflect as a group or lie silently stargazing under the expansive desert sky, you'll see clearly why Sandra chose this ancient, spiritual space as the setting for her horse-guided soul sessions.

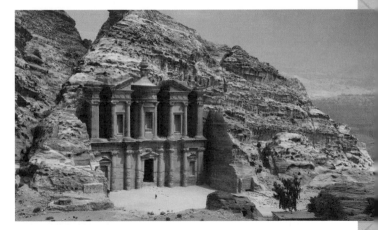

ON YOUR DOORSTEP
Sandra's retreats are situated in the south of Jordan. Set aside a few extra days to spend some time trekking the trails in the ancient city of Petra, take a dip in the Dead Sea, or snorkel in the Red Sea.

$ *Approx US$445 for a 3-day retreat. Longer retreats and shorter workshops are available*
|◉| *Local meat, vegetables, bread, rice*

☞ *Available in Little Petra and Wadi Rum, Jordan* **www.pinkspiritjordan. com**

MEXICO
HARAMARA RETREAT

● *Feel the spirit of the jungle, beach and ocean at this hideaway paradise*
● *Open your chakras in the outdoor yoga space wrapped in nature*

Imagine beach bungalows with ocean views, warm air gently breezing through the outdoor yoga *shala* (studio) and an infinity pool over an ocean. This is Haramara, emanating relaxation and deserted-island vibes, and designed with the environment in mind. Every structure has been hand-built and the space feels comfortably untouched to take advantage of the surrounding natural landscape of jungle, beach and sea.

The cabanas here are immersed in nature for guests to take in the enticing ocean views and jungle canopy – even the open-air showers come with views. Yoga classes are taught in the equally nature-enveloped yoga *shalas*, especially designed to take advantage of the breathtaking sunrises and sunsets. Enjoy a blissful, four-hand massage in the wellness centre and feel your cares drift off on the horizon.

ON YOUR DOORSTEP
Celebrated as a relaxed, surfer town that honours and maintains Mexican culture, Haramara's home, Sayulita, is well known for its eco-tourism and evolving yoga scene. Surfers of all levels are invited to catch waves in a place famous for producing some well-known surfing pros.

$ *All-inclusive Sample Package with deluxe cabana (double) US$1786*
🍽 *Mostly vegetarian, nutritious cuisine prepared by local chefs*

☛ *Sayulita, Nayarit*
866 801 4084
www.haramararetreat. com

MEXICO

YÄAN TULUM

● *Yoga and meditation classes overlooking the jungle canopy*
● *Ancient Mayan therapies and treatments*

It is fed by crystalline waters from the region's famed *cenotes* (sinkholes where limestone rock has collapsed to reveal exceptionally clear groundwater beneath). It is flanked by the tawny Caribbean on one side and by jungle on the other. You can begin your day with a plunge in the ocean or with yoga and meditation sessions on a treetop yoga *shala* with superb jungle views. Suffice to say that Yäan's wellness and healing spa in Tulum helps you to re-attune with nature.

Along with the usual treatments, the spa also uses ancient Mayan healing techniques to give guests an understanding of the culture that once ruled this wild region of Central America. Here you can sample a traditional *temazcal*: a Mayan sweat lodge used for centuries to cleanse the spirit and engender a closer connection to Mother Earth. Ceremonies are held according to certain phases of the moon and come with a fair bit of ritual chanting. Intensify the inner healing with an Aztec chakra-balancing massage, or by having hot obsidian stones, sacred in Mexican culture and a crucial trade commodity in the Tulum of yore, placed on your body.

A rooftop garden planted with herbs and flowers provides a basis for the treatments, with therapists selecting different plants to include in their therapies daily. Garden herbs are infused in the tea and the scrub you are offered as part of the luxuriating process.

ON YOUR DOORSTEP
Tulum, in Quintana Roo province, has some of the most interesting Mayan ruins in Mexico, stretching from the jungle to the beach and sea. Whether you like lounging on beaches, cycling to nearby cenotes for an invigorating swim, or trekking into jungle, this part of the Yucatán has plenty to do. The mega-resort of Cancún is 80 miles (130km) northeast along the coast.

$ *1 week of treetop yoga M$1845*
🍴 *Myriad Mexican and international offerings along the strip in Tulum*

☛ *Tulum*
+52 1 984 179 1530
http://yaanwellness. com

THE TEMAZCAL: SWEATING IT OUT, MAYAN STYLE

In the Maya Civilization, health was perceived as balance and sickness as imbalance. The Mayan temazcal, or sweat lodge, was about getting balance back. The temazcal was an important permanent structure in a community, usually constructed from volcanic rock. The sweat-out, particularly popular after battle or a ceremonial ball game across Mesoamerica, was thought to realign the self with Mother Earth.

YOGA STYLES

HATHA

Hatha is the umbrella term for any yoga that is based in the physical, differentiating it from traditional spiritual practices that did not involve any movement. Hatha yoga therefore is any kind of practice that involves yoga asana (poses). However, today the term is often used colloquially to describe a more traditional, simple practice of basic asana, pranayama (breathing exercises) and meditation.

IYENGAR

Developed by the late Indian guru BKS Iyengar, Iyengar yoga consists of around 200 classical yoga postures and 14 breathing exercises (pranayama). Iyengar is a practice based on meticulous alignment, often with the assistance of yoga props to find precision in each pose. Teachers must undergo comprehensive training to teach this practice, and classes are focused, traditional and disciplined.

KUNDALINI

This style uniquely stands out from the crowd with its highly energetic and spiritual practices. Kundalini yoga is an integration of traditions including hatha yoga, kriya yoga (pranayama, chanting, meditations and energy exercises) and other practices oriented towards the 'awakening of kundalini' – a primal energy said to be located at the base of the spine that, once awakened, leads to union with the divine.

BIKRAM

Although controversial given its competitive nature, trademarked sequence and sexual assault allegations against its founder, Bikram yoga devotees swear by this popular practice developed by Bikram Choudhury. Bikram yoga is a series of 26 poses practised sequentially in a room usually heated to between 95–107°F (35–42°C), and students can expect a strict, physical practice that's sweaty and challenging.

ASHTANGA

Ashtanga yoga is based on traditional teachings and is an ideal practice for busy minds and fitness-focused bodies. Popularised by K Pattabhi Jois, ashtanga follows a specific sequence of poses, and as students continue to advance they are given options to advance in 'series' (which ultimately become very rigorous). The practice encourages a deeper understanding of yoga's philosophies and students often become committed yogis as a result.

VINYASA

A recently popularised practice, vinyasa classes are known for their fast-paced fluid movements that are creatively linked with the breath. It's often physically similar to ashtanga, and vinyasa teachers structure their classes to smoothly move from shape to shape in a dance-like flow. Vinyasa appeals to students looking for an entertaining and physically challenging experience that's also accessible to new yogis.

Yin

Yin yoga is growing in popularity due to its focus on relaxation and slowing down – providing balance to our fast-paced, Yang-dominated lifestyles. Based on the philosophies of both Western science and Chinese medicine, yin yoga classes are mostly floor-based, with poses held for much longer than usual (anywhere from two to 10 minutes), allowing students to release deeply held tension in the body.

Restorative

Similar to yin, restorative yoga classes aim to encourage the deep relaxation of their students through long holds in relaxing poses. There's very little physical exertion and often props are used to allow students to completely release into shapes without any sense of effort or strain. If taught and practised correctly, it's not uncommon for students to be so deeply relaxed that they fall asleep.

Pranayama

Unlike many of today's popular yoga practices, pranayama involves very little physical effort. In fact, pranayama means, simply, to control the breath, and a practice can be done sitting in a meditative posture or lying down. Pranayama is often taught at the beginning or end of a regular yoga class and involves different breathing exercises designed to clear blockages and allow life force energy (prana) to move freely.

PORTUGAL

VAL DE MOSES

● *Yoga retreats in the foothills of the Serra da Estrela mountains* ● *Early-morning forest walks through eucalyptus trees, plus swimming and mud bathing in the Rio Zêzere*

This family-run retreat was founded by husband and wife Andrew and Vonetta Winter in 2007 when, on a motorhome holiday, they stumbled across an abandoned family farm that just happened to have the same name as their dog (Moses). Andrew, whose first job was as a chef, has a special interest in the ayurvedic philosophy around digestion, and Vonetta previously had a yoga and massage clinic in London. And it's here, in the remote Portuguese mountains, where they have combined their talents to set up a unique retreat.

Yoga classes are held twice daily in the rustic wooden yoga *shala*, plus there are silent meditation morning walks, philosophical teachings and deep tissue Chinese Tui Na Massage.

The highlight of a retreat here is most definitely the mid-week trip to Rio Zêzere for a wild swim and slathering on of the riverbank mud. And while there's plenty of scheduled quiet time for contemplation and reflection, more swimming or walking, there's also a Friday-night party with music and dancing.

Retreats held across the year by various practitioners are predominantly yoga based, though some will emphasise other wellness aspects, such as sleeping. Most focus on expanding yoga practice through classes, meditation sessions and massage, adding in elements such as acupuncture and pilates, depending on the retreat. A range of accommodation options are available for all of these, from shared stone cottages to farmhouse bedrooms or forest 'soul pads'.

ON YOUR DOORSTEP
If you're looking to give back to the local community, a nearby olive farm, Quinta da Corga, is usually on the lookout for volunteers in return for accommodation. Tasks could involve gardening, cooking, picking olives, or even soap-making with the excess olive oil.

$ *1-week retreat from €800 per person*
🍽 *Vegetarian/ vegan with fresh local produce and an ayurvedic focus*

☛ *Amieira, Oleiros* **+351 (0) 272 634006 www.valedemoses. com**

BENEFITS OF
mud bathing

People have believed in the healing powers of mud for many years (how many mud face masks do you see on the shelves?). Mud is believed to have anti-inflammatory properties, due to the presence of minerals such as sodium, magnesium and potassium. It may also help relieve symptoms of psoriasis and rosacea, so long as the mud is not too grainy and abrasive.

● Yoga　● Nature　● Meditation

SPAIN
CAL REIET HOLISTIC RETREAT

● *Transformational yoga retreats for all levels* ● *Guided meditation, breathing sessions and mantra singing* ● *Situated in the rural heart of Mallorca*

Cal Reiet is a fantastically smart, cream-coloured Mallorcan manor house set in the rural heart of the island in a luxuriously flowering Mediterranean garden. Here wellness-focused travellers and yogis can find a like-minded community seeking a healthy, holistic lifestyle.

Throughout the year, top-notch international wellness gurus set up shop here, running retreats that aim to deliver life-changing experiences. The retreats are engagingly diverse – ranging from detox cleanses to breath practice, guided meditation and even leadership coaching – which means returning guests can explore different practices or build on their existing experiences.

Nourishing food is also a big part of the offering. The focus is on raw, vegan and vegetarian cooking and guests are welcome to participate in culinary workshops, which arm them with new ideas that will support their changed lifestyle when they return home.

ON YOUR DOORSTEP
Santanyi, the closest village, is a five-minute walk. There's a market twice a week and plenty of cafes, restaurants and boutique shops. The beach is a 10-minute drive away.

$ *1½-hour Lomi Lomi Nui massage €155*
|O| *Caffeine-, wheat- and dairy-free vegetarian dishes*

☛ **Mallorca**
+34 971 947 047
http://calreiet.com

SPAIN

Suryalila Retreat Centre

● *Rest and rejuvenate on an olive farm with a mountain backdrop*
● *Quirky yurts and yoga spaces overlook the Spanish countryside*

Located in picturesque southern Spain, this retreat is also a working olive farm surrounded by rolling hills, lakes, sunflower fields and a stunning mountain range which combine to create an ideal backdrop for yoga and meditation. You can choose to participate in one of the many retreats or trainings offered throughout the year, or create your own yoga holiday, which gives you the option of joining in on some daily yoga classes and activities.

The main yoga hall is a magnificent, light-filled geodesic space that overlooks lush hills and an atmospheric ruined convent, and is the centrepiece of one person's desire to create the most beautiful yoga space in Europe. The visionary behind the project is a yoga teacher who dreamed of incorporating all of her favourite things from retreat centres around the world, and the retreat was created by a group of long-time friends.

Accommodation is eccentric and cosy, with furnishings and decorations from India, Morocco and Bali. Visitors can choose from a number of options, including glamping-style yurts.

For relaxation, the salt-water swimming pool, set amidst the stunning Spanish countryside, is a soothing place to while away the hours, and the mud-brick sauna is a spa lover's dream come true.

ON YOUR DOORSTEP
Andalusia is celebrated for its mountains, sleepy towns perched on rolling country hills, wondrous natural coastlines and cities rich in history. An hour's drive away from Suryalila lie historical cities, empty beaches and quaint mountain towns.

$ *Rooms start from €115 per night single, or €220 double (inclusive of meals and yoga)*
🍽 *Buffet-style, colourful, gourmet organic vegetarian fare*

....

☛ *Cortijo La Fabrica, Cadiz*
+34 856 023 631
www.suryalila.com

OLIVES OF Suryalila

Suryalila is home to an olive oil grove with over 350 ancient trees, providing guests with cured olives and organic olive oil. The retreat owners have lovingly maintained the farm, and original oil urns and carts remind visitors of the grove's rich history. During olive season, local villagers harvest the olives for oil, as they have been doing for generations.

● Yoga　● Nature　● Meditation

SRI LANKA
Barberyn Reef Ayurveda Resort

● *Twice-daily classes held on a rooftop with ocean views*
● *Learn meditation techniques and the Buddhist philosophy*

Set in a luscious landscape on the Sri Lankan coast, Barberyn Reef is billed as a place where visitors come to 'listen to their bodies' with the aim of healing through ayurveda therapies. An in-depth consultation is carried out upon arrival and guests are assigned a personal ayurveda doctor or therapist for the duration of their stay.

Ayurveda therapies are believed by their adherents to be effective at improving a range of health-related illnesses and issues, from allergies to insomnia – though you're unlikely to have any trouble getting to sleep at Barberyn, particularly if you're in one of their stilted Beach

Front rooms, where the subtle white noise of the ocean drifting through should gently carry you off to the land of nod. And if that doesn't work, yoga is held each morning and evening on a rootop with ocean views, and there are often dharma talks explaining the philosophy of Buddhism, along with meditation classes.

ON YOUR DOORSTEP
Located in the popular beach spot of Beruwala (above), you can while away plenty of time just lazing on the beach. If you need a bit of culture, the resort is close to a number of temples, including 12th-century Galapota Temple.

$ *From €160 per night for a double room. Mandatory ayurveda treatment €80 per day* **🍽** *Nourishing meals prepared to suit individual* **doshas**

**☞ Beruwela, Sri Lanka
+94 34 227 6036
www.barberyn
resorts.com**

SRI LANKA

NILAMBE BUDDHIST MEDITATION CENTRE

● *Retreats for beginners and advanced practitioners looking to deepen their practice*
● *Located on a secluded hillside above a beautiful tea farm*

Upul Nishantha Gamage, resident Meditation Instructor at Nilambe, says of *anāpānasati* (mindful breathing), 'It may seem to be the most straightforward of meditation techniques, but it is also the most profound.' Though the practice of meditation is ancient and simple, for those of us wrapped up in the trappings of the modern world, the greatest challenge lies in finding the time and space in which to practise. The Nilambe Centre provides both of these things, billing itself as an 'authentic Buddhist meditation retreat'.

While the course itself involves guided meditations beginning at 5am and continuing at scheduled intervals throughout the day, Nilambe's program is not as rigorous nor dogmatic as that of the traditional 10-day Vipassana meditation course (which employs similar teachings and philosophy and is offered widely in other Buddhist retreats). Though both share the precepts of vegetarianism,

separation of genders and practice of silent sitting meditation, participants at Nilambe are offered shorter courses (of between five, seven and 10 days). In addition, students may study in the library and are permitted to bring their own (vegetarian) food to supplement the two daily meals, and to practise yoga at the centre.

Though not a typical holiday camp, there is an air of camaraderie that develops among participants during mealtimes and shared chores (called 'working meditation'). The retreat centre and surrounding area are so beautiful that serenity comes easily to those making the trip. Those doing the work will leave with profoundly useful life skills.

ON YOUR DOORSTEP
Communal areas and meditation halls made of stone are connected by winding cobblestone paths enfolded by lush rainforest. The surrounding hills, valleys and tea farms are lovely to look at.

$ *Payment is on a donation basis*
|●| *Vegetarian Sri Lankan breakfasts and lunches daily*

☛ **Nilambe, Sri Lanka**
http://nilambe.net

THE SPIRITUAL PATH

"*There are three steps of the spiritual path: Knowing, Learning, Living. We have to know what to do by reading books and listening to teachers. Then we have to learn how to do it. After knowing and learning, we have to apply the knowledge and practice into our life. The realisation happens only then.*"
Upul Nishantha Gamage, Meditation Instructor, Nilambe Buddhist Meditation Centre

● Yoga ● Nature ● Meditation

THAILAND
BHUD'S XHALE YOGA RETREAT

● *Yoga classes are inclusive, with all levels in mind* ● *Chanting and laughter meditation* ● *Excursion to nearby thermal pools*

The healing power of laughter is strong at this week-long yoga retreat, where groups differ in their mix of nationalities and skills but are brought together by the vivacious Bhud, an ex-Bangkok resident who disarms everyone with her self-deprecating happiness – even the most standoffish participants bond soon enough.

Bhud has built her retreat to make the most of its natural surrounds. The yoga *shala* (studio) and separate dining spaces are open to the lush gardens – the sound of tropical rain, insects and birdsong may enter your evening meditation, if you let them. The food is freshly prepared

and delicious; it far outstrips expectations at this simply furnished, low-key retreat, and a morning is set aside to learn about nutrition and healthy cooking skills such as home fermenting and vegan cooking. A request for total silence before midday forces you to properly unwind and find your inner peace.

ON YOUR DOORSTEP
Pai is a small but popular town surrounded by beautiful mountains. If you feel the need to escape the peacefulness and let your hair down a bit, the downtown area has plenty of nightlife and restaurants.

$ *5-night yoga and meditation retreat from US$425–485pp*
⦿l *All vegetarian, fresh food, made on-site*

☛ *Mae Hong Son, Pai*
+66 89 758 3635
https://xhaleyogapai.com

THAILAND

KAMALAYA

● *Take your yoga practice to the next level with personal guidance* ● *Soak up picturesque views of tropical Thailand* ● *Meditate in an ancient monk's cave*

The energy of Kamalaya is profoundly spiritual, despite (or perhaps facilitated by) its five-star luxury. The essence can be found in its name. In Sanskrit, Kamal means lotus and Alaya means realm – an ancient symbol for the unfolding of the human spirit, or healing and growth from within. And the retreat easily delivers on this promise, as it's almost impossible not to gain some spiritual insight amidst the still serenity.

The luscious hillside location, overlooking Thailand's pristine tropical beaches, invites the kind of inner tranquillity you rarely access within the chaos of everyday life. Visitors can choose from one of the many wellness programs available – from detox, weight loss and yoga to comprehensive optimal fitness and more – or simply indulge in the luxurious accommodation, which includes a wellness consultation and access to the scheduled holistic activities (think yoga, cooking classes, fitness and meditation).

The team of health professionals and therapists includes Traditional Chinese medicine experts, ayurvedic consultants, naturopaths, nurses, nutritionists and spiritual mentors (to name a few), affording guests a holistic approach to health and wellness that they can take away with them. The Monks' Cave is at the heart of Kamalaya's philosophy, and is the perfect space for quiet contemplation at any time of day.

ON YOUR DOORSTEP
Koh Samui abounds with picture-perfect beaches, waterfalls, exotic spas and fine dining. A day trip around the island will introduce you to small villages, temples and secluded beaches that offer some insight into what life was like here before the tourism boom.

$ *Hillside room THB10,400 double per night (high season)*
🍽 *East-meets-West healthy fusions*

☞ **Koh Samui, Suratthani**
+66 77 429 800
www.kamalaya.com

THAILAND

THE YOGA RETREAT

● *Daily ashtanga practice* ● *Guided meditation and pranayama (breath control)*
● *Thailand in a nutshell: tropical beaches, jungly hills*

Early morning and all is quiet in the *shala* (studio) except for the creak of floorboards as supple limbs stretch in warm-up. Hoots and warbles reverberate in the jungle and a whisper of a breeze rustles the prayer flags as dawn creeps across the canopy and the sun rises on another day at the Yoga Retreat. With everyone in perfect lotus position, the class opens with Sanskrit mantras and sun salutations – the morning yoga sequence to switch on all the major muscle groups. Then the novices are talked through the primary series of *asanas*, or postures, while more experienced yogis familiar with the drill contort their bodies into improbable shapes. It's the kind of flexibility that comes with hard practice alone.

Dangling off Thailand's southeast coast, Koh Pha-Ngan is perhaps better known for its rollicking Full Moon parties and glossy-brochure beaches, but it can do peaceful too. And nowhere more so than at this nicely chilled retreat, with simple hut lodgings, a spiritual atmosphere and vegetarian and raw food to fill the gut and nourish the soul. Stay for several weeks for the full benefit of daily ashtanga yoga, guided meditation and *pranayama* (breath control) and – if you dare – liquid-only detoxes. Ashtanga yoga's rightful home might be Mysore in India, but this Thai retreat is wholly in tune with its philosophy, and you'll leave looser, lighter and with a heightened sense of self-awareness.

ON YOUR DOORSTEP

It's a jungle out there… Some 90% of Koh Pha-Ngan is tropical rainforest and a world apart from the Full Moon madness of Haad Rin in the island's south. Go north for beach time and joint-cracking, post-yoga massages overlooking the Gulf of Thailand's flour-soft sands and cerulean seas.

$ *6-day yoga retreat and accommodation 9400THB*
❙⦿❙ *Vegetarian, vegan, raw, Thai and delicious*

☛ **Koh Pha-Ngan, Surat Thani**
+66 77 374 310
www.yogaretreat-kohphangan.com

ASHTANGA *yoga*

Ashtanga yoga, deemed the highest 'classical' or 'royal' form of yoga, means 'eight limbs', referring to the eight elements of yoga as set forth in Patanjali Yoga Sutras (300–250 BC). Only one of these eight aspects involves asanas, or postures. The others are concerned with taming the impulsive 'animal nature', mastering control over consciousness (through meditation, for instance) and joining the individual with the divine.

● Yoga ● Nature

TURKEY
HUZUR VADISI

● *Retreats for all levels led by high-calibre practitioners*
● *Deliberately isolated in an idyllic, unspoilt mountain valley*

Huzur Vadisi means 'peaceful valley' in Turkish, and the idyllic tranquillity of the setting here, with its rustling pine trees and tinkling goat bells, is a fantastic bonus to the world-class yoga retreats run at Huzur Vadisi between May and September.

Led by renowned practitioners, the week-long retreats cover all manner of styles from yin and yang yoga by Simon Low to the fluid Scaravelli-based style of former dancer Catherine Annis. Sessions are held in a lovely open-sided *shala* (studio) alongside supplementary t'ai chi, meditation classes and night walks.

Although the practice is physically demanding, almost all the retreats are adaptable to varying skill levels. Accommodation is in luxurious yurts while shared meals consist of tasty Turkish vegetarian dishes created from vegetables grown on site. It's a perfect place to detox.

ON YOUR DOORSTEP
The retreat is a 15-minute drive from the small yachting resort of Göcek, with its seafront cafes and restaurants. A boat excursion around the surrounding Göcek Islands is lovely, and near the retreat there are plenty of mountain walks.

$ *Week-long retreat £875 double/twin yurt*
🍽 *Flavourful Turkish dishes based on kitchen-garden vegetables*

☛ *Göcek Ovacik Mah, Göcek*
www.huzurvadisi.com

UNITED KINGDOM

FINDHORN FOUNDATION

● *Reconnect with nature and yourself* ● *Tend the gardens, chop the firewood, participate in the eco-projects, feel the spirit of the place*

Any aspect of mindfulness, meditation or spirituality you can conceive of has probably been tried and tested at the pioneering Findhorn Foundation at some point, because where retreats are concerned, this community sequestered away on the Aberdeenshire coast at the mouth of the River Findhorn has been a leading light for decades. What began as a garden that flourished against all the odds in the dry, sandy coastal soil of western Scotland, drawing horticulturalists from miles around, later started attracting spiritually inclined types. Today, it constitutes Britain's largest intentional community, and is a thriving eco-village.

The first step to becoming part of the Findhorn community is completing an Experience Week: living in the community and discovering how it ticks. During this time you will help tend the community garden, work in the kitchens, and begin a journey of inner discovery. After this, an array of courses open up. Interconnectedness with nature is an overriding philosophy behind all programs, as is attunement with self.

The Findhorn Foundation probes the boundaries of spiritual learning through mediums as diverse as painting and permaculture. But it pushes other boundaries too. It has developed trailblazing architecture with a low ecological footprint,

and is one of northern Scotland's leading producers and retailers of organic food. There is plenty of time outside of the community participation to wander the lonely shorelines nearby.

ON YOUR DOORSTEP

This stretch of the Aberdeenshire coast is lined with dune-flanked sandy strands. Within easy driving distance east is Elgin with its magnificent 13th-century ruined cathedral, while west is Inverness, gateway to the fabulous hiking and climbing opportunities of the Scottish Highlands.

$ *Week-long community experience from £250*
🍽 *Quinoa and mixed bean salads, home-made hummus*

☛ *The Park, Findhorn, Forres*
+44 (0)1309 691 653
www.findhorn.org

UNITED KINGDOM

GAIA HOUSE

● *Silent walking and sitting meditations in a historic, listed building*
● *Peaceful strolls amid blooming gardens in the South Devon countryside*

The first surprise at Gaia House is that a silent meditation retreat isn't strictly silent. Or, as one of the coordinators puts it: 'No one will mind if you quietly ask someone in the kitchen where the vegetable peeler is.' The second surprise is that the silence doesn't begin from the moment you arrive. Of course, conversations are involved when retreat guests arrive and register (generally between 2pm and 5pm) and settle in to their rooms. These are usually shared, dorm-style, but requests on health grounds for single rooms are considered. Some teachers will encourage 10 non-stop minutes of chat as a way of preparing and then perhaps say something like 'now let's introduce silence'. And you're off. Into your own head space. Which might sound daunting in a new and strange environment, where you don't know where things are…but…

The third surprise is how well this is catered for at Gaia House: there are labels and instructions on everything you could think of. You can leave notes for teachers and vice versa. There is still a sense of connection and communication. In fact, on group retreats there are regular (verbal) teachings and guidance as part of the program, which is especially helpful for newcomers. Schedules are posted of timetables for sitting meditations, walking meditations through the beautiful grounds, duty rosters (there's a one-hour work period each day to help look after the house and grounds) and meal times. Ease yourself in with the one-day Meditation Day: Finding Peace in a Changing World, then build up to the six-day Meditation and Mindfulness in Daily Life.

ON YOUR DOORSTEP
The point of the silent meditation retreat is to not go exploring out into the louder world (there is a gradual transition at the end of the retreat), and the grounds around Gaia House make for delightful walks.

$ *6-day Meditation & Mindfulness in Daily Life retreat from £280pp*
|◉| *Choice of vegetarian, vegan and dairy- and gluten-free options*

☛ *West Ogwell, Newton Abbot, Devon*
+44 (0) 1626 333613
www.gaiahouse.co.uk

WHY PRACTISE SILENT MEDITATION?

"Spending time on a silent retreat creates the space to let go of the everyday habitual ways of thinking and acting that perpetuate stress. We have a chance to learn how we can make life difficult for us and those around us, and so develop resilience and a kinder approach to ourselves and our relationships, allowing for greater ease and contentment."
Devin Ashwood, Director, Gaia House

UNITED KINGDOM

SHARPHAM HOUSE

● *Learn about mindfulness in a Palladian villa*
● *Mindful singing, cooking and walks in nature*

As you take the first steps towards achieving inner peace and harmony through cultivating a mindfulness practice, it certainly helps to be surrounded by a naturally beautiful, inspiring and calm environment. Ticking all these boxes, and more, is Sharpham House, a late 18th-century Palladian villa sitting elegantly in Capability Brown–designed gardens and offering commanding views over the Dart Valley.

Straight from a Jane Austen novel, this grand house offers a magnificent central stairwell twisting up to a domed ceiling and a superb selection of private rooms (most sharing bathrooms). It belongs to the Sharpham Trust, a charity that strives to connect people with nature, and foster mindfulness and wellbeing. Throughout the year a series of retreats and courses, each with a foundation in teaching mindfulness, are hosted at Sharpham House itself, in the more modest, but still comfortable Barn (used for week-long retreats with a focus on meditation and community living), or in tents within the estate's lush woodlands.

Retreats can be focused purely on mindfulness but Sharpham's speciality is applying the practice's principles to a range of activities including yoga, writing, vegetarian cooking, choral singing and appreciation of nature. Among the most popular of the themed retreats are the ones where mindfulness is paired with hikes through the estate (which includes a vineyard, farm and serene natural burial ground), along the rugged Devon coast and across the stark majesty of Dartmoor.

ON YOUR DOORSTEP

Sharpham borders the picturesque market town of Totnes where the high street climbs to a hilltop castle and medieval priory, and a new age, alternative vibe is cultivated. A free-thinking, creative attitude also reigns at the nearby Dartington Hall, which has splendid gardens.

$ *Mindfulness retreats £375–450*
¶●¶ *Locally sourced, seasonal vegetarian food*

☞ *Ashprington, Totnes, Devon*
+ 44 (0) 01803 732542
www.sharpham trust.org

THE ART OF MINDFULNESS

"Mindfulness encourages awareness of ourselves and all that surrounds us. When we walk with that greater awareness, we notice our increased levels of fitness and wellbeing. With a steady focus on our senses, we might hear and see more than we would normally. This often leads to a greater appreciation of and a reconnection to our natural world."
Linda Vincent, Walking Retreat Leader, Sharpham House

UNITED STATES
LUMERIA MAUI

● *Meditate to the rising sun* ● *Enjoy the benefits of therapeutic, devotional yoga*
● *Relax in the seaside hills of the Hawaiian countryside*

Lumeria has at its heart a vision to capture the true essence of Hawaii by providing a mindful alternative to the conventional resort holiday. The property, which was completed in 1910, has been beautifully reconceived from the sugar plantation era and blessed by shamans, providing an ideal backdrop for the retreat's offerings – from yoga and hula classes to sound therapy and horticulture, as well as island-wide adventures like riding and cycling.

Its inland location in the verdant hills above Maui's North Shore creates an inclusive, interactive group dynamic at the retreat. Guest rooms are modern and earthy, and the on-site restaurant boasts a farm-to-table gourmet menu, with much of the produce sourced on the resort. The yoga classes take advantage of expansive ocean and valley views, and sunrise meditation provides a perfect start to an enlightened day.

ON YOUR DOORSTEP

Lumeria sits between the historic plantation towns of Paia and Makawao. A rustic seaside town, Paia is a favourite among artists, off-the-beaten-path travellers and locals. Makawao, known as Upcountry Maui, is famous for its Hawaiian cowboys.

$ *Garden King Room from US$256 (inclusive of organic breakfast and access to all classes and activities)*
|◉| *Clean, nutritious, farm-to-table cuisine*

☛ *Makawao, Hawaii*
+1 808 579 887 724
www.lumeria
maui.com

● **Yoga** ● **Meditation**

UNITED STATES
KRIPALU CENTER FOR YOGA & HEALTH

● *Retreats focusing on different meditation practices*
● *Variety of yoga forms offered, from therapeutic to kundalini*

Kripalu is located in the forested hills of the Berkshire Mountains in Massachusetts and offers a raft of programs and workshops incorporating yoga, ayurveda, self-discovery and meditation. It is more a school than a spa resort, and offers training in ayurveda nutrition and yoga teaching. If you just want to relax and do a little yoga for a few days, it also offers a basic R&R Retreat that includes meals, yoga classes, workshops and evening events.

Kripalu provides a daily schedule and you can stick to it as much or as little as you want. So, for example, you might do a morning yoga class, an afternoon workshop on ayurveda, the noontime Kripalu YogaDance class, then an evening cookery class. Meanwhile, to make your retreat as spa-like as possible, you can enjoy the sauna, fitness room, hiking trails and lakefront beach in the summer.

ON YOUR DOORSTEP

Amid the Berkshire Mountains, Kripalu is a good base for the Tanglewood Music Festival, Jacob's Pillow dance centre and the Berkshire Theater Festival, which are all booming in summer when there are also lots of options for lake swimmers and hikers. In the winter, the mountains are criss-crossed with ski trails.

$ *Weekend stay, private bath (includes all retreat programs) from US$636*
|◉| *All-natural buffet with ayurvedic choices*

☛ *Stockbridge, Massachusetts*
+1 866 200 5203
https://kripalu.org

UNITED STATES
SIVANANDA YOGA RANCH

● *Sivananda classical yoga classes for beginners to advanced*
● *Silent meditation, mantra chanting and contemporary spiritual lectures held twice daily*

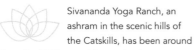

Sivananda Yoga Ranch, an ashram in the scenic hills of the Catskills, has been around since the 1970s, providing a classic yoga retreat for people interested in meditation, contemplation, rest and relaxation. At Sivananda, you practise not just hatha yoga (the physical postures that make up a yoga class), but karma yoga or the yoga of good works. While it isn't a requirement, visitors may choose to volunteer at the ashram: cooking, cleaning, gardening, or even just answering the phone and maybe sweeping the temple.

There are 28-day yoga teacher training courses, although the majority of visitors come for either a week or a weekend. Yoga and meditation are offered twice a day, though no activity is mandatory, so you can feel free to take things at your own pace and just relax.

The Yoga Ranch is strictly vegetarian: meat, poultry, fish and eggs are not allowed on the grounds. Neither are garlic and onions, which are not part of the yogic diet. If you want to immerse yourself in your yoga practice with other devoted yogis, while minimising the distractions of electronics and the modern world, then Sivananda is an excellent choice for a wellness break. Simple, humble, calm and pure, it is truly mindful.

ON YOUR DOORSTEP
The Catskill Mountains, famous for family resorts in the 1950s and '60s, remains a destination locale for hikers, climbers, rafters and skiers, depending on the season. This is the place to be outdoors!

$ *1-night stay in a single room approx US$130*
❙❍❙ *Local produce, all-vegetarian cuisine*

☛ Woodbourne, New York
+1 845 436 6492
https://sivananda yogaranch.org

ASHRAM
in the Catskills

"Every day at Sivananda has been structured the same since the beginning. In this ashram, we know how well yoga in its classical way works. We don't have any need to change because it is suitable for all people of all ages in all conditions. It always works."
Swami Paramananda, Manager at Sivananda Yoga Ranch

UNITED STATES
SPIRIT ROCK

● *Sitting, walking, eating and working meditation* ● *Mindfulness and dharma talks*
● *Mindful yoga and yoga teacher training*

Spirit Rock sits a 45-minute drive and a world away from San Francisco: ditch the hectic metropolis for the quiet, oak wood-coated hills and learn to look into your inner self at this leading California meditation retreat. The 166-hectare (411-acre) bucolic tract of West Marin County provides plenty of space for introspection and reflection, and offers teachings, talks and courses subscribing to Buddhist thinking. All technology, and even wearing fragrance or reading a book, are discouraged at Spirit Rock in an effort to get guests focusing on just being.

Meditation, practised in various guises and settings from walking through to eating, provides the thrust of the day's activities. At the heart of your training and development here is dharma, the Indian principle of being, in relation to life and universe as practised in Buddhism and Hinduism. Yoga teacher training is also offered, as are in-depth day-long and multi-day courses, combining meditation techniques with mindfulness, breathing exercises and spiritually oriented lectures and debates.

Guests, or 'retreatants', as they are known here, are invited to help out with the day-to-day duties of running Spirit Rock, such as cooking and cleaning. Spirit Rock comes as close to the way of thinking and living of an Asian Buddhist monastery as is possible in California and accordingly, the longer you stay here and stay switched off from the grid, the more enriched your spirit could become.

ON YOUR DOORSTEP
'Frisco is close by for the complete antidote to Spirit Rock. The pulsing city by the bay, where hippie counterculture was born in the flamboyant Haight-Ashbury district, is flanked by the iconic Golden Gate Bridge, the island-prison of Alcatraz and a liberal smattering of urban restaurants, museums and shops.

$ *Day-long mindfulness courses US$30–100*
🍽 *Meals provided on retreat programs; healthy fruit-and-veg-led food*

☛ **Woodacre, San Francisco, California**
+1 415 488 0164
www.spiritrock.org

Healthy

NUTRITION

NATURE

SPA TREATMENTS

● **Nature** ● **Spa Treatments**

ARGENTINA
ARAKUR

● *Hydrotherapy pools filled with glacial meltwater*
● *Admire the end of the world from this spa perched in the wilds of Patagonia*

The world's southernmost city, Ushuaia, where the ragged, brooding, snow-dusted mountains of Tierra del Fuego give way to the notoriously rough waters of the Southern Ocean and, beyond, the eternal whiteness of Antarctica, is not where you might expect to find a luxury hotel and spa. Then along came Arakur in 2014. Dramatically perched above the city, built according to an ultra-modern aesthetic in natural stone and plate glass, and with views out across the Beagle Channel, the hotel looks the business.

Better still, post-hike or pre-cruise, you can take in said view in unhurried fashion from the spa, with its open-air hot tubs and hydrotherapy pool filled with heated rainwater and glacial meltwater – a bizarre feeling indeed this far south. Those intrepid Antarctic explorers of yore certainly never had it this good.

ON YOUR DOORSTEP
Arakur backs on to the quiet trails of the Reserva Natural Cerro Alarkén, a beautiful expanse of *lenga* (southern beech forest), waterfalls and mountains, which tops out at Cerro Alarkén. Strike out alone or hook on to the hotel's guided walks.

$ *Double rooms from US$250*
🍽 *Go for poolside snacks, Argentinian asado (barbecue) or fresh spider crab*

☛ **Ushuaia, Tierra del Fuego**
+54 2901 44 2900
www.arakur.com

AUSTRALIA

GAIA RETREAT & SPA

● *Spa treatments using own-brand products*
● *Organic cooking classes* ● *Subtropical hinterland hideaway*

Over a decade in operation and Gaia is still winning international awards for its holistic wellness programs. Tucked in a pocket of subtropical rainforest near Byron Bay – Australia's wellness hotspot – the retreat is situated in a tranquil spot humming with cicadas. Treatments here make use of the retreat's own organic skincare products, which feature native ingredients such as Kakadu plum, the world's highest-known natural source of vitamin C.

Stay in cabin-style rooms as part of a retreat package or just visit for the day. There's a packed roster of activities offering the flexibility to be as busy or as blissfully still as you wish, and a small army of naturopaths, fitness trainers and other practitioners at hand to guide you through your wellness journey. Be sure to make the short hike to the Samira Yoga Lookout – a favourite of co-founder Olivia Newton-John.

ON YOUR DOORSTEP
The small hamlet of Newrybar is a few minutes' drive away, with its award-winning restaurant, Harvest. Just beyond is the quaint town of Bangalow, while a further 15-minute drive will land you in the famous surf town of Byron Bay.

$ *AU$1145*
for a standard 2-night retreat
I◉I *Homegrown or locally sourced produce*

☛ *Brooklet, NSW*
+61 2 6687 1216
https://gaiaretreat. com.au

IN THE WORDS *of the founder*

"Gaia is my healing place. It's an unpretentious retreat; a place of heart to reconnect with the land and yourself."
Olivia Newton-John
Co-founder and Director, Gaia Retreat & Spa

AUSTRALIA

GWINGANNA

● *Largest spa in the southern hemisphere* ● *Surrounded by ocean and mountain views* ● *Bush walks in subtropical rainforest*

Perched on a forested plateau surrounded by towering trees, Gwinganna's idyllic location is the first hint of this multi-award-winning wellness haven's philosophy. Cocooned from the outside world – and its distractions and vices – the luxurious, eco-certified retreat isn't just designed to help you relax and de-stress, but to evaluate your lifestyle habits, and take conscious steps towards improving them.

Whether you opt for a restorative two-night escape or a seven-day lifestyle reboot, a typical day begins by watching the sun rise over the Pacific Ocean while practising the ancient meditative art of qigong. Guests can then take a hike alongside Gwinganna's resident botanist on one of the 16 trails that lace the 495-acre (200-hectare) property. Following a nourishing organic breakfast, guests are encouraged to choose from a range of yin (inwardly focused) and yang (outwardly

focused) activities before embracing one of the fundamental elements of wellbeing after lunch: rest. You might want to relax in your stylish eco-suite or take a dip in the pool, but for most people, this time is spent in the 33-room spa indulging in a raft of therapies ranging from organic facials to Japanese 'rockupuncture' (acupuncture combined with hot stone massage) to life-coaching sessions.

With guests requested to leave personal food, alcohol, caffeinated drinks, cigarettes, newspapers and ideally also electronic devices at home, Gwinganna sets the stage for the ultimate detox.

ON YOUR DOORSTEP
While it might seem a world away from the tranquillity of Gwinganna, the Gold Coast with its stunning white-sand beaches, countless cafes and emerging gastronomic scene is just a 25-minute drive from the retreat.

$ *2-night all-inclusive retreat AU$1045*
◉ Organic produce from the kitchen garden; menus designed with a nutrionist

---

● *Gold Coast,* **Australia**
+61 7 5589 5000
http://gwinganna.com

WHY EMBARK ON A *wellness escape?*

"There's no set prescription for wellness that works for everyone. Embarking on a wellness retreat, however, provides an opportunity to re-evaluate lifestyle habits that are preventing you from living your best life, and with the help of supportive professionals and a few healthy boundaries, discover sustainable changes you can apply to your own daily routine to get back on track."
Sarah Reid, eco-travel writer and wellness retreat convert

AUSTRALIA

Waldheim Alpine Spa

● *Tranquil spa set in the heart of Tasmania's Cradle Mountain wilderness*
● *Private treatment rooms overlooking mountain streams and King Billy pine trees*

The only spa in Tasmania's remote World Heritage–listed Cradle Mountain–Lake St Clair National Park, Waldheim Alpine Spa is ideal for nature lovers. *Waldheim* is German for 'forest home', and was the name of lodgings built in this area by Austrian naturalist and conservationist Gustav Weindorfer, who emigrated to Australia in 1899. He and his Australian wife strongly campaigned for the government to endorse the area as a national park. And now, if there's anywhere in the world you might spot a wombat shuffling past while relaxing in the spa, this is it.

Treatments can either be incorporated into an overnight accommodation package (the spa is part of the Peppers Cradle Mountain Lodge) or just a casual visit, but definitely book well in advance for the latter. There are a variety of packages that are both invigorating and restorative: Alpine Revival and Tension Tonic or the evocative Deeper Than Deep Hot Stone Massage. The Mountain Dreaming package is popular for its massage, superfood pro-radiance facial and scalp therapy, but treat yourself to the peaceful beauty of the Private Sanctuary for your very own dry-heat sauna, wet steam room, cool plunge pool and exclusive views across Pencil Pine river. Time your trip for winter for the cosiness of the open fireplace in the foyer and the chance to see snow fall while relaxing in a private outdoor hot tub.

ON YOUR DOORSTEP

Take a self-guided walk around Cradle Mountain and Dove Lake, with the opportunity to glimpse Australian wildlife: wallabies, wombats, echidnas and perhaps even a platypus. The lodge also offers guided walks for guests, such as the Native Animal Night Viewing Tour.

$ *90-min Private Sanctuary AU$170*
🍽 *Decadent add-ons include Tasmanian sparkling wine and chocolate-dipped strawberries*

☛ *Cradle Mountain, Tasmania*
+61 3 6492 2133 (spa)
www.cradlemountain
lodge.com.au/
waldheim-alpine-spa

THE HEALTH BENEFITS OF NATURE

Exposure to nature is renowned for its mood-boosting properties. Evidence suggests that it can alleviate symptoms of depression, and improve memory and focus. Studies also show it can have a beneficial effect on hypertension and respiratory problems. The psychological benefits of mountain air and forest environments in particular are said to be significant, especially for reducing stress levels.

AUSTRIA

Ayurveda Resort Sonnhof

● *Ayurvedic massage, scrubs and oil treatments* ● *Austria meets Southern India in ayurvedic wellness cooking* ● *Mood-lifting hikes in the Tyrolean Alps*

Ayurveda might hail from Mother India, but this chakra-cleansing resort has brought it home to the Austrian Alps, adding its own luxurious rifts. Spirit-lifting mountain views, a Garden of Five Elements where you can walk among roses; Buddha statues and ponds; and cooking that utilises spices, garden herbs and produce from the Mauracher family's own farm, all speak of a place in tune with nature. The vibes are good, too: the minute you set foot in this plateau-perched hotel, breathe in the incense and sip a tea tailored to your ayurvedic *dosha* (constitutional type), the stress slides away.

One of Europe's leading centres for ayurvedic medicine and detox, the Sonnhof has a team of therapists specialising in practices such as acupuncture, manual medicine and kinesiology. There is also an on-site 'near-psychic' who will help you determine your balance of *doshas* (*vata*, *pitta* and *kapha*).

With individual therapy plans, no two stays are alike. A day of treatments might involve a relaxing *vishesh* (deep-tissue massage), an invigorating Himalayan salt scrub and a hypnotic *shirodhara* – a procedure where warm oil is poured in a continuous flow across the forehead. In between, there's time to chill in the candlelit Ayurveda Centre, with its moon and sun saunas, indoor pool, infrared cabins, *dosha*-inspired steam chambers and meditation

rooms. There are also classes in practices such as mindful spirit yoga and qigong.

ON YOUR DOORSTEP

Der Berg ruft! The mountain calls! This is Austria's Alpine heartland, with walking trails and skiing galore. Year-round, the trip into fortress-topped Kufstein, set against the mighty backdrop of the Kaisergebirge, is worthwhile. In summer, you can swim in nearby Lake Thiersee.

$ *Day spa €30; double rooms from €260 in low season* ⦿*l Ayurvedic, Austrian, wholesome and healthy*

☞ **Hinterthiersee, Tyrol**
+43 5376 5502
www.sonnhof -ayurveda.at

AUSTRIA
Hotel Theresa

● *Feel the healing powers of the Alps in the Tyrol's Zillertal* ● *Alpine-inspired treatments using herbs, honey and hay* ● *Slow food and all-natural, seasonal produce*

What could be more relaxing than gazing up to Austria's Zillertal Alps from Hotel Theresa's open-air, saltwater hydrotherapy pool? And the meadows where bell-clanging cows graze in summer and cross-country skiers glide through pristine snow in winter never look more beguiling than from a bubble bed pummelling your tight spots. It's a serene prospect and one that fits in neatly with the nature-inspired wellness ethos here.

Waking up each day to the Alps is bound to put a spring in your step. As will the rather fabulous spa with its jetted pools, hot tubs, relaxation areas warmed by open fires, mountain-facing saunas, herbal-scented steam rooms and infrared room. There's a definite nod to the Tyrol in the treatments, from the tension-banishing massages with herbs, arnica and joint-soothing marmot oil to the honey-pine and Alpine hay baths that Heidi would surely have adored.

ON YOUR DOORSTEP
Zell am Ziller is as Tyrolean as villages come, with hiking trails heading off in all directions, slopes swishing with downhill skiers in winter, as well as all kinds of adventurous pursuits – from white-water rafting on the Ziller to paragliding and canyoning.

$ *Day package (including treatments) €149*
🍽 *Healthy, well-balanced buffets with a nod to the Alps*

☞ *Zell am Ziller, Tyrol*
+43 528 222860
www.theresa.at

AUSTRIA

PARK IGLS

● *Mayr fasting and healthy, seasonal meals* ● *Massage and water therapies*
● *Nordic walking, hiking and skiing in the Tyrolean Alps*

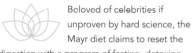

Beloved of celebrities if unproven by hard science, the Mayr diet claims to reset the digestion with a program of fasting, detoxing and relaxation. This clinic, located high in the Austrian Alps, has the bonus of a sensational view across to the Nordkette massif which flings up above the Tyrolean capital, Innsbruck.

Spread across quiet parkland, the open-plan spa adheres to a clean, modern aesthetic that reveals the purist tendencies of its origins as a sanatorium for the elite back when it opened in 1908. The approach is holistic, and guests' diet, physical activity and therapies are carefully monitored and measured. Following a consultation, you're allotted an individual plan that defines your days.

A morning might begin, say, with Epsom salts, a 'detox' breakfast, a warm liver compress and circulation-stimulating Kneipp water treading. Then it's on to treatments, which reach from manual abdominal therapy (a Mayr classic) to acupuncture, sleep diagnostics, deep-tissue massage, thalasso exfoliation and seaweed wraps. Exercise is an integral part of the Mayr philosophy, so the spa aims to get you moving in its indoor pool, panoramic fitness room (check out the muscle-toning kyBoots) and with daily activities from Pilates to Nordic walking. Or you could just opt for a sauna and steam.

ON YOUR DOORSTEP
Embrace the Alps on trails and cross-country tracks leading deep into the mountains and forest. In winter, there's downhill skiing at the local peak of Patscherkofel (7369ft; 2246m). Regular buses go from Igls to Innsbruck, where a medieval Old Town spirals around a Habsburg palace.

$ *1-week basic package €977 for treatments, check-ups and activities*
🍽 *8-stage Mayr diet and light Austrian cuisine*

✈ *Innsbruck-Igls*
+43 512 377305
www.park-igls.at

BHUTAN

COMO UMA PUNAKHA

● *Vistas on to one of Bhutan's lushest valleys, the serene Punakha valley*
● *Smooth heated river-stone massage*

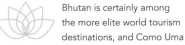

Bhutan is certainly among the more elite world tourism destinations, and Como Uma Punakha has a very exclusive feel. It's the most strikingly located of two Como spa hotels in the country, found tucked away in the unspoilt Punakha valley. This getaway's huge windows maximise the lurid light of the pine-stippled mountainside outside, the scene churned through by the Puna Tsang Chu river. And it is the riverbed stones, heated and pressed into the back for a massage or, in keeping with Bhutanese tradition, dropped into a bath whereupon they supposedly 'release'

their nutrients into bathers' bodies, that are the most locally representative therapies on offer. Afterwards, revel in an exquisite meal at the complex's Bukhari restaurant, with its terrace giving a bird's-eye view of the valley.

ON YOUR DOORSTEP
Unforgettable treks such as the Druk Path trek fan out around the hotel. The Mo Chhu and Samdingkha rivers have sensational white-water rafting. The Gangtey valley, famous for its dwarf bamboo and rare birdlife, is close by too.

$ *Bhutanese blessing ceremony with hot stone massage and dinner US$2424*
🍽 *Bhutanese cuisine, strong on vegetables*

☛ *Botokha Kabesa, Punakha*
+975 8 279 999
www.comohotels. com/umapunakha

BHUTANESE *stone bath*

Many would agree there is nothing better than a long, hot soak to rid yourself of the aches and pains of a hard day. In traditional Bhutanese culture, the most healing water is thought to be fresh river water, known as menchu, which is heated with hot riverbed stones that, upon heating, purportedly release their mineral nutrients. Followers believe it can soothe ailments from stomach disorders to joint complaints.

BRAZIL

LAPINHA

● *Calorie-curated plans based on individual goals* ● *Scenic walking trails on 1360 acres (550 hectares) of land* ● *Alternative medicine-based therapies*

An epic and luxurious destination retreat in the gorgeous Brazilian countryside, Lapinha sits about 55 miles (88km) southwest of Curitiba in green and pleasant grounds edged by striking Araucaria groves. The area is flush with walking trails, organic gardens and meadows complete with grazing cows. A first for its time, the centre was founded by a German immigrant and has been doing its thing since 1972. The ethos here is all about organic food and natural remedies, and the experience begins and ends with an assessment of health and fitness. These are used to tailor five- to seven-day goal-based programs which may include a mix of diet and gastro-, hydro-, biorhythmic- and physio-therapies – to name but a few. It's Brazil's only Mayr clinic as well.

The spa has won numerous destination awards and in Brazil has become the go-to retreat in which to trash bad habits, and churn out a 'new you'.

Highlights include mealtime, where the low-fat, low-salt, vegetarian versions of *feijoada* (Brazil's national dish, but usually loaded down with pork, salt and fat), the outstanding pinion gnocchi, locally produced honey and scrumptious soups are a revelation in both portions and satisfaction. Classes (yoga, Pilates et al) and treatments (over 40, ranging

from traditional massages to water-based therapies) are optional but encouraged.

ON YOUR DOORSTEP
Tiny Lapa, founded in 1769, is one of Paraná's oldest colonial towns. Its cobbled, 14-block historical centre is a lovely, off-the-beaten-path piece of bucolic tradition making for a fun and pleasant place for a stroll. The town is 0.6 miles (1km) north of Lapinha.

$ *5-day packages from US$1615*
🍽 *Organic vegetarian. No caffeine or alcohol*

....

☛ *Lapa, Paraná*
+55 41 3622 1044
www.lapinha.com.br

CANADA

THE AUGUSTINIAN MONASTERY

● *A monastic wellness experience in a 17th-century hospital*
● *Wholesome menus designed to promote mindful eating*

The Augustinian Monastery forms part of Québec City's Hôtel-Dieu complex, a teaching hospital founded in 1637 – one of the oldest in north America. Carrying on the work of the original Augustinian Sisters, the not-for-profit 'healing hotel' invites you to regain balance and stillness through a program of yoga, massage, meditation and nutritious and mindful eating, sometimes in complete silence.

With a well-balanced restaurant menu full of dishes made with fresh, organic ingredients, your body (as well as your soul) will soon feel nourished. By night, rest easy in the restored rooms that once served as cloisters. Bedding made from natural fibres, along with large windows providing peaceful views, make this a supremely comfortable monastic stay.

ON YOUR DOORSTEP
Located in the historic Old Town of Québec City, a Unesco World Heritage site, the retreat is surrounded by 17th-century buildings and streets – perfect for exploring on foot.

$ *4-night Regeneration Stay from $252 per night*
🍽 *Well-balanced, nutritional meals created with contemporary and traditional methods*

☛ *77, rue des Remparts, Québec City*
+1 418 694 1639
www.monastere.ca

WHY PRACTISE
mindful eating?

At the Augustinian Monastery you're encouraged to take your time while eating, whether observing silence during breakfast or enjoying a slow lunch with other guests. Eating slowly and mindfully has been linked to improved digestion, greater satisfaction and lower overall calorie intake.

● **Nature** ● **Spa Treatments**

COLOMBIA
Volcán de Lodo el Totumo

● *Immerse yourself in a natural vat of volcanic mud*
● *Relax with a mud massage and wash-down in the river afterwards*

You guessed correct. A '*volcán*' in Spanish is indeed a volcano, and in this caldera north of Cartagena you can clamber into a natural vat of lukewarm volcanic mud. There are numerous supposed health benefits to doing so, depending on which of the locals congregated about the volcano approach you listen to, but your skin will feel wonderful at the end of it all. A 20-minute immersion in silt is rendered infinitely quirkier by the extra 'treatments' available. On offer are a massage, a mud scrape-off as you leave and a river wash-off at the end, all conducted by attendants who approach you as you descend into the mud. Be warned: the local ladies will insist on you baring all for the scrub-down. The haphazardness with which proceedings are conducted is quintessential South America, but the experience is good fun and, whatever the actual health benefits, you'll feel great.

ON YOUR DOORSTEP
The nearest city is Cartagena (above), one of Colombia's prettiest, most popular destinations. The walled 16th-century Old Town, once one of the Spanish Empire's most treasured strongholds, makes for a magical stay.

$ *Mud bathing in volcano as part of round-trip from Cartagena COP$40,000*
l◉l *Snack stands around the volcano entrance*

☛ *Via al Volcán el Totumo, Santa Catalina, Cartagena*

FINLAND

HERRANKUKKARO

● *Steam off in the world's largest underground wood-smoke sauna*
● *The surrounding islands are Finland at its balmiest*

Herrankukkaro, a traditional wood-built fishing village on the dreamy scattering of islands southwest of Turku, is as quirky and sauna-heavy as Finnish communities get. The sauna has been an essential element of Finnish wellbeing for centuries, used for everything from giving birth to diplomatic negotiations, and the wood-smoke sauna is the First Class of all Finnish saunas: the most traditional kind and atmospheric with birch smoke.

This is the world's largest underground wood-smoke sauna, with a 124-seat capacity and six levels of benches cosily positioned around a pile of wood smoking in the middle. The Finnish believe the benefits of this style of sauna are many – not only is the steam said to be detoxifying, apparently it can even calm your soul! The sauna is one highlight of a settlement proud of its homegrown and foraged food culture, invigorating island activities and peaceful maritime location.

ON YOUR DOORSTEP
Herrankukkaro and the Turku archipelago are a beguiling region of Finland. Take a boat trip between the myriad islands or explore the lonely coastline on foot.

$ *Day package including food, island activities and wood-smoke sauna entry €159 for groups of 10+*
IOI *Homemade Finnish fare*

☛ *Herrankukkaro, Luotojentie, Naantali Rymättylä*
+358 2 515 3300
www.herrankukkaro.fi

LÖYLY: THE SPIRIT *in the steam*

When the Finn next to you tosses water on to the sizzling stones to buffet out steam across the sauna room, there is more to the action than you might think. The steam of a sauna has near-mythical properties in Finnish culture: a cleanser of ills, sure, but a resolver of lovers' dilemmas and a precipitator of spiritual contemplation, too. In fact, the word 'löyly' means both 'steam' and 'spirit' in Finnish.

FINLAND
LÖYLY

● *Practising 'aloneness' in the communal sauna* ● *Embracing nature with a freezing plunge in the Baltic Sea* ● *Responsibly caught fish and reindeer burgers on the menu*

Make no mistake, Mother Nature dictates life in the Finnish capital of Helsinki, where winter brings long hours of darkness and summer endless sunshine bouncing off the surrounding Baltic Sea. Only the custom of the sauna regulates life through the seasons. The ritual – both an embracing of nature and a defiant fist-shake in its face – reflects the affinity Finns have for their environment. Similarly, Helsinki's contemporary public sauna, Löyly, keeps you close to the elements. The angular hill-like structure is made from silvery birch wood and sits crouched on the shoreline of the up-and-coming neighbourhood of Hernesaari. Here in the soothing gloom,

stripped of clothes and status, and embraced by tendrils of steam (*löyly*), you can gaze out at the shimmering Baltic and practise your *omissa oloissaan* ('aloneness with one's thoughts').

ON YOUR DOORSTEP

Helsinki enjoys 80 miles (130km) of coastline and over a third of the city is given over to green spaces. Summer's white nights can just as easily be spent swimming at Hietaniemi beach as attending a symphony at the Music Centre in Töölönlahti.

$ *2-hour sauna session €19 (swimwear required)*
!◉! *Lean, mean reindeer-meat burgers*

☛ *Helsinki*
+358 9 6128 6550
www.loylyhelsinki.fi

FRANCE
Sofitel Quiberon Diététique

● *Rejuvenating seawater treatments, luxurious massages and saltwater immersion*
● *Rooms with sea views* ● *Low-calorie seafood-based meals*

Warming up saltwater to unleash the magic of the sea has long been en vogue in France, and the country's premier spa retreat is best known for its elite roster of clientele that reads like the guest list at George Clooney's wedding. Strung along a craggy promenade on the Presqu'île de Quiberon (Quiberon Peninsula), the Sofitel has two neighbouring properties that champion thalassotherapy – the practice of using seawater to promote wellness.

Guests on the sea and spa side of the complex enjoy more resort-like pursuits; those with a more rigorous approach to spa-ing head to the so-called Centre Diététique for a wholly immersive health experience that aims to recalibrate the body from head to toe.

A cream-coloured bathrobe is your de facto uniform as you move between appointments, all of which make use of the trademark seawater. Try a cleansing hose-down, a shallow pool massage or just a nice long soak in a salt-water jacuzzi. There are also skincare consultations and hypnotherapy is available for clients hoping to curb bad habits.

Afterwards, guests are sent to the dedicated restaurant serving low-calorie fare. The tenets of French cuisine – bread, butter and cream – aren't the stars of the dinner table here. Instead, perfectly prepared seafood is the main attraction. Although calories and protein-to-veg ratios are carefully calculated for meals, diners hardly feel as though they're sacrificing taste for the sake of getting trim.

ON YOUR DOORSTEP
In addition to the famed 'Thalassa' retreats dotting its mid-Atlantic shores, Brittany is known for its dramatic tides and purple-tinged twilight that has long lured artists to its coastline. Pont Aven, nearby, was Paul Gauguin's stomping ground before he ventured to Tahiti.

$ *Approx €300 per night; €3000 for a 6-day package*
🍽 *Seafood that's full-flavoured but low in calories*

☛ **Quiberon, Brittany**
+33 2 97 50 20 00
www.sofitel.com/gb/hotel-0562-sofitel-quiberon-dietetique

GERMANY
FRIEDRICHSBAD BADEN-BADEN

● *Thermal water and invigorating soap scrubs in opulent Roman-Irish baths*
● *Rambles in the fresh air of the Black Forest on the fringes of Baden-Baden*

As Mark Twain put it, 'after 10 minutes you forget time; after 20 minutes, the world'. As you slip into the regime of steaming, scrubbing, dunking and hot-cold bathing at this Roman-Irish bath in Baden-Baden – the chic spa town in southwest Germany whose very name encourages you to strip off and bathe with reckless abandon – you'll soon be feeling the same. The hot springs here bubble 3937ft (1200m) to the Earth's surface at temperatures of between 132.8°F (56°C) and 155.8°F (68.8°C) and have been used for bathing since the beauty-conscious Romans liked to splash around in them some 2000 years ago.

Modesty? Leave it in the changing room. The Germans are famously nonchalant about nudity and, trust us, no one bats an eyelid at bare bottoms and wobbly bits here. There are 17 carefully timed steps to spa-going heaven at the Friedrichsbad, whisking you on a circuit from ice-cold plunge pools to jetted tubs, mist-filled rooms tiled in exquisite Majolica

(painted ceramic) and a steam room fired entirely by geothermal energy – cool or what? Then there's the icing on the cake: a whopping great neoclassical dome of a pool, buttressed by marble columns, where you can float as sunlight filters softly down, just as genteel folk did when the bath first opened 140 years ago.

ON YOUR DOORSTEP
On the fringes of Germany's Black Forest and close to the French border, Baden-Baden is a cultured town, with art-nouveau villas spread across its hillsides, a riverside park for strolling, a palatial casino and Museum Frieder Burda showing Picasso, Pollock and Miró originals.

$ *3½-hour spa entry including soap-brush scrub €37*
I◉I *Nearby Kaffeesack does great coffee and snacks*

☛ *Baden-Baden,*
Friedrichsbad
www.carasana.de
+49 7221 275920

SCRUB-A-DUB-DUB

No visit to the Friedrichsbad is complete without the famous Seifenbürstenmassage. Don't go expecting some relaxing treatment, however: this is eight minutes precisely of vigorous, circulation-boosting scrubbing with soap and a bristle brush – all performed unceremoniously on a marble slab by confident, matronly hands. You'll leave feeling loose all over and with skin so clean it squeaks.

GERMANY

VILLA STÉPHANIE

● *Medical therapies delivered by some of the best German specialists*
● *Bespoke, balanced diets devised by qualified nutritionists*

Part of the hyper-exclusive Oetker brand, Brenners Park Hotel is a grand five-star spa hotel in Germany's most famous spa town. More recently, the hotel opened Villa Stéphanie, an intimate, 15-bedroom sanctuary dedicated to detoxing over-achieving global nomads who flock here for the state-of-the-art medical facilities and top-notch practitioners.

Dr Harry König leads the Formula 1 team of medical specialists who conduct a 360-degree assessment of your overall health. Then guests are dispatched for appropriate treatment with cardiologists, gynaecologists, physiotherapists and even aesthetic dentists. Complementing the hard sciences are alternative therapies aimed at combating stress, anxiety and fatigue.

As the focus is very much on preventative healthcare, personal trainers help to devise fitness programs that guests can integrate into their daily lives back home. Activities include not only yoga, but also kickboxing, Nordic walking, strength and figure training, and mental training. In fact, simply swimming in the delightful pool overlooking the hotel's private park through the floor-to-ceiling windows is detox enough for many guests.

But before it all starts to sound too clinical and demanding, consider the spoiling spa menu. Rather than being seen as an indulgence, bespoke massages (always with the same therapist), facials and therapeutic

stretching sessions are considered an essential feature of each wellness package.

ON YOUR DOORSTEP

Baden-Baden is an affluent, culturally rich town. You can see stunning contemporary art at the Museum Frieder Burda and, in autumn, the town hosts the world-class Festspielhaus music festival. The Black Forest is also on the doorstep and a perfect place for walks and bike rides.

$ *7-night Classic Detox retreat £2930pp full-board*
🍽 *Fine, innovative European dining*

☛ **Schillerstraße 4/6, Baden-Baden**
+49 7221 9000
http://oetker collection.com

GREECE

OUT OF THE BLUE, CAPSIS ELITE RESORT

● *Consultation with a clinical nutritionist*
● *Rejuvenating heat treatments in the hydrotherapy pool*

While spending time on a Greek Island might conjure up images of sun-soaked indulgent splendour, why not reset your intentions and dedicate your time away to healthy self-improvement. Just looking at Crete's exotic Out of the Blue, Capsis Elite Resort, set on its own private peninsula, might have you thinking cocktails rather than smoothies, but the resort specialises in several wellness aspects that promise an uplifting experience.

The Euphoria Rejuvenating Spa experiences allow for your treatments to be taken outside in the lush botanical garden settings. There's also a clinical nutritionist at hand for a consultation or you might just want a Cretan chocolate treatment (it involves you being wrapped in a carob and honey mask). And if you couldn't escape the family on this trip, there's even a nutritional program for kids and adolescents, which involves a medical examination with a pathologist, daily activities and cooking lessons with the whole family. The six-day Yoga & Organic Food retreat is popular. It includes all organic meals (most vegetables and herbs are grown on site), two daily outdoor yoga classes, a body massage, a wellness capsule session and three heat treatments in the hydrotherapy pool and hammam, along with nutritional consultations and access to the weekly fitness program.

ON YOUR DOORSTEP
A little further around Crete's coast (about a half hour's drive east) is Peskesi restaurant, founded by Dr Panagiotis Magganas, a researcher of Cretan gastronomy for over a decade. This restaurant champions the nutritional value of products from the Cretan land.

$ *6-day Yoga & Organic Food retreat from €999 per person (excluding accommodation)*
!●! *Organic, locally sourced produce; optional 2-day raw food program*

☛ **Heraklion, Crete**
+30 2810 811 112
www.capsis.com

BENEFITS OF *yoga outdoors*

It might seem counter-intuitive to practise yoga outdoors – isn't nature distracting? – but, on the contrary, fans say it can actually heighten awareness. Studies have also shown that spending time in nature can restore your energy reserves and attention span.

GREECE

PORTO ELOUNDA GOLF & SPA RESORT

● *Locally inspired scrubs with Cretan sea salt and olive oil*
● *Outside the window, the Med fans out with Crete's best watersports possibilities*

On Greece's largest island, Crete, stands one of the country's biggest and best wellness resorts. Close to the coastal village of Elounda, patronised by celebrity holidaymakers including the Saudi Arabian Royal Family, Porto Elounda stands out even by the area's luxurious accommodation standards. In this enclave, comprising a golf resort flanked by villas, suites and spacious rooms with terraces gazing out to sea, it is possible to have a seaside workout at the gym, scuba dive, yacht, waterski or wakeboard, play tennis or recline on the resort's own expanse of sandy beach.

But perhaps more than any other aspect of Porto Elounda, it is the Six Senses spa that has won the greatest acclaim. The spectrum of wellness offerings is broad, and often accompanied by first-class fitness instruction. The spa uses Apivita products made with extracts from Greece's native plants such as jasmine, fig, olive oil and Cretan sea salt. There's also the chance to have a Cleopatra-style bath with added aromatherapy oils and salt in with the milk. There are olive stone exfoliations, too. The spa is also big on ayurvedic therapies: marma massage, shiatsu and abyhang fusion. Or try an enriching dabble in algotherapy: deep cleansing using algae, in which you can be wrapped if you so desire.

ON YOUR DOORSTEP
Crete is a large island, and Elounda, nearby, is a gorgeous destination with plenty to amuse. The harbour and restaurants will waylay you long enough, and the nearby former leper colony at Spinalonga retains striking vestiges from its stints under Venetian and then Ottoman rule, including an impressive fortress.

$ *3-day Sense of Detox program including algotherapy €250*
◉| *8 restaurants to choose from at the complex*

....

☞ *Elounda, Crete*
+30 2841 068 000
www.porto elounda.com

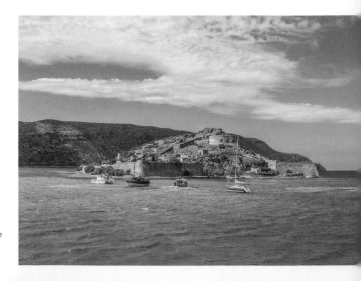

● **Nature** ● **Spa Treatments**

HUNGARY
Hotel Spa Hévíz

● *Rejuvenating mud wraps and medical massages*
● *The world's largest geothermal lake set in a national park*

Lake Hévíz is the largest active geothermal lake in the world and sits in a volcanic crater atop a bacteria-rich peat bed. Fed by hot and cold springs, the lake maintains a soothing 77–96°F (25–36°C) between winter and summer. Locals believe the water's rich mineral content – including carbonic acid, calcium, sulphur and magnesium – and its blue and green algae (including spirulina major) have a healing effect. Whether that's true or not, noone can deny it certainly feels nice.

Hungarians have been coming here since Roman times, and in the 12th century a balneotherapy spa and health centre was established. St Andrews Hospital perches in the middle of the lake on stilts. Here you can seek out massages, mud wraps and hydrotherapy treatments or just join the ageing clientele sunbathing on the deck.

ON YOUR DOORSTEP
The nearby city of Keszthely is one of the most charming bordering Lake Balaton with a baroque-style castle to explore along with the aristocratic home of Earl György Festetics, the originator of the first Hévíz medical centre.

$ *All-day admission to the lake 3700HUF*
🍴 *Local Hungarian restaurants in Hévíz town*

☛ *Lake Hévíz,*
+36 83 501 708
http://hotelspaheviz.hu

HUNGARY

Széchenyi Baths

- ● *Thermal pools of increasing hotness*
- ● *Deep-tissue Swedish massage by experienced therapists*

The largest spa city in Europe, Budapest sits atop a cauldron of 120 thermal springs, which feed 160 public baths. The most famous of them is Széchenyi Baths, which looks like a baroque palace. It houses 15 indoor pools and three enormous outdoor pools, one of which is for swimming while the other two steaming thermal pools feature jacuzzi jets and a pounding massage waterfall. Here you'll find Hungarian retirees passing the hours playing games of chess on floating boards.

Interior pools vary in temperature up to 104°F (40°C), although the hottest bath is only recommended for 20 minutes. Alongside are saunas and steam cabins and you can book a variety of massages with experienced therapists.

ON YOUR DOORSTEP

Budapest is a beautiful *fin de siècle* city rich in baroque, neoclassical and art-nouveau architecture. Of particular note are the Great Synagogue, the Hungarian National Museum and the views from the dome of St Stephen's basilica.

$ *Admission, cabin and 60-minute Royal Thermal massage €87*
🍽 *There's a canteen or you can bring a picnic*

☛ *Budapest*
+36 1 363 3210
www.szechenyibath.hu

ICELAND

BLUE LAGOON

● *Spa bathing in mineral-rich water amid a black lava field*
● *Skin-nourishing white silica mud masks* ● *Massages on a floating mattress*

There is something surreal about the scene: bathers caked in white-silica mud masks bobbing around in a vast milky blue pool while lifeguards stand by clad in balaclavas and goose-down jackets. But then again, everything is extraordinary at the Blue Lagoon.

The spa is fed by piping hot water from the futuristic Svartsengi geothermal plant, its silver towers blowing clouds of steam above you. There's hardly a tree in sight and the scarred black lava fields contrast dramatically against the bright blue of the pools, which are superheated to 100°F (38°C). Rich in blue-green algae, mineral salts and fine silica mud, the water is purportedly nourishing for the skin. Slather yourself in the silica and algae mud masks and you emerge with cheeks as soft as a baby's bum.

Beside the pools, an enormous modern complex houses hot-pots, steam rooms, a sauna and a piping-hot waterfall that delivers a powerful hydraulic massage. A VIP section has its own wading space, lounge and viewing platform; and, for extra relaxation you can lie on a floating bed and have a deep-tissue massage.

There's a swim-up lagoon bar and a cafe serving light bites, as well as the fine dining LAVA restaurant where you can nibble on birch-and-juniper-cured arctic char. Imminent is the opening of The Retreat, a new five-star hotel with an underground spa carved out of an 800-year-old, moss-covered lava flow.

ON YOUR DOORSTEP

Downtown Reykjavik is an easy 45-minute drive away and offers one of Europe's hippest city scenes with creative dining and wild nightlife. Don't miss the excellent Reykjavik Art Museum and whale- and puffin-watching trips are available at the Old Harbour.

$ *Ticket including mud mask, algae mask and reservation at LAVA restaurant ISK9990*
❢❶❙ *Fish-focused contemporary Icelandic cuisine*

☛ *Grindavik*
+354 420 8800
www.bluelagoon.com

INDONESIA
Como Shambhala Estate

● *The entire spectrum of treatments from massage to crystals*
● *Lush jungle setting* ● *Nutritionally balanced dining*

Tucked away from Bali's tourist crowds in a tranquil 56-acre (23-hectare) rainforest, Como Shambhala Estate is the ultimate wellness oasis. A 'retreat for change' by its own definition, the luxury hotel brand's flagship property, which combines holistic wellness with state-of-the-art facilities, is still considered one of the world's finest heath resorts more than a decade after opening. You can book a beautifully appointed suite in one of the stunning freestanding 'residences' by the night if you wish, which includes access to the estate's spa facilities, fitness centre, and participation in daily scheduled activities – from Pilates to guided nature walks, yoga to aqua circuit training – but Como's real star is its individually tailored wellness programs.

Available for three to 14 nights, Como's six programs range from an intensive cleanse including targeted nutrition, daily therapies and specific exercises, to an oriental medicine regime using techniques such as acupuncture, herbal medicine, nutritional therapy and meditation.

With fresh, nutritionally balanced dining available at two on-site restaurants – all-day dining restaurant, Glow, and Kudus House where breakfast and dinner are served in a 150-year-old former Javanese residence – you needn't leave the property during your stay. Once you stumble upon the natural springwater pool hidden amongst the luscious tree ferns, you might not even want to.

ON YOUR DOORSTEP
It's just a 10-minute drive south to Bali's cultural heart of Ubud with its temples, art galleries, boutiques and excellent cafes and restaurants. The crowds can be a little confronting after leaving the serene sanctuary of the Estate, however.

$ *US$600 for 1 night*
❍ *Opt for light and nutritious or more indulgent Indonesian-inspired cuisine*

....

☛ *Ubud, Bali*
+62 361 978 888
www.como
shambhala.com

● **Nutrition**   ● **Spa Treatments**

INDONESIA

FIVELEMENTS

● *Gourmet raw food packed with flavour and nutrients*
● *Slather your skin in superfood-powered facials*

Fivelements is a luxury wellness resort in Bali. The retreat packages here are rooted in the principles of raw vegan cuisine, and the rituals and sacred arts of traditional Balinese culture.

Banish any ideas of boring salads, the award-winning Sakti Dining Room elevates raw vegetables into gourmet dishes that are as beautiful and tasty as they are nutritious. The show-stopping lasagna features pasta-thin layers of zucchini, mushrooms and tomatoes smothered with dairy-free cashew cheese, pesto and tomato sauce. There's also fresh juices and guilt-free desserts. If you're inspired, sign up for a culinary lesson to learn the secrets of the raw food chefs. You might never crave cooked food again.

Continue your renewal at the spa. It takes classic treatments to the next level, concocting facial serums out of superfoods, and offering luxurious massages with the added touch of a traditional Balinese energy healer. Rigorous body scrubs start with a foot bath ritual and end with a soak in a flower-filled tub overlooking the Ayung river.

You can try out more creative arts such as Aikido, painting and, of course, yoga practice. And, if you fancy seeing all your earthly cares and worries go up in smoke, you can also participate in a traditional Balinese fire blessing ceremony.

ON YOUR DOORSTEP
Property-wide meditation music (projected from speakers discreetly tucked into stones along the footpaths) sets a soothing background for lingering strolls around the lush, riverside property, which blooms with medicinal herbs and plants.

$ *5-day Signature Rejuvenation Retreat from 56,830,000Rp*
🍽 *Plant-based, mostly raw foods*

☞ **Mambal, Bali**
+62 361 469 260
www.fivelements.org

● **Nutrition** ● **Spa Treatments**

INDONESIA
ONEWORLD AYURVEDA

● *Ayurvedic diet customised for each client*
● *A mind-boggling array of treatments based on ayurvedic tradition*

Ayurveda believers advocate maintaining harmony between body, mind and spirit through a proper combination of the elements of air, fire, water and earth. Diet programs at this spa are specifically crafted to balance these elements

Days begin with a gong and some ayurvedic medicine, followed by meditation and yoga practice, all before breakfast. In between meals and spa treatments, guests are invited to take part in cooking demonstrations, meditation classes, guided walks through the surrounding rice paddies and discussions about health and wellbeing. Rooms are exquisite, each with private balconies overlooking the surrounding jungle and rice terraces. The overall vibe at Oneworld is one of serenity and healing, and the staff do their best to ensure each visitor experiences maximum relaxation.

ON YOUR DOORSTEP
Oneworld sits next to the Tegallalang rice fields, about 5 miles (8km) from the town of Ubud. The grounds contain a permaculture herbal garden, a yoga *shala* (studio) and swimming pool, as well as bamboo forests and several tropical gardens.

$ *10-day all-inclusive Panchakarma Retreat 51,480,000Rp*
🍽 *Fully ayurvedic meals with flavours combined to promote balance*

☛ *Ubud, Bali*
+62 361 289 752
www.oneworld
ayurveda.com

● **Nutrition**   ● **Nature**   ● **Spa Treatments**

INDONESIA
Ubud Sari

● *Raw-food classes and tropical-juice fasting* ● *Dawn walks and herb-education trails in the resort's gardens* ● *Therapeutic massage and traditional treatments*

Raw food proponents claim it's no fad diet, more a way of life, and on tropical Bali there's such an overflowing swag bag of fresh fruit and veg that it's easy to see why raw food has become a trend in island homes and restaurants.

Ubud Sari designs its retreat programs to give participants the practical know-how to achieve a raw-food lifestyle, complemented by colonics, juice fasting, energising yoga and submersion in nature and Balinese culture. Although this comfortable health resort is within walking distance of Ubud's lively centre, you'd never know it: Mother Nature looks

like she's on steroids in Sari's lush gardens, cocooned within a heavenly circle of paddy fields, palm trees and rainforest. Nutrition is the main focus at Sari – above all, come for the hands-on classes in raw-food preparation.

ON YOUR DOORSTEP
Ubud is the beating heart of Balinese culture, with crumbling temples to explore, a surprising local food scene and scores of artisan shops. It lies within the island's jungle-cloaked interior, woven with emerald-coloured paddy fields and serene walking trails.

$ *Raw Health Rejuvenation Week package US$1500*
🍽 *Raw food and vegan*

☛ *Ubud, Bali*
+62 361 974 393
www.ubudsari.com

IRELAND

KILCULLEN'S SEAWEED BATHS

● *Seaweed and saltwater steam baths in faded Edwardian grandeur*
● *Bracing, spirit-lifting hiking and surfing on Ireland's wild Atlantic coast*

You've most likely heard of the benefits of seaweed in the context of fancy, new-fangled spa treatments, right? Well, you might be in for a surprise in Enniscrone on the wave-battered northwest coast of Ireland. The Kilcullen family proudly opened the doors of their whitewashed bathhouse on the seafront in 1912, and five generations later here they still are, harvesting the wrack from the beach at low tide and pumping in water fresh from the Atlantic every day. The Edwardian baths might have been the height of modernity at the time, but now they are a glorious blast from the past, with their huge cast-iron tubs and tiled chambers.

Flash it isn't, but this good old-fashioned treatment is grand for giving the body a spring clean. And unlike most spas, there's no looking at the clock here: take all the time you wish, soaking at leisure in the hot, green, saltwater bath after emptying in a bucket of seaweed. Slimy? 'Silky' is perhaps more the word you're looking for. Such briny bliss is rivalled only by the steam chamber: a glorified cupboard with a cut-out hole for your head so you can inhale the clouds of salt vapours. So far, so relaxing. But this is Ireland, after all, so don't think you're getting off that lightly. Before you leave, it's time for a freezing-cold saltwater shower to leave you as soft as a newborn's bottom and tingling from head to toe.

ON YOUR DOORSTEP
This is a cracking corner of Ireland for coastal rambles along the wind-lashed Wild Atlantic Way (www.wildatlanticway.com). With big horizons and bracing air, all the joy here is outdoors, whether you're striding along clifftops, kitesurfing or horseriding along Enniscrone's 3-mile (5km) arc of sandy beach.

$ *Seaweed and steam baths €25*
🍽 *Try Clare Island organic salmon at Áit Eile*

☞ *Enniscrone, Co Sligo*
+353 963 6238
www.kilcullen seaweedbaths.net

● Nature ● Spa Treatments

IRELAND
VOYA SEAWEED BATHS

● *Long soaks in vitamin-rich water* ● *Seaweed-filled tubs providing skin treatments*
● *Find some calm staring at the windswept beach town of Strandhill*

Voya's bathing products are found in boutique hotels all over Ireland, but the family business is headquartered in tiny Strandhill near the town of Sligo.

Its day spa offers a variety of wellness treatments, but specialises in a signature hour-long seaweed soak. In a private bathing chamber, guests' pores are gently opened with generous amounts of steam, then they take to their claw-footed bathtub where they cover themselves in a steeping vegetal assortment of ochres, browns and greens, emerging an hour later with dolphin-like skin.

The marine plants are certified organic and sustainably harvested by hand along the most remote recesses of Ireland's western coast. Voya claims the plants leach nutrients into the bath, creating a vitamin-rich bathing experience that supposedly provides improvements to the texture and suppleness of skin and hair.

ON YOUR DOORSTEP
A laid-back California beach town plunked down on windswept Irish waters, Strandhill is perfect for a spot of surfing at the local wave-riding school, followed by lunch at Shells Cafe.

$ *Baths from €28*

☛ **Strandhill, Co Sligo**
+353 71 916 8686
www.voyaseaweed
baths.com

Shake it up: Smoothie Recipes to Get your Day Started

Smoothies are a great way to pack in some nutrients when you're short on time, as long as you're limiting sugar intake and including healthy natural ingredients. Try these delicious recipes for a quick breakfast or afternoon pick-me-up. Just add all ingredients to a blender and whiz them up.

01

Choc Berry Protein Shake

1 cup (250mL) coconut water

½ banana

½ cup (125mL) frozen raspberries

1 tbs chocolate-flavoured protein powder

1 tsp chia seeds

1 tsp raw honey

1 tsp LSA mix (ground linseed, sunflower seeds and almonds)

02

Green Machine

handful chopped kale (stems and veins removed)

handful chopped cucumber (with skin)

handful chopped Granny Smith apple (with skin)

handful chopped celery

ice cubes

squeeze of lemon

drizzle of raw honey

03

Carrot & Ginger

2cm piece ginger, roughly chopped

½ carrot chopped

1 cup (250mL) frozen mango

½ cup (125mL) orange juice

juice of 1 lime

04

Coco Matcha

1 cup (250mL) coconut water

1 tbs protein powder

1 tsp high-quality matcha tea

½ cup (125mL) ice

½ frozen banana

¼ avocado sliced

1 tsp tahini

05

Blueberry Heaven

½ cup (125mL) frozen blueberries

½ avocado sliced

½ frozen banana

1 large handful fresh baby spinach

1 tsp raw honey

1 cup (250mL) water

ITALY
TERME MERANO

● *A vast spa park overlooked by mountains*
● *Saunas, steam rooms, fango wraps and a snow room*

Locally born architect Matteo Thun breathed new life into this ageing spa town with his swanky revisioning of the city's central spa into a glittering glass cube. It houses a staggering array of thermal pools, baths, steam rooms, saunas and thermal inhalation rooms.

Vying with the architecture are the stunning views. Swim through the sluice gates from the 13 indoor pools and you're met by a vision of palm-studded gardens tumbling down the valley flanked by the snowy peaks of the Ötztal Alps. Here there are a further 12 pools, including a spring bath, a swirling flume, an underground steam bath, a Kneipp pool to turbo-charge your circulation and a bathing trail.

Afterwards warm up in the (all-nude) Finnish or Tyrolean organic hay sauna where the calming scent and essential oils of hay and herbs relax and energise. More targeted treatments and private thermal baths require a prior appointment, but massages and wraps are open to all. Try the White Gold wrap with fine marble particles and edelweiss or the oil massage with warm herbal bundles.

ON YOUR DOORSTEP

In-the-know Mitteleuropeans often combine a visit to Merano with skiing or hiking in Merano 2000. You could also give over a few days to exploring the botanical gardens at Castel Trauttmansdorff or wander the Waalweg trails, which follow ancient water channels.

$ *White Gold body wrap €66*
|●| *Light, fresh bistrot-style meals*

☛ **Merano**
+39 0473 252000
www.termemerano.it

ITALY

Vair at Borgo Egnazia

● *Nouveau Roman-style baths and divinely scented Pugliese treatments* ● *Walks in citrus and olive groves and swims off the Adriatic coast*

 Wafts of lemon and jasmine in the olive groves, the Adriatic glimmering on the horizon and hundreds of candles lighting up a stage set of a Pugliese citadel built in the pale local tufa stone – Borgo Egnazia could just be heaven. Heaven of a holistic kind, of course, as the cherry on the five-star cake is its spa, which consistently ranks as one of the best wellness escapes in the world. Why? Well, beyond the utter gorgeousness of this fantasy *borgo* (village) of sorts, spread across 40 acres (16 hectares) of grounds, with sea views and often-flawless blue skies, the treatments are unlike anything you'll ever have experienced.

Vair is the spa's name and its aim is to heal and transform you – physically, emotionally and spiritually. The way it goes about this is a poem to Puglia. Here you can bathe and steam by candlelight like a Roman god(dess). There are olive-oil massages with vibrational water like the rhythm of the sea, and facials using almond milk and homegrown garden herbs such as sage, rosemary and mint. Its therapists comprise artists, musicians and dancers as well as the more standard practitioners – there is even an on-site shaman! Stays begin with a private consultation to design your personal program of treatments, which might range from iyengar yoga to olfactory memory recall, and music and dance therapy.

ON YOUR DOORSTEP
Rewind several centuries exploring the nearby Greco-Roman remains of ancient Egnazia or master your stroke on the 18-hole San Domenico golf course. A short drive inland brings you to the Valle d'Itria, with its distinctive *trulli* – beehive-shaped, whitewashed, conical-roofed houses.

$ *Spa days (including treatments) €210–400*
⦿ *From wood-fired pizza to season-driven Pugliese cuisine*

☛ *Savelletri, Fasano*
+39 0802 255455
www.vairspa.it

JAPAN

KINOSAKI

● *Piping-hot geothermal waters bubbling up from underground to soothe aches and pains*
● *Arab-themed saunas and private onsen baths*

An integral part of Japanese culture, onsen are natural hot spring baths found all over the country – thanks to its sizeable amount of volcanic activity – and the minerals in these waters are said to be beneficial for overall health and wellbeing, from aiding skin issues to boosting circulation. The naked communal bathing and etiquette can be a little daunting for foreigners but it's well worth losing your inhibitions to partake in this relaxing cultural experience.

Kinosaki, a two-hour train ride from Kyoto, is one of the best places to get your gear off and take a soak in the soothing geothermal waters. It's home to seven individual onsen spread about, and the town is a pleasant walkable size. It's best to spend the night in one of Kinosaki's delightful ryokan (traditional lodging), and then, in the early evening, join the throngs of Japanese clip-clopping in *geta* (wooden sandals) and *yukata* (light cotton kimono) along the town's willow-lined canal and from onsen to onsen. Nishimuraya Honkan ryokan is the pick of the lot and has two beautiful onsen.

Kinosaki onsen highlights include the outdoor cypress barrel bath at Mandara-yu; the 'cavelike' bath at Ichi-no-yu onsen; the rooftop *rotenburo* (outdoor hot spring bath), Arab-themed saunas and Penguin sauna (ice sauna) at Sato-no-yu onsen; and the lovely garden bath at Kou-no-yu, the town's oldest onsen. Don't miss the two-level *rotenburo* at Gosho-no-yu located on the town's main street.

ON YOUR DOORSTEP
It's hard to imagine wanting to leave Kinosaki, but if your skin is turning prunelike from all the onsen time, take a trip 3 miles (5km) south to Genbudō. This collection of caves is rippled with basalt lava formed 1.6 million years ago.

$ *Yumeguri day pass to all onsen ¥1200*
◉ *Local delicacy* kani *(crab) fresh from the Sea of Japan during winter*

☛ *Kinosaki, Hyōgo Prefecture*

JAPAN
Takaragawa Onsen

● *Geothermal mineral waters help to relax the mind and body*
● *Riverside outdoor onsen among the forest*

 An onsen has to be pretty special to be dubbed one of the best in Japan, and Takaragawa is just that. Located in the northern Gunma Prefecture, this natural hot spring bath is superbly isolated among the region's beautiful forests and mountains and upstream from the Tone-gawa. Gunma's natural surroundings are the perfect playground for outdoor adventurers while Takarawaga is the ultimate spot to soothe and restore tired, aching muscles after a ski or hike.

Part of the charming Ōnsenkaku ryokan (traditional lodging), Takaragawa onsen has four large rock pools (one women-only) that sit in the open-air amidst the leafy forest by the gushing river. It's a truly magical spot to let the minerals in the water do their work.

ON YOUR DOORSTEP
The surrounding mountains and river provide endless outdoor opportunities year-round, from white-water rafting in spring to canyoning, mountain biking and hiking in the warmer months, and off-piste skiing and snowboarding come winter. Exercise caution when hiking as bears are in the area.

$ *¥1500 entry for non-guests*
Japanese cuisine incorporating local mountain vegetables and freshwater fish

☛ **Minakami Onsen-kyo, Gunma Prefecture**
+81 278 75 2614
www.takaragawa.com

MALDIVES
Huvafen Fushi

● *World's first underwater spa experience*
● *A wealth of watersports in the clear waters of the Indian Ocean*

Huvafen Fushi's only neighbour, the huge turquoise ocean, has provided this classy adult-only spa resort with much of the inspiration for its pampering sessions. Spread across and around an atoll with thatched accommodation on stilts above or abutting the iridescent water, Huvafen Fushi has one wellness claim that elevates it into a league of its own: the complex boasts the world's first underwater spa. The facials, using Teresa Tarmey treatments, are famous, but, best of all, you also get to watch clownfish and stingray going about their business on the reefs right outside. Developed a hankering for more under-ocean action? You're in luck, with superb diving and snorkelling on hand.

ON YOUR DOORSTEP
The isle on which Huvafen Fushi sits is one of the more isolated of the Maldives, but the shimmering Indian Ocean provides five dive sites, snorkelling, sailing trips and Huvafen Fushi's dreamy saltwater pool.

$ *Beach bungalow with private pool US$1700 per night*
Italian, Japanese, seafood, wine flights; under- and over-water dining

☛ **North Malé Atoll**
+960 664 4222
www.huvafenfushi. com

MAURITIUS
Shanti Maurice

● *Huge list of body treatments and massages*
● *Idyllic, tropical, beachside setting*

Set amid a sea of sugar cane on a wild stretch of beach between Blue Bay and Le Morne, Shanti Maurice is the epitome of a tropical paradise. If it weren't enough to be lulled to sleep by the sound of surf crashing on the beach outside your private villa or dining in the jasmine-scented evening air on zingy Mauritian cuisine, the award-winning Nira Spa will plunge you into an ayurvedic trance of blissed-out wellbeing.

The day starts with a grounding session of hatha yoga and progresses to mind–body balancing activities including meditation, Pilates, hydrotherapy and tailored aquafit or other fitness activities. In addition, there are dozens of massages, including a magnesium sleep massage, a chakra-balancing marma massage and an ancient Indian Mukha Lepa herbal facial.

ON YOUR DOORSTEP
If you can tear yourself away from the resort's picture-postcard private beaches and tropical gardens, you can hike the Unesco World Heritage–listed Le Morne Brabant mountain, visit nearby tea plantations or go diving amid the coral gardens that ring the island.

$ *Marma massage 90 minutes 5,500MUR*
▢ *Mauritian cuisine using ingredients from the herb and vegetable garden*

☞ *Chemin Grenier, St Felix*
+230 603 7200
https://shantimaurice. com

● Nature ● Spa Treatments

MEXICO
Ixchel Jungle Spa

● *Intense full-body therapeutic massage and facials*
● *Birdsong and blooming flowers on the forest edge*

Where Cancun hotel spas have piped-in music and aromatherapy misters, Ixchel Jungle Spa, less than an hour down the highway, has the same in natural form. Birds chirp in the trees, and the scent of flowers drifts in on the breeze – because this 'spa' is hosted under the thatched roof of an open-sided *palapa* tucked on the edge of the forest. Better still, the massage therapists at this local cooperative are all Mayan women who use techniques that they've practised since childhood. A massage under the *palapa* here is not about pampering, it's a full-body tune-up and draws many loyal repeat guests. Combine a muscular massage with a soothing aloe vera moisturising treatment and facial – great after being on the beach.

ON YOUR DOORSTEP
A designated nature reserve, the vibrant coral reef off Puerto Morelos is a good destination for snorkelling. Or head inland into the forest to visit a number of cenotes, the freshwater-filled caverns and swimming holes that dot the Yucatán Peninsula.

$ *4-handed full-body massage US$100*
▢ *Fresh juices from local fruits and greens*

☞ *Puerto Morelos, Quintana Roo*
+52 998 180 5424
http://mayaecho.com

MEXICO
LOS COLIBRIES MAYAN JUNGLE SPA

● *Open up to the sounds and surrounds of the Mexican jungle*
● *Sulphur mud scrubs, milk baths, Mayan sweat lodge*

There are far fancier wellness retreats, but there is something immensely peaceful about the scaled-down simplicity of Los Colibries, where treatments are carried out in rooms opening out to the lush jungle all around. Spa service has surely never been friendlier as guests are scrubbed with sulphuric mud, bathed in milk, massaged and treated to a session in the *temazcal*, an ancient Mayan sweat or steam lodge believed for centuries to be the secret to spirit cleansing. The best bit, though, is how close the jungle is to the treatment tables. Do not close your eyes for too long as you relax in your outside milk bath, or you will miss the spider monkeys cavorting overhead.

ON YOUR DOORSTEP
Puerto Morelos is the nearest sizeable town (11 miles; 18km), although it's a pleasantly quiet resort compared to nearby Cancún. The offshore reefs and cenotes (flooded sinkholes) are the area's big draws.

$ *Mayan massage and temazcal M$1300*
I●I *Restaurants in Puerto Morelos and along the road to the spa*

☛ *Puerto Morelos, Quintana Roo*
+52 998 105 2016
http://loscolibries.mx

NEW ZEALAND

SPLIT APPLE RETREAT

● *Tailored wellness programs* ● *Overlooking Tasman Bay and the Abel National Park*
● *Flavourful fusion cuisine with a low glycemic index*

Built on the twin expertise of retired physician Dr Lee Nelson and his wife, chef Anne Pen Lee, Split Apple Retreat offers wellness programs that combine diet, exercise, effective stress management and individually tailored, health-boosting supplements. All that plus a truly spectacular Mediterranean-Asian fusion menu.

The truth is, it isn't hard to be healthy at Split Apple. Stunningly located on a cliff overlooking the Tasman Bay and the fern-filled Abel National Park, days here are lost in a soothing round of coastal hikes, long sea swims and meditative mornings spent reclining on the panoramic terrace entranced by Lee's specially devised meditation audiotapes

The Japanese spa, meditative rose garden, gym, yoga hut and FAR-infrared sauna and steam room barely seem necessary in such a beguiling setting although they do, of course, promote a deep sense of relaxation and rejuvenation. More critical is Anne's fantastic fusion menu, created using ingredients sanctioned by Lee for their nutritional value and low glycemic index. Far from the austere health menus of many medical spas, the evening's multi-course dinner packs a serious flavour punch and leans heavily on locally sourced vegetables and fish. As a final treat, guests get to take home a complimentary cookbook.

ON YOUR DOORSTEP
Situated on the doorstep of the Abel Tasman National Park where you can enjoy easy hiking trails, sea kayaking, fishing, boating, stand-up paddle boarding, cycling and horse riding. Arty Nelson, the oldest town on South Island, is just over an hour's drive away.

$ *3-night Taste of Wellness package from NZD6700*
🍽 *Nutritious, gourmet, Asian-Mediterranean cuisine*

☛ *Kaiteriteri, Motueka, Tasman*
+64 3 527 8377
www.splitapple.com

PERU
CASA DEL SOL MACHU PICCHU BOUTIQUE HOTEL

● *Inca stone massage and coca leaf scrubs*
● *The thrilling mist-swaddled peaks of the Valle Sagrado (Sacred Valley) rear outside*

Travellers have been recovering from the aches of the Inca Trail in the thermal waters of Machu Picchu Pueblo for centuries, indeed the settlement's Spanish name, Aguas Calientes, means 'hot waters'. But there hasn't always been a boutique spa on hand to recover in after a romp about the ruins. You can be soothed here by treatments the Inca themselves may well have relished.

During the hotel's Inca stone massage, hot stones are used to alleviate taut back muscles. Alternatively, try their coca leaf exfoliation, where the coca leaves used by indigenous people since time immemorial – to treat everything from altitude sickness to rheumatism – get rubbed into the skin. Quinine from the Andean Cinchona tree is also incorporated in treatments. The hypnotic Vilcanota river crashes outside: do not pass by the hydrotherapy pool, which handily has panoramic views.

ON YOUR DOORSTEP
Ahem, South America's most popular visitor attraction, the magical Inca ruins of Machu Picchu are close by. However, the Valle Sagrado has hundreds of other Inca ruins, hikes and climbs in less-trampled locales.

$ *Inca stone massage S80*
🍽 *Peruvian-international; meat and veg from local communities*

☞ ***Machu Picchu Pueblo, Cusco***
+51 84 211 118
http://casadelsol hotels.com

Coca leaf's
CURATIVE EFFECTS

Coca, better known for its extract used to make cocaine, has been chewed all across South America for centuries. The leaf is used as an antidote to altitude sickness and fatigue. It is also soaked in hot water as a curative tea (mate de coca). Coca leaves are rich in nutrients such as calcium and potassium.

PERU
COLCA LODGE, SPA & HOT SPRINGS

● *Soak in mineral-rich hot springs* ● *Hike to secluded pre-Incan ruins*
● *Enjoy a massage with Colca Valley views*

Found at the end of a series of dusty roads that snake their way around the spectacular Colca Canyon, visitors to the Colca Lodge are rewarded with a high-altitude retreat that makes the most of its secluded locale.

Outdoor adventures and nature are the name of the game in this part of the world, with hiking, horse riding, cycling and exploring nearby alpaca farms all on the agenda. Thankfully, relaxing is also a priority at Colca Lodge.

Home to four open-air mineral pools of varying temperatures, this is the ideal place to rest weary muscles. Rich in lithium, the riverside pools are landscaped with locally sourced, natural materials such as stone, earth and straw. The views from the hot springs are impressive, whether gazing upon terraced farmland during the day or a splatter of southern hemisphere stars at night.

Hot stone massages and other treatments provided by the day spa will have you sighing with delight, as will the on-site restaurant's Peruvian cuisine and the picturesque landscaped gardens that surround the series of low-rise guest rooms located around the sprawling property.

ON YOUR DOORSTEP
Southern Peru's show-stopping Colca Canyon is a popular spot for hiking, rafting and birdwatching. Home to the impressive Andean condor, this scenic part of Peru is also populated by plenty of llamas and alpacas.

$ *From US$178 per night*
|◉| *Traditional Peruvian delicacies and international dishes feature on the menu*

☛ *Valle del Colca, Arequipa*
+51 54 282 177
https://colca -lodge.com

● Nutrition ● Spa Treatments

THE PHILIPPINES
THE FARM AT SAN BENITO

- *A broad range of treatments on offer, from Hilot massages to coffee scrubs*
- *Dine on tasty raw food at the award-winning vegan restaurant*

Less than a two-hour drive from Manila's traffic-choked streets and bustling megalopolis lies the paradise that is The Farm at San Benito, tucked away in the jungle near Lipay City. It has been attracting wellness seekers and big-name celebrities for years and it's not hard to see why. This is a temple to clean living with guided detox programs, and spa treatments running the gamut from colon hydrotherapy and traditional Hilot massages to chlorophyll body wraps and coffee scrubs. Spend downtime relaxing in your bamboo-thatched villa or get active with a daily yoga class or qigong, or opt for some guided meditation.

Another reason for the popularity of The Farm is the award-winning Alive! restaurant, which serves incredible raw-food vegan meals using ingredients picked from the on-site organic garden.

ON YOUR DOORSTEP

Get moving on a sunset power walk around the farm's grounds or take a short trip to visit the world's smallest volcano, Taal Volcano in Tagaytay, with its breathtaking panoramic views of Taal Lake (above).

$ *4-night Detox D'Lite retreat from US$2620*
🍽 *Delicious farm-to-table vegan raw food*

☛ **Lipay City**
+632 884 8074
www.thefarmat
sanbenito.com

PORTUGAL

São Lourenço do Barrocal

● *Incredible stargazing in the Alqueva Dark Sky Reserve* ● *Susanne Kaufmann–endorsed spa*
● *Alentejo menus and single-estate reserve wines*

The golden plains and vineyard-covered hillsides of the Alentejo offer up the kind of spiritual communion with nature that inspired Romantic poet William Wordsworth. Scattered with mystical prehistoric dolmens (megalithic tombs), menhirs (upright monumental stones) and Palaeolithic carvings, it is an ancient landscape and a perfect place for this serene spa set within José António Uva's 1927-acre (780-hectare) family wine and olive oil estate.

The Barrocal community was once a thriving village, and over 12 years Uva determinedly brought it back to life in his reimagining of the estate as an exclusive retreat respectful of the area's unique ecology and history. Hence the collaboration with organic skincare specialist Susanne Kaufmann, whose eponymous products use plant extracts from the Alpine Bregenz forest. Here, they are deployed in a variety of massages and skincare treatments, including a sesame-and-apricot-kernel scrub combining lymph drainage and acupressure, and stimulating facials.

Food from the estate is similarly simple and nourishing: salads tossed in estate olive oil and flame-cooked Alentejo black pork from acorn-eating Iberian pigs are typical. Food is both delicious and energising, setting you up well for weekend trail running, cycle rides around Lake Alqueva and scenic horseback hacks through the oak forests. When the deep velvet of night falls, decamp to the Alqueva Lake Observatory for stargazing with an astronomer. Wordsworth himself would be lost for words.

ON YOUR DOORSTEP
The Alentejo is one of Portugal's most unspoilt rural regions. Nearby is Lake Alqueva and a number of historic medieval villages, including the walled hilltop town of Monsaraz and the Unesco World Heritage town of Évora.

$ *1-day active regeneration including light lunch €250*
🍽 *Communal farm-to-table eating on healthy Mediterranean produce*

....

☞ **Monsaraz**
+351 (0) 266 247140
www.barrocal.pt

PORTUGAL

Six Senses Spa Douro Valley

● *A team of tree-climbing specialists (yes that is a real job) will help you scale the heights of the on-site enchanted forest* ● *Ten treatment rooms with views over the valley*

Six Senses Spa, in Portugal's stunning Douro Valley, can be found by descending a Gothic candlelit staircase inside a restored 19th-century mansion. Rooms here feature modern styling and views of woodlands or the Douro river below.

Integrated wellness programs offer guests a customised plan of fitness and nutrition goals to work towards. You'll also have the chance to try a variety of yoga styles with in-house yoga masters. Enjoy a drink or two on the patio overlooking the swimming pools and verdant valley, before taking a stroll through the aromatic organic vegetable and herb gardens. Expect to find local flavours on offer at meal times in a choice of al fresco or upscale indoor restaurants, including the wine library where you can sample vintages from the region.

Treat yourself to a range of indulgent face and body treatments on offer at the spa, including the luxurious rose diamond facial, which uses real diamond dust to exfoliate the skin. As night falls, turn your attention to the much-neglected facet of a balanced wellness program – quality sleep. Six Senses offers a sleep regime to help guests adopt healthy relaxation techniques leading to better rest. Handmade mattresses and sleep consultants offer customised solutions to help you develop healthy sleep habits.

ON YOUR DOORSTEP
Play at being a winemaker for the day with a tour of local vineyards, and you'll even get a chance to stomp the grapes yourself, season permitting. The Douro river also provides many recreation opportunities, including wine cruises, canoeing and water skiing.

$ *Rooms from €270 a night*
⦿l *Local fresh flavours of the region and abundant seafood*

....

☛ *Duoro Valley*
+351 (0) 254 660600
**www.sixsenses.com/
resorts/douro-valley/
destination**

PORTUGAL
Vilalara Thalassa Resort

● *Thalassotherapy and holistic health packages* ● *Fresh Portuguese seafood and 'detox' menus*
● *Lovingly tended gardens with astonishing Atlantic views*

The lure of the sea hooks you the minute you pass through the gates and into the 30-acre (12-hectare) estate of Vilalara, which staggers down to a lovely scoop of cliff-backed golden beach and the deep-blue Atlantic on Portugal's Algarve coast. It ranks as one of the world's best thalassotherapy spas and the term really comes into its own here, with uplifting ocean views on repeat, the rhythmic sound of waves, saltwater pools and treatments. With villas, cabana beds and sea-facing terraces snuggled away in lush gardens of palms, bougainvillea and lemon trees, all drenched in pure Atlantic light, it's private and serene.

Then, of course, there is the spa itself, which offers packages designed to give body and mind a complete spring clean. During your time here, you might, say, have consultations with osteopaths, nutritionists, mindfulness guides and craniosacral therapists, join aqua Pilates, yoga, and Tibetan bowls classes. Or you could just opt for some much-needed R&R, or maybe a skin-smoothing thalassotherapy treatment which range from warm seawater baths to seaweed therapy and mud treatments. Private consultations ensure that every stay is individual and tailored. The holistic approach is reflected in the food, too, which swings from juice fasting detoxes to gourmet, locally sourced Portuguese cuisine.

ON YOUR DOORSTEP
If you can tear yourself away from those fabulous Algarve beaches, factor in a day trip to nearby Albufeira's medieval walled old town, or head into Portimão for simply grilled fish fresh from the Atlantic at a humble waterfront tavern.

$ *Thalassa Wellness Day €100; thalassotherapy bath €40*
🍽 *Detox diets and gourmet Algarvian seafood*

....

☛ *Porches, Lagoa*
+351 (0) 282 320196
www.vilalararesort.com

● **Nature**   ● **Spa Treatments**

SLOVAKIA
AQUACITY

● *Huge waterpark with indoor and outdoor geothermal pools* ● *The High Tatras mountains, one of Eastern Europe's premier outdoor playgrounds, soar above the complex*

Outdoor enthusiasts have been gravitating to the mountainscapes of the High Tatras for over a century, but lovers of luxuriating only really began to descend since the advent of AquaCity. This eco-resort, powered on geothermal energy channelled from underground pools deep below the mountains, has been a byword for wellness in Slovakia since its completion in 2008. Most of AquaCity is about good old-fashioned fun: a monolithic waterpark splash-about with nine indoor and outdoor geothermal pools and eight sorts of sauna and inhalation rooms (including salt, herbal and eucalyptus).

But there is also a long list of massage therapies available – from relaxation massages to sport, hot stone, chocolate, Hawaiian, Indian and bamboo massage where the poles are rolled along your body to supposedly boost circulation. There's also tons to keep the kids entertained.

ON YOUR DOORSTEP
The peaks of Slovakia's High Tatras swoop up directly above AquaCity, and trailheads and mountain resorts are accessed from Poprad via electric railway. Hiking, climbing and skiing are the main activities in the mountains.

$ *All-day waterpark entry and wellness area excluding treatments €34*
🍴 *Restaurant and cafes; options aplenty in central Poprad*

☛ *Poprad*
+421 527 851 111
www.aquacity.sk

SOUTH AFRICA

Aroma Boma

- *Get a taste of African ritualistic healing*
- *Spy the big five on safari in the savanna*

Game for the very definition of South African luxury? Then board a plane for Ulusaba, a game reserve perched on a *koppie* (rocky outcrop) towering above a vast tract of bushland adjacent to Kruger National Park. You come here primarily for some of the planet's most sensational wildlife viewing: the crag providing a vantage point for watching animals no other location hereabouts can rival. But, this being Richard Branson's private reserve, indulgence is a good reason to stop by too, invariably appreciated after rising early for safari. And Ulusuba indulgence takes on a unique African theme.

In such a biodiverse area, ingredients for treatments naturally embrace what grows in the vicinity. Local flora that could turn up in your pampering session include rooibos (a nutrient-rammed plant commonly used as a tea), marula (the extract from a lowland South African tree, known as Africa's 'miracle' oil for its supposed anti-ageing properties) and aloe (an immune booster also effective at soothing wounds). In one signature treatment that harks back to time-tested tribal healing techniques, African mud is slathered on to your body and marula oil is then massaged into your head and scalp.

But wellness is sometimes, well, just about being. And Ulusuba is a place to be, to sample a vintage from the wine cellar and then gaze out at the wilderness from the inviting terraces, or to stargaze from the reserve's observatory and enjoy nature at its most thrillingly immense.

ON YOUR DOORSTEP

Sabi Sand Reserve is in the middle of nowhere, adjacent to another wondrous middle-of-nowhere, Kruger National Park. The isolation is great, for this is where big game animals roam free: lions, elephants, buffaloes, black rhinos and leopards.

$ *Zambian healing ritual (herbal infusion then massage) R1200*
🍽 *Braai (barbecue)*

....

☛ **Ulusaba, Sabi Sand Reserve, Mpimalanga**
+27 11 325 4405
www.virginlimited edition.com/en/ ulusaba

● Nutrition ● Nature ● Spa Treatments

SRI LANKA

Santani Wellness Resort

● *Ayurvedic, spa and wellness programs to soothe both mind and body* ● *Luxurious accommodation built in harmony with the surrounding tea plantations and paddy fields*

Just as the name Santani ('in harmony with') suggests, it's all about balance at Sri Lanka's only purpose-built, luxury wellness retreat. Santani's minimalist design, pristine green setting and holistic approach – using modern practices as well as traditional ayurveda – invite you to treat your body and train your mind. Join a group retreat or opt for an individual program tailored to your wellness goals. Stretch your body with yoga and expand your mind with a riverside meditation. Wander the forests of this tranquil former tea plantation or descend deeper and indulge in a treatment at the tri-level spa, built into the hillside. Refuel on natural foods, chef-selected specifically for you. Whatever you choose, your best bet is to follow Santani's laid-back lead and let the silence, spectacular views and well-trained staff inspire you to find your best balance.

ON YOUR DOORSTEP
This secluded sanctuary is situated on a 48-acre (19-hectare) former tea plantation, surrounded by rice paddies and jungle vegetation that visitors are free to explore. Kandy, the cultural centre of Sri Lanka and a Unesco World Heritage site, is about a 1½ hour's drive away.

$ *1-week mindfulness retreat approx US$3200*
⦿| *Personalised wellness cuisine designed by an ayurvedic practitioner*

☛ **Arantenna Estate, Werapitiya, Kandy**
+94 76 399 1919
www.santani.lk

● **Nutrition** ● **Nature** ● **Spa Treatments**

THAILAND
KEEMALA

● *Sleep in treehouses nestled in the forest canopy*
● *Holistic wellness, beauty and bodywork therapies* ● *Tailored health-food menus*

You'll soon be feeling free as a bird in the jungle as you make yourself at home in one of Keemala's extraordinary treehouse villas. The treetop accommodation is beautifully finished with teak, bamboo and rush matting and – in the more luxurious Bird's Nest villas – comes complete with a private pool overlooking the bay.

If you can tear yourself from the view, you'll be placed in the hands of expert wellness practitioner Khun On, who runs the Mala Spa. Here, you can dip in and out of a menu of one-on-one wellness sessions, daily yoga, Thai Bodywork, Raindrop Healing Therapy, muscle-thawing massages and soothing facials deploying all-natural Siam Botanicals. Guest practitioners include reiki specialists, chiropractors and shiatu masseurs. The whole experience is a welcome, if trippy, escape from reality.

ON YOUR DOORSTEP
Keemala is a 40-minute drive northwest of Phuket Town and 20 minutes north of Patong, both of which will take care of your shopping and entertainment needs. Otherwise, the resort runs a shuttle to the Kamala (above), Surin and Layan beaches.

$ *3-night Purify Program THB41,000pp*
🍽 *Spicy Thai and Indian cuisine*

☛ *Kamala, Kathu District, Phuket*
+66 76 358 777
www.keemala.com

THAILAND

THE SANCTUARY

- ● *Beautiful setting on the quiet, jungle side of Koh Pha-Ngan*
- ● *Yoga classes and yoga teacher-training* ● *Popular fasting and 'detox' programs*

In a forested enclave of Koh Pha-Ngan, The Sanctuary started life in 1989 as a private escape for friends. It has since gained a reputation for its friendly atmosphere, picturesque location and excellent yoga teachers.

Many visitors come to The Sanctuary especially for the detox package whereby participation begins with a lengthy interview with a resident nutritionist. Depending on the results of the interview (the nutritionist might recommend a day or two *easing in* period), the fasting portion of the detox begins the next morning with herbs, followed by the first of four daily 'purification shakes'. Following a 3pm juice and the third 'shake' is what to some will be the most anticipated and to others the most dreaded ritual of the day: the 4pm colonic.

Fasters are welcome to do yoga classes, enjoy the sauna and of course swim in the blue waters of Hat Rin bay.

ON YOUR DOORSTEP

No roads lead to The Sanctuary, just a jungle trail over a hill or a quick long-tail boat ride from Hat Rin. The beachfront resort is nestled between a quiet, sandy beach and a hillside jungle filled with coconut trees.

$ 9-night 'detox' package with Thai-style room THB45,630–50,340
◉ Shakes, probiotics, veggie broths, coffee colonics

☛ Koh Pha-Ngan
+66 81 271 3614
www.thesanctuary thailand.com

TURKEY

Pamukkale & Hierapolis

● *Some of the planet's most divine natural pools to paddle and plunge in*
● *Hierapolis' hot mineral-rich waters have been sought out since antiquity*

Viewed from above, Pamukkale resembles agate slices: sparkling cyan and aquamarine pools rimmed by travertine rocks that fall away in terraces down a hillside. And wading barefoot through these heavenly waters would be enough to entice visitors in their droves. Combined with the close-by Greco-Roman ruins of Hierapolis, however, it constitutes Turkey's most visited attraction. And Pamukkale and Hierapolis have to be seen to be believed: as people have clearly thought for several millennia. It was doubtless the dreamy travertine cooling-off spots that prompted the construction of Hierapolis, a celebrated spa since the 2nd century BC. A lot of ancient wellness advice pointed the afflicted in this direction because of its mineral-abundant 97°F (36°C) waters believed to cure rheumatism and high blood pressure, as well as other ailments.

Splash your way up through Pamukkale to Hierapolis, on the crest of the hill above. Here, besides the stupendous ruins, is the highlight for bathers: an immersion in the same waters the city's inhabitants once used. Float over ancient columns and amongst the remnants of temples in the Antique Pool, commanding a separate entrance fee to Pamukkale. It is ideal to enjoy the whole experience without the day trippers that descend in the afternoon, so stay over in Pamukkale village, and take the waters in the morning, bringing a picnic lunch to munch pool-side.

ON YOUR DOORSTEP
Discover the ancient Phrygian cities of Laodicea ad Lycum, in Denzili 30 miles (48km) southwest of Pamukkale, and Tripolis, near Yenicekent 27 miles (44km) northwest of Pamukkale; the Seljuk caravanserais of Hanabad and Akhan; and cloth handicrafts at Buldan.

$ *Entry including access to pools at both sites ₺67*
🍽 *Pamukkale village has several restaurants*

☞ *Denzili province*

UNITED KINGDOM

ISLE OF ERISKA HOTEL

● *Hebridean seaweed wraps and sea-salt scrubs*
● *Roam free on a private Hebridean island*

In stark contrast to the rugged surrounds of western Argyll, the gentle Isle of Eriska offers you a far easier time of it. On this verdant, flower-bedecked little island – exclusively the domain of the hotel and its grounds – it is nigh-on impossible not to unwind. Recline in your room, either in the 19th-century castellated main mansion or in suites that sport their own private gardens and hot tubs, take to the fairways of the 9-hole golf course or follow one of the island trails to spy otters and grey seals cavorting on the shoreline.

The Stables Spa is all about taking the best of the hotel's photogenic environs and condensing them into pampering form. One thing in particular abundance hereabouts is seaweed: revered for its therapeutic properties for centuries. Utilising the Ishga range of Scottish seaweed-based skincare products, this is the only luxurious place to grab a Hebridean seaweed treatment with a stunning Hebridean sea view thrown in. Sea-salt scrubs, marine-mud envelopment and algae wraps add to the treatment line-up.

For more energetic guests, taking to the waters, from where this sea-bashed, loch-riven landscape is best appreciated, is a must: the hotel can arrange yacht cruises and kayaking trips.

ON YOUR DOORSTEP
Nearby Oban is a chocolate box town known as the sea gateway to the Inner Hebrides: an alluring archipelago of quirky islands full of moody history and fabulous wildlife watching. The gorgeous island beaches are not all seaweed-covered either – prepare for dreamy sands and fairy-tale coves.

$ *Ishga seaweed body wrap £75*
🍽 *The hotel's restaurant is Scottish fine dining strong on seafood and steak*

☛ **Benderloch, Oban, Argyll**
+44 (0)1631 720 371
www.eriska-hotel. co.uk

HEBRIDEAN SEAWEED

Seaweed flourishes in the cold, nutrient-rich water off the coast and islands of Scotland and it was traditionally used in these parts as a way to perk up the listless and fertilise the land. An industry has been made from seaweed harvesting on Scotland's remoter coasts for centuries. Today, near the Isle of Lismore, there are plans to reignite the once-lucrative industry and open the UK's first dedicated seaweed farm.

UNITED KINGDOM

Green Ayurveda Spa

● *Customised treatments and packages*
● *Ayurveda practitioners, counselling and dietary advice*

You won't be the first person seeking out Green Ayurveda Spa who thinks their navigation system has totally led them astray. While the name brings expectations of verdant isolated splendour, the reality is far from this. It's… in…an…industrial estate? Once you're in the spa, however, walking across a bridge to the sound of a bubbling water, inhaling oils and wood from India (that'd be the 2200lb (1000kg) Keralan massage tables) you could be anywhere. Dr Majosh Jolly, owner and Managing Director, has seen this reaction before. 'We are known very well in Yorkshire as the spa in the industrial estate, but some people are surprised,' he smiles, pointing out that the overnight accommodation for retreats come is in the form of luxurious cottages that overlook several acres of countryside nearby.

The key draw for visitors here is Dr Jolly (and his team)'s Keralan provenance and traditional training in ayurvedic practices. Many of the spa's clients have had experience of ayurveda in India and respect the spa's authenticity. All clients have an individual consultation with an ayurveda practitioner to determine their *dosha* (body type) prior to treatment, whether that be a visit to the day spa for, say, a Holistic One Day Rejuvenation, or a more intensive retreat. The traditional Panchakarma Detox & Weight Loss retreat is the most popular.

ON YOUR DOORSTEP

Green Ayurveda Spa is located between Harrogate, one of Yorkshire's finest Victorian spa towns, and York, with its medieval magnificence and 13th-century walls. It's about a 30-minute drive to each if you'd like to bookend your treatment with some historical exploration.

$ *Panchakarma Detox & Weight Loss retreat, minimum 5 days from £1350pp (excluding accommodation: £50pp per night at nearby Priory Cottages)*
🍽 *Ayurvedic food, based on recipes from Kerala, India*

☛ **452 Thorp Arch Estate, Wetherby**
+44 (0) 1937 541 177
www.ayurveda inyorkshire.co.uk

The power of Ayurveda

"The beauty of ayurveda is that we treat the body as a whole. Health, according to ayurveda, is a happy body, a happy mind and a happy soul. Mind, body and soul unites together in your mother's womb to form a life. So it's important you keep these three things happy and healthy all the time."
Dr Majosh Jolly BAMS BNYT, Owner & Managing Director, Green Ayurveda Spa

UNITED KINGDOM
THE CLOVER MILL

● *Eco-friendly ayurvedic health spa in a renovated 17th-century water mill*
● *Tranquil, themed retreats in the countryside to rebalance body, mind and spirit*

Turning on to the narrow lane towards The Clover Mill, expanses of green countryside on the Worcestershire–Herefordshire border seem to be yours alone. Or not quite. Along the gravelled entrance towards this 17th-century water mill and the nearby three (soon-to-be five) luxury eco-lodges, your first welcome could come from an alpaca (Ted, Monsoon, Ben or Archie), otherwise you'll be greeted by rescue dog Millie, your new best friend on starlit walks along the ancient weir and meadows of this peaceful 11-acre (4.5-hectare) property. Founder Julie Dent won't be far away, unless she's harvesting wild garlic, putting an apple cake in the Aga or brewing tea of cloves, cardamom, cinnamon and pepper in her cosy, aromatic kitchen.

Julie opened The Clover Mill in 2013 as a boutique ayurvedic retreat and spa, following a transformative personal experience on a retreat in Sri Lanka in 2005.

She later found there was a frustrating lack of similar holidays locally in the UK.

The six treatment rooms spiral out in the mill's rustic structure, and lighting is used to great effect, with a yoga studio on the top floor. While you could visit on a casual basis, the intimate (maximum 10 guests) residential retreats are best to truly unwind. These begin with a personalised ayurvedic *dosha* (body type) diagnosis and customised treatments. The annual knitting yoga retreat regularly sells out, and the Rest & Digest retreat involves ayurveda-inspired meals and hands-on cooking classes.

ON YOUR DOORSTEP
The nearby Malvern Hills Area of Outstanding Natural Beauty lives up to its name, with 9 miles (14km) of ancient volcanic hills. Hikes promise forts, castles and priories.

Malvern water (a natural spring water available at public wells) has been consumed in the area since Victorian times.

$ *5-day Rest and Digest retreat from £1721pp, twin room* **|◎|** *Freshly harvested, pre- and pro-biotic seasonal vegetarian food*

....

☛ **Cradley, Malvern, Worcestershire**
+44 (0)1886 880 859
www.theclovermill. com

THE IMPORTANCE OF 'REST & DIGEST'

"If you are often in fight-or-flight mode living on adrenaline, then this retreat will help you activate your parasympathetic nervous system to switch to rest-and-digest mode. Indirectly, via stress-relieving lifestyle techniques we can rebalance our whole body, mind and spirit."
Julie Dent, Founder, The Clover Mill

UNITED KINGDOM

Thermae Bath Spa

● *Soothing waters from Britain's only natural thermal spa* ● *Hydro-massage, steams and scrubs in historic-meets-ultramodern spa, with views over Georgian rooftops*

The Romans knew they were on to a good thing some 2000 years ago when they frolicked around in Bath's steaming waters – emerging, surely, with the body of Venus and the complexion of Cleopatra. Today, they are the only place in Britain where you can float in natural thermal baths fed by hot springs, which pump up 264,170 gallons (1 million litres) of the mineral-rich water every day. And it gets even better at Thermae Bath Spa. From the open-air pool you can gaze wistfully out across the historic skyline of Bath – over the rooftops of its honey-coloured Georgian houses and up to the tower of its medieval abbey – all while being pummelled into a blissful state of relaxation by hydro-massage jets. It's at its most atmospheric when illuminated by night. The indoor Minerva Bath is pretty impressive, too, with its flowing curves, fluted columns, whirlpool and lazy river.

Housed in a shell of local stone and plate glass, the spa has more intimate areas, too, like the oval-shaped Cross Bath, a sacred site where the Celts once worshipped their goddess, Sul. The Wellness Suite is quite lovely, with its sweet-scented Roman steam room infused with botanicals; misty, menthol-infused ice chamber for cooling off; and starlit relaxation room, where heated loungers send spa-goers drifting ever so softly to slumberland.

ON YOUR DOORSTEP

Besides its Roman heritage, Bath is famous for its gold-hued Georgian architecture. If it's your first visit, you won't want to miss stunners such as the Royal Crescent, a grand sweep of townhouses, and the elegantly columned Pump Room (go for afternoon tea).

$ *2-hour Thermae Welcome from £36*
🍽 *Salads, sandwiches and locally sourced specials at Springs Café*

☞ *Bath, Somerset*
+44 (0)1225 331 234
www.thermae bathspa.com

A Bath
and a half

Fancy a little extra pampering? Thermae Bath's signature treatments include Watsu aqua therapy which involves a combination of shiatsu massage and acupressure, performed in the water; the 85-minute Roman Trilogy, a salt-and-coffee body scrub followed by a vanilla-ylang-ylang massage and a revitalising rose-and-geranium facial; and the Vichy Experience where guests are pummelled with hydromassage showers, aromatherapy essences, exfoliating scrubs and hot stones.

UNITED KINGDOM
SUNNY BROW HOLISTIC RETREAT

● *Body-and-soul-focused holistic therapies connecting with nature*
● *Whole food cookery classes using macrobiotic principles*

The tasty home cooking at Sunny Brow Holistic Retreat is but one of many reasons to visit this enchanted location deep in the heart of England's Lake District. Founder Suzy-Anne Saunders' studies with the International Macrobiotic School led to her interest in holistic counselling and it's the melding of various treatments and techniques that create a unique environment for anyone looking for relaxation or personal inquiry.

Come for a day or stay in one of the converted five-star barns overlooking sheep-filled pastures on this 33-acre (13-hectare) Cumbrian farm. You may learn the significance of spotting a deer en route to the yurt, you may learn more about your past life, you may gain a new respect for Mother Earth and the five elements, or you could simply just relax and rejuvenate. The latter takes no effort whatsoever: a walk along the stream among the native oak, hazel, hawthorn and silver birch trees will start that journey.

The eclectic mix of experiences here (especially in nature) is the big drawcard, and you could easily return to this restorative woodland several times to try experiences with such intriguing names as Feel The Rhythm Djembe Drumming, Remarkable Meetings With Trees, a Healing Food Retreat, or Inner Sacred Dance. Those seeking a deeper spiritual experience go for the Soul Healing Retreat.

ON YOUR DOORSTEP

England's Lake District is nirvana for hikers, and Sunny Brow Farm's proximity to Ambleside puts you in prime position to enjoy the best of the scenery. Wander the fells and the forests, discover the 1st-century Roman Fort, or just picnic beside Lake Windermere.

$ *4-night Soul Healing Retreat from £300pp for shared double/twin room* 🍽 *Organic, whole foods, unprocessed, using macrobiotic principles, primarily plant-sourced*

☛ *Outgate, Near Ambleside, Cumbria* **+44 (0)1539 436 288** **www.sunnybrowfarm.co.uk**

"Our Soul Healing Retreat has been formed in a shamanic style, with healing yoga, ritual and ceremony, soul reading and soul healings. A retreat in this deeply connected space will allow for more flow, freedom and happiness within your life."
Suzy-Anne Saunders, Founder, Sunny Brow Holistic Retreat, BA, Shamanic practitioner, yoga teacher, holistic therapist, macrobiotic chef

Indulged

Spa Treatments

Food & Drink

Luxury

ARGENTINA
Cavas Wine Lodge

● *Savour Malbec and Torrontés through wraps, scrubs and baths*
● *Amidst Mendoza's best vineyards, the wine pairing and degustation here are superb*

Owning your own 50-acre (20-hectare) vineyard is nothing to boast about in the fertile Andean foothills of Argentina's wine mecca, Mendoza: here wine is a way of life, and over 1500 wineries cluster in the shadow of the mountain range. Cavas Wine Lodge serves up something a little different to your standard wine flight, however – wine by the bathload.

Wine wellness has been growing in popularity for several years and here, in one of South America's foremost boutique spas, it is ripe for sampling. Descend to the lodge treatment rooms to bathe in the red stuff, get lathered up with a scrub made from Malbec grape seeds, or help your muscles unknot with a grape seed oil massage. Many products also combine herbs and flowers grown in the garden outside.

Conclude your day's indulging with a drop more in the privacy of the sumptuous bedrooms; each has its own plunge pool, outside shower and a wood-burning fireplace. Just make sure you give yourself the time to appreciate the view. All rooms face west offering spectacular sunsets and star-gazing opportunities. Take your glass of Mondoza Malbec out on to the balcony and raise a toast to the distant mountain peaks rising out of a sea of vineyards, all bathed in that singular Andean light.

ON YOUR DOORSTEP
Visitors would be hard-pressed to resist the allure of the great wineries in the Mendoza region, most within a 30-minute drive of Cavas Wine Lodge. For a romantic winery tour, try horse riding between vineyards. The Andes, with innumerable outdoor activities, are a 30-minute drive away.

$ *Crushed Malbec scrub AR$810*
|◉| *Andean-Argentinian classics garnished with homegrown herbs and veg*

☛ Alto Agrelo, Mendoza
+54 261 410 2697
www.cavaswine lodge.com

AUSTRALIA
Hepburn Bathhouse & Spa

● *Mineral-salt body treatments and aromatic steam rituals*
● *Private mineral baths infused with thermal mud or Royal Moroccan Milk*

Set in Victoria's 'spa centre' around 90 minutes from Melbourne, Hepburn Springs has been attracting city slickers looking to improve their health with the aid of the area's mineral springs since the late 1800s. These days, the Hepburn Bathhouse is the crowning jewel in this wellness getaway hotspot situated among the scenic Central Highland's hills, lakes and forests.

Mineral water is drawn straight from the source and pumped into the communal pools in the super-chic main bathhouse where large windows provide bush views for soaking guests. The Sanctuary offers mineral bathing, along with a steam room, salt and magnesium pool, outdoor creekside pool and hammam. Private pools and other spa treatments are available in a lovely historic building. The Thermal Mineral Mud Bath helps relieve muscle pain and leaves you with baby-soft skin, or try the Mineral Detox body exfoliation using ground mineral salts and a spirulina algae body mask.

ON YOUR DOORSTEP
Don't miss the Convent Gallery, a 19th-century convent-turned-art-gallery. Book in for a sensational meal at the Lake House restaurant.

$ *Day retreat package from AU$245; main bathhouse entry from AU$37*
🍽 *Pastries and light meals in the Pavillion cafe*

☛ **Hepburn Springs, Victoria**
+61 3 5321 6000
www.hepburn bathhouse.com

● Spa Treatments ● Luxury

AUSTRALIA
Injidup

● *Ocean views from the villas' private plunge pools*
● *Marine wraps, kodo massages and a range of facials*

Most people head to Margaret River for epicurean pursuits – filling the belly with some of Australia's best gourmet produce and getting sloshed on the region's much-lauded wine. After all that indulging you might need to recoup, rejuvenate and tend to the mind and body. That's where Injidup comes in. Situated on a quiet slice of beach in the heart of wine country in the little town of Yallingup, Injidup is a stunning adults-only hideaway perfect for recharging the batteries.

Panoramic ocean views and private plunge pools await in the villas, of which there are just 10, ensuring an atmosphere of privacy and seclusion. If you can tear yourself away, Injidup Spa retreat by Bohdi J offers a menu of pampering treatments. The signature Li'tya Kodo Rock Massage is a rhythmic body massage inspired by Australian Aboriginal techniques.

ON YOUR DOORSTEP
Injidup Beach is a 15-minute walk away. Yallingup has some great dining options if you don't want to stray far, but be sure to make time for exploring Margaret River's wineries and artisan food producers.

$ *Villas from AU$650 per night; Li'tya Kodo Rock Massage AU$230*
🍽 *Breakfast hampers full of local produce on arrival*

☛ **Yallingup, Western Australia**
+61 8 9750 1300
www.injidup sparetreat.com.au

AUSTRALIA

PENINSULA HOT SPRINGS

● *Secluded private bathing with lavender-milk-infused water* ● *Kodo massage inspired by traditional Australian Aboriginal techniques* ● *Organic mineral mud wraps*

The Mornington Peninsula has long been attracting visitors to its calm Port Phillip Bay waters and the powerful crashing surf of the Bass Strait–facing beaches. But in recent years, visitors are heading here to plunk themselves in different waters – the thermal mineral water bubbling up at, quite literally, the peninsula's hottest attraction, the Peninsula Hot Springs.

It is the vision of founding brothers Charles and Richard Davidson, who were inspired by visits to hot springs in Japan. Set in an Australian bush hideaway setting, the water in the pools is high in mineral content – magnesium, potassium and boron – and according to the brothers helps relax your muscles and de-stress.

Divided into two main areas, the Bathhouse is a family-friendly area with over 20 hot spring pools spread out, including the popular hilltop pool with panoramic views. The Spa Dreaming Centre is for those looking for less chatter and more serenity – where adults only don fluffy white robes and duck in and out of pools and wooden barrel baths, before lounging on deck chairs.

If you need to up your blissed-out state, the spa offers kodo massages, mud wraps and sea-salt exfoliation, or you can choose a private bathing session. And for a bit more fun try the Clay Ridge Experience, where you'll be given clay mixed with thermal waters to paint on your face and body.

The ever-expanding hot springs will soon have a new bathing area, amphitheatre, ice cave and accommodation.

ON YOUR DOORSTEP

If you can drag yourself out of the hot pools there is plenty of great wine tasting to be had in nearby Red Hill, excellent art exhibitions at the Mornington Peninsula Regional Gallery, and miles of beaches surrounding it all.

$ *Bathhouse entry from AU$40; Spa Dreaming Centre entry AU$75*
🍽 *Cafe-style meals and picnic area*

☞ *Fingal, Mornington Peninsula*
+61 3 5950 8777
www.peninsula hotsprings.com

● Spa Treatments ● Food & Drink ● Luxury

CANADA

Balnea Spa & Thermal Reserve

● *A rejuvenating thermal experience* ● *Indulgent tailored facials and body treatments* ● *Delicious gourmet meals from some of Montréal's top chefs*

Journey only an hour from Montréal to discover Balnea Spa, situated above a stunning private lake, in a forest of pine trees. On arrival, the staff will take you on a tour of the gorgeous facilities before you step into your robe for a day spent luxuriating in the many hot and cold thermal baths, saunas, ponds, relaxation areas and, of course, the lake.

Balnea also offers a wide selection of massages and facial treatments for men and women. You can even opt for a mini treatment to add on to your thermal bath experience. If you're after something a little more vigorous, book in for a yoga or boot camp class.

At the end of your day, enjoy a healthy meal, juice or a glass of wine at Lumami, Balnea's restaurant which has a seasonal health-focused menu. Visit on a Sunday in summer and enjoy food cooked by some of Montréal's top chefs, with a different chef visiting each week.

ON YOUR DOORSTEP
Wind your way through the forest setting on one of the many bicycle routes in the grounds of the spa. If you prefer to explore on foot, take to nearby hiking trails.

$ *Thermal spa $70 ($45 when booked with a treatment)*
|◉| *Health-conscious gourmet seasonal menu*

☞ **Bromont-sur-le-lac, Québec**
+1 450 534 0604
www.balnea.ca

CANADA
Bota Bota

- *Nordic water circuit aboard a floating spa*
- *Indulgent facials, massages and body treatments*

A repurposed ferry is the unlikely home of this haven of relaxation and tranquillity floating in Montréal's Old Port. Step on deck and prepare to be luxuriously pampered.

Decorated in chic black and white, the ferry is uber stylish inside with guests dressed in bath robes as white and fluffy as a bag of bunnies. The main feature at Bota Bota is the Nordic water circuit. Start with a sauna then plunge your body into one of the icy pools. Try the eucalyptus steam room, the outdoor whirlpools, cold baths and then a shower and then do it all over again. Don't let the Montréal frost deter you; winter is one of the best times to enjoy the spa.

Take your relaxation to the next level and book in for a facial, body treatment, massage or even a manicure or pedicure. You're unlikely to find a massage menu like this anywhere else in the city. Splurge on a massage with a live harpist to serenade you, because – well, why not?

ON YOUR DOORSTEP
Explore Montréal's stunning Old Port with a walk along the waterfront or wander through the many laneways and explore the shopping, food and seasonal activities.

$ *Water circuit from $70*
|◉| *Delicate dishes made from fresh local produce*

☛ **Old Port of Montréal**
+1 514 284 0333
http://botabota.ca

CANADA

SCANDINAVE SPA

● *Finnish-style sauna and plunge pools*
● *Restorative Swedish massage in stunning surrounds*

If bathing outside in subzero temperatures doesn't sound like the most relaxing way to spend a day, you need to experience Scandinave Spa in Whistler, British Columbia's premier ski destination. This haven of hydrotherapy is perched on the edge of the Lost Lake forest with views across the spruce- and cedar-covered hills. In winter, enjoy the view across the glistening snow-covered forest from the comfort of one of the many outdoor baths.

The Finnish tradition of raising the body's temperature before plunging it in cold water or snow is renowned for its muscle-relaxing and soothing benefits. Purchase a hydrotherapy package and you will find yourself hopping from warm pools to ice-cold and then sliding into an armchair around a crackling fire before repeating the process. The warm baths and saunas are supposed to cleanse the skin and improve circulation, while the cold dipping pools are said to release endorphins and increase the heart rate.

Visitors can also book a massage with one of the Scandinave massage therapists. The Swedish or Restorative massages make a great complementary treatment to your hydrotherapy experience. If all the relaxation has left you hungry, visit the bistro to refuel your rejuvenated body.

Scandinave is only open to patrons 19 years and older, and silence is encouraged; the trickling pools and wind in the pine trees are ample sound track.

ON YOUR DOORSTEP
Visit in winter for the chance to ski the famous slopes of Whistler. In summer, explore the national parks on a hike or mountain bike ride.

$ *$70 bath access*
🍽 *Light meals and snacks in a bistro setting*

☛ **Whistler, British Columbia**
+1 604 935 2424
www.scandinave.com/whistler

CZECH REPUBLIC

CHODOVAR

● *Bathe in beer or hops* ● *Revel in all things beer with a stay in West Bohemia's oldest brewery*

If you do not fall in love with beer after a stay at Chodovar, you never will. Chodovar's history of brewing liquid gold dates back at least to the 1570s, but the brewery today, also a hotel and fun wellness centre, has tapped into every possible beery way to charm you.

In a yellow edifice dating from the mid-19th century, brewery tours and tastings are supplemented by a 'beerarium' restaurant, housed in the former malthouse and storehouse and surrounded by the workings of the brewery. Here, 10 made-on-the-premises brews can be sampled, ranging from dark beer to Pilsen and Radler. And if your taste buds aren't in to it, maybe your body will be. Beer wellness at Chodovar involves bathing in a tub of beer, or, for beery couples, a double bath. Fear not beer-fans, baths come with a chilled glass of lager on the side. For more conventional relaxation, try the whirlpool or Finnish sauna afterwards.

ON YOUR DOORSTEP

Chodová Planá has a brewing tradition dating back five centuries and also boasts a baroque castle and pretty parklands. Nearby, Mariánské Lázně (above) is fabled for its hundred-odd iron-rich mineral springs.

$ *Beer bath CZK690*
🍽 *'Beerarium' restaurant serving hearty Czech food in a former malthouse*

☛ *Chodová Planá*
+420 374 617 100
www.chodovar.cz

● **Spa Treatments**　● **Food & Drink**　● **Luxury**

FRANCE
LES SOURCES DE CAUDALIE

● *Vinotherapy spa treatments using grape-based products* ● *Michelin-starred dining in Le Grand Vigne* ● *Five-star country-style accommodation*

This is not just any spa, this is the original Caudalie Vinothérapie Spa, where the grape-based French skincare range was born. The spa is housed in a collection of six rustic-chic structures with massive old beams that look like they've been there for centuries. The spa has its own natural hot spring and there are 20 treatment rooms where you can enjoy such wine-based fun such as crushed cabernet scrubs, wine-and-vine-flower wraps, Pulp Friction massages (geddit?) and barrel baths of grape marc.

Outside the spa, you can join the grape harvest, visit the vineyard and cellars, partake in guided wine-tasting sessions and dine in Chef Nicolas Masse's Michelin-starred restaurant, La Grande'Vigne.

ON YOUR DOORSTEP
It's hard to see why you'd leave this idyllic estate where you can spend days cycling, swimming, learning to cook and wine tasting. If you must, Bordeaux (above) with its flash wine museum and grand squares is a 30-minute drive north and the beaches of Arcachon are an hour west.

$ *Half-day grape ritual €290*
🍽 *Michelin-starred gourmet French dining*

☛ *Bordeaux*
+33 5 57 83 83 83
www.sources-caudalie.com

● **Spa Treatments** ● **Luxury**

FRANCE
NOLINKSI SPA

● *High-end treatments in a subterranean candlelit spa*
● *Five-star hotel in the centre of Paris' sightseeing area*

There's no other city in the world quite so ripe for indulging in than Paris, and hotel Nolinski is the epitome of indulgence. Housed in a stunning Haussman building on Avenue de l'Opéra, just steps from some of the city's most iconic landmarks (the Louvre, Jardin des Tuileries), Nolinksi perfectly blends glamour and classic Parisian chic thanks to its Carrara-marble-lined lobby, plush carpets, art-deco details and colour scheme ranging from burnt orange to inky blues.

Descend underground into the flickering candlelit spa where a showpiece granite-walled pool is reflected in the mirrored ceiling.

Treatments focus on repair for the whole body from anti-jet-lag eye treatments to a 'hair detox'. Opt for the Nolinski Signature Ritual that starts with a soothing foot bath and sauna before a candle back massage and hot volcanic stone treatment.

ON YOUR DOORSTEP
Nolinski's prime location means the best of Paris is at your feet as soon as you step out the front door. Spend hours lost in some of the world's greatest art collections at the nearby Louvre, the Musée de l'Orangerie and the Musée d'Orsay.

$ *Nolinski Signature Ritual by La Colline €270*
❏ *French fare and delicious desserts in Brasserie Rejane*

☛ *Paris*
+ 33 1 42 86 10 10
http://nolinskiparis. com

GERMANY

HOTEL BAREISS

● *Hydrotherapy, herbal steams and facials deep in the beautiful Black Forest*
● *Three-Michelin-starred restaurant, one of Europe's best*

A twisting road leads over fir-tree-cloaked hills and into the deep valleys of the Black Forest to Hotel Bareiss – a rustic-chic, five-star address, renowned the world over for its three-Michelin-starred restaurant. Head chef Claus-Peter Lumpp walks the culinary high-wire with his exquisitely composed, French-inflected, seasonal menus.

So far, so indulgent, but Bareiss will spoil you in more ways than one. Its stylish spa is one of the finest in this neck of the woods – trust us, you'll want snow to fall in winter just so you can hole up here for the entire day. With its relaxation rooms warmed by open fires, indoor and outdoor hydrotherapy pools, saunas, herbal steam rooms and treatments from marine-mineral facials to silk glove massages and ayurvedic *shirodhara* (oil anointing), forest escapes don't get any more decadent than this.

ON YOUR DOORSTEP

Hotel Bareiss is a terrific base for a leisurely road trip along the B500 Schwarzwald Hochstrasse (Black Forest High Road), which leads you over hill and dale and deep into the lushly forested, lake-speckled heart of the Black Forest National Park.

$ *50-minute full-body massage €84*
🍽 *From pool bar snacks to the pinnacle of haute cuisine*

☞ *Baiersbronn*
+49 7442 470
www.bareiss.com

GREECE
AMANZOE

● *Full-moon yoga sessions held in an amphitheatre*
● *Hilltop marble pavilions fit for a Greek god* ● *Fine dining with a focus on local produce*

Resembling a modern-day Acropolis, Amanzoe sits like a tufa-coloured temple on a hilltop amid an ancient olive grove, the Saronic Islands dotting the spectacular sea views that the resort commands. As the sun sets, the whole scene turns soft shades of pink and mauve – in fact, the view from Mt Olympus could hardly be better.

Though undeniably glamorous, the focus here is on health rather than good times. There are tennis courts, a 25-metre pool (plus three more down at the Beach Club), a gym and a vast spa where practitioners run programs combining diet, gymnastics, Pilates, yoga, massage and sea bathing.

The open-sided yoga pavilion, which looks out on that heavenly view, hosts hatha, vinyasa flow and ashtanga sessions with world-class teachers, while full-moon yoga sessions take place in an amphitheatre to great dramatic effect. The Watsu aquatic therapy sessions combine elements of the Alexander Technique, craniosacral therapy and sound therapy.

The spa also offers a variety of massage and skin treatments using natural ingredients such as organic honey, Himalayan salt and nutrient-rich clay.

After a day or two of care here, combined with an endless supply of divine food, you'll both look and feel as good as any Greek god.

ON YOUR DOORSTEP
Below the resort there's a very exclusive Aman beach club and speedboats for island-hopping excursions. Otherwise, important archaeological sites can be found at Epidaurus and Mycenae, and the picturesque islands of Spetses and Hydra are just offshore.

$ *1-hour aquatic bodywork session €220*
🍽 *Japanese and Greek cuisine from locally sourced suppliers*

☞ **Peloponnese**
+30 2754 772 888
www.aman.com

● Spa Treatments   ● Food & Drink   ● Luxury

ITALY

PETRA SEGRETA

● *Romantic five-star escape high in Gallura's rugged hinterland*
● *Homegrown meals with a gourmet Sardinian touch*

Slip down a lane twisting into the craggy granite hills of Gallura and there, on a rise, is Petra Segreta. Taking in the full sweep of the Costa Smeralda and the glimmering sea, this five-star retreat is pure rustic romance. It's designed like a *stazzo* (a traditional Sardinian shepherd dwelling), with low-slung stone buildings, wood-lined, candlelit spaces and gardens heady with the scent of myrtle, mastic and juniper. This is a hideaway with serious style and off-the-radar privacy.

The intimate vibe segues into the Bali-style spa, with a Roman sauna, Turkish bath and a waterfall cascading into an outdoor pool, with jets and microbubble geysers. Lusciously scented local essential oils are used in massages and treatments such as Padma reflexology and Hawaiian Mana Lomi that, like the setting, border on the divine.

ON YOUR DOORSTEP
Gathered around a piazza, the hill town of San Pantaleo is an authentic slice of Sardinian life. It's a short, scenic drive to the Costa Smeralda, indented with some of Sardinia's loveliest white-sand, turquoise-water bays, such as Aga Khan favourite, Spiaggia dei Principe.

$ *Doubles from €169*
|●| *Own-farm produce, organic homegrown vegetables, Sardinian seafood*

☛ *Sardinia*
+39 0789 1876441
**www.petra
segretaresort.com**

JAPAN

Aman Tokyo

● *Deep soaking tubs with views of the Tokyo skyline*
● *Traditional kampo herbal therapies and customised programs*

More commonly known for their rural retreat, Tokyo Aman is the Aman chain's first luxury urban hotel, located at the top of the cloud-nudging Ōtemachi Tower. The huge minimalist rooms blend natural materials with lots of smooth blonde wood, dark stone walls and white *washi*-paper. Wow factors are everywhere from the *furo* stone baths looking out on the Tokyo skyline to the nothing-is-too-much-trouble service and the chic Black Bar with its black-menu concept including items such as black sesame grissini and the signature black espresso martini.

The luxury continues in the spa where traditional kampo herbal therapies are used as inspiration in treatments. The Aman Tokyo Signature Journey uses Japanese clay, fine camphor and *kuromoji* powder in a full-body scrub to boost circulation, followed by a massage.

ON YOUR DOORSTEP
Stroll around the expansive Imperial Palace Gardens stopping in at the lovely Ninomaru Grove in the East Garden with its pretty pond and teahouse. The nearby National Museum of Modern Art (MOMAT) houses an excellent collection of art from the Meiji period onwards.

$ *Aman Tokyo Signature Journey (150 min) ¥56,000*
🍽 *Creative Italian at restaurant Arva, afternoon tea in The Lounge, French cuisine in The Café*

☛ **Tokyo**
+81 035 224 3333
www.aman.com/ resorts/aman-tokyo

JAPAN

BETTEI OTOZURE

● *Soak in the mineral-rich waters of the ryokan's grand onsen*
● *Sample traditional* kaiseki *cuisine incorporating local specialities*

Tucked into the mountains of this hot-spring-rich country, the sleek Bettei Otozure ryokan (traditional Japanese inn) in the Yamaguchi prefecture is worth the detour from Japan's cultural capitals. The standout here is the ryokan's grand onsen, a commanding set of natural baths fed by the mineral-laden thermal waters that surround this traditional (in sensibility) yet modern (in aesthetic) inn. Onsen are a requisite element in Japanese self-care, similar in concept and experience to public baths in other cultures. Like a Scandinavian sauna, they are egalitarian in spirit, intended as a communal practice. True believers will attest that the alkaline spring water has healing properties, serving as a balm to joint and muscle pain.

The experience at this family-owned inn is enhanced by the beauty of the surrounding woodlands – and by the gracious design of the cedar-wood onsen itself, which offers areas for quiet reflection, conversation and whirlpools. The open-air space in the grand onsen, open until 12.30am, allows for relaxation under the stars – as do the private whirlpools found on the balconies of some private rooms. A separate spa complex offers massages and body treatments.

This ryokan's rural setting might suggest a rough-hewn approach to its on-site dining – and yet the inn's traditional *kaiseki* (Japanese haute cuisine) menu offers a masterful take on this rigorous Japanese dining concept. Expect local additions such as *uni* (sea urchin) or even *fugu* (puffer fish), as well as a selection of local sakes.

ON YOUR DOORSTEP

The rugged Sea of Japan coastline offers opportunities for hiking and exploration by boat – hitch a ride from one of the tour operators based in nearby Nagato for a close-up look at the 'Sea Alps' of Oumi-jima, a collection of rock formations on the island towering above the azure-blue water.

$ *From ¥40,000 per night*
🍴 *Kaiseki (Japanese haute cuisine) using vibrant local ingredients*

☛ *Yumoto Onsen, Yamaguchi*
+81 837 25 3377
http://otozure.jp

JAPAN

PARK HYATT TOKYO

● *Luxurious treatments with Tokyo city views*
● *Egyptian cotton sheets and gold-dust facials*

Even Bill Murray and Scarlett Johansson can't upstage the exceptional Park Hyatt Tokyo – it stole the scene at every chance in Sofia Coppola's *Lost in Translation*. Its sky-lit swimming pool, contemporary chic rooms and 52nd-floor New York Bar, which somehow impossibly looks down on most of Tokyo's endless skyline, look as amazing off-screen as they do on.

The hotel takes up the 39th to 52nd floor of a glass tower building designed by Pritzker Prize–winning architect, the late Dr Kenzo Tange. All of its guestrooms and suites feature original artwork, design touches and modern amenities – splurge on a room with a view if you too, like Scarlett's character Charlotte, wish to contemplate your life while perched on the windowsill staring at the skyscraper-filled horizon.

Work off the Kobe sirloin steak you tucked into over dinner at the New York Grill with a trip to the hotel's Club on the Park gym and aerobic studio for circuit training, aqua exercise, yoga, sauna, or to just relax with a guided Good Night Sleep Stretch. But before you hit your bed (and those luxurious Egyptian cotton sheets), be sure to book in for a treatment at the spa. Get those knots worked out with Japanese oils in a Tokyo Massage, relieve tension and stress with a hot-and-cold-stone facial, or feel like a movie star yourself with a Golden

Body Treatment complete with a gold sugar scrub and oils enriched with gold particles.

ON YOUR DOORSTEP

This is Tokyo. What's not on your doorstep? Head to The Imperial Palace or Yogoyi Park for a bit of greenery and people watching; check out the Shintō shrine, Meiji-jingū; slurp down some soba at a stand-up noodle bar and have a night out in Shinjuku.

$ *Deluxe rooms from ¥75,000 per night; gym & pool access ¥4000*
|◉| *Prime steaks at the New York Grill*

☛ *Tokyo*
+81 353 22 1234
https://tokyo.park.hyatt.com

JORDAN

Mövenpick Resort & Spa Dead Sea

● *Enjoy the Dead Sea's soothing properties as wellness-wishers have done since antiquity*
● *Tranquillity lounge with sea views*

Elements of the Dead Sea's singular make-up have been sought-after for medicinal and indulgent purposes for millennia. The bituminous deposits found in the waters have long been used as a curative and the balsam that grew around the shoreline was the prime source for fragrance in the ancient world. For these reasons, it is said, Mark Anthony conquered the Dead Sea region for Cleopatra. It is in peace that people come to the sun-baked stretch of Dead Sea shore straddled by the Mövenpick Resort today. But they still come seeking cures and pampering.

This is one of the most singular amongst Mövenpick's 83-strong collection of resorts worldwide: unique in Jordan and amongst the foremost wellness addresses in the Middle East. The complex boasts 64,583 sq ft (6000 sq metres) of space dedicated to luxuriating. The five main pools include two with percentages of Dead Sea water, and there is a tranquility lounge (relaxation room) with to-live-for sea vistas. The main ingredient in the treatments offered is the Dead Sea's nutrient-packed black mud, prized for its cleansing and purifying properties.

The resort itself is as welcome to the eye as its treatments are to the body. Designed on a traditional stone-built Jordanian village and set amidst beautiful gardens, many of the 346 rooms boast balconies gazing out over the sea.

ON YOUR DOORSTEP

Once done with the complex's nine restaurants, bars, spa and idyllic Dead Sea beach, nearby adventures outside include a trip to Mt Nebo, supposed burial place of Moses, and the spectacular Hammamat Ma'in natural hot springs.

$ *Dead Sea view rooms with breakfast from JOD99*
❢❂❢ *Juice bar, grilled meats, restaurants from oriental to Italian*

....

☛ *Amman*
+962 5 356 11 11
www.movenpick.com

Dead Sea healing

Seawater: good. Dead Sea water: very, very good. Since Roman times, the afflicted have sought cures here. The Dead Sea has eight times the minerals of normal seawater and the high salt content also means it's a ready-made flotation tank. What's more, the higher levels of potassium and calcium, along with the salt and the region's generous showing of sun, are attributed to the soothing of skin complaints.

MAURITIUS

THE OBEROI

● *Africology and ayurvedic therapies* ● *Dine in the Gunpowder Room, housed within a colonial battery* ● *Long, private white-sand beach*

The Oberoi on Mauritius ups the ante in the battle to be the most luxurious hotel on the island. Its long stretch of private sandy beach certainly helps, as do the thatched villas overlooking a sub-tropical garden. The property also contains a listed national monument, a colonial fortification now lovingly refurbished for guests' dining pleasure, and this helps too.

At the spa, 'Africology' (the practice of using Africa's natural ingredients to create treatments) and ayurvedic techniques predominate, although there is also Thai and other types of therapy available. The signature African Hypoxis Body Experience begins with application of a purifying mask using African plant extracts and marula oil, followed by a soothing African foot massage and a bathing ritual. Alternatively, try having hot lava shells gently glided over your body. Geranium, neroli, rooibos and lavender are among the bountiful African botanicals enhancing the treatments here.

Outside, there are two dreamy pools with ocean views, and it would be wrong not to have a float in them when the rest of the pampering day is over. Hatha yoga, t'ai chi, meditation and breathing techniques are offered alongside floodlit tennis courts and a fitness centre looking out on the Oberoi's rather inviting sub-tropical garden.

ON YOUR DOORSTEP
Port Louis, the capital of Mauritius, is 9 miles (15km) away. It sports attractive French architecture and has decent shopping. In Pamplemousses, 6 miles (10km) east, stop by L'Aventure du Sucre, a sugar museum housed in a former factory with displays on the island's history.

$ *African Hypoxis Body Experience €175*
🍽 *Creole, Asian and international; dine beachside or in a colonial French battery*

⸺⸺⸺⸺⸺⸺⸺⸺

☛ **Turtle Bay, Pointe aux Piments**
+230 204 3600
**www.oberoihotels.
com/hotels-in-mauritius**

MEXICO
CHABLÉ RESORT

● *Villa accommodation in a 19th-century hacienda* ● *Mayan mysticism and an on-site cenote* ● *Organic Mayan menus listed among the best in the world*

Wrested back from the verdant jungle and restored to its original stately grandeur, this 19th-century hacienda and one-time sisal factory is now a world-class destination spa with 750 acres (300 hectares) of steamy Mayan jungle to lose yourself within. Centred around its own cenote – a natural limestone sinkhole celebrated by Mayans as the entrance to the sacred world – the spa has 12 modernist treatment rooms and three sweat lodges devoted to *temazcal* ceremonies conducted by visiting shamans.

Mornings start with conventional complimentary fitness classes: biking, yoga, combat fitness, Pilates and animal motion. Then hardcore spa acolytes progress to bespoke programs utilising chakra therapy, reiki, sound cleansing, Mayan rebirth massages and hypnotic three-hour *temazcal* rituals, where mind and body are stretched to their limits amid copal-infused steam clouds and shamanistic chanting all inside the intense darkness of a sweat lodge. Phew.

Besides the extraordinary treatments on offer, the beauty of Chablé's crumbling walls, snaking tree roots and dense forest hung with lanterns contributes greatly to a general feeling of bliss. It's a feeling that is further enhanced by the exceptional cooking of chefs Jorge Vellejo (of Quintonil in Mexico City, one of the best restaurants in the world) and Luis Ronzón.

Sourcing the best local ingredients, they serve up a modern Mexican menu that is thrilling to the tastebuds – pork cooked underground in spices and bitter orange, carpaccio of grilled mamey fruit, venison tartare with habanero-chilli vinaigrette. It's simply out of this world.

ON YOUR DOORSTEP
Just down the road is the quaint village of Chocholá, where you can pick up local produce such as honey. Otherwise, visit the Yucatán capital, Mérida, with its wonderful museums, art galleries and restaurants.

$ *Mayan herbal compress massage US$240*
🍽 *Mayan-inspired cuisine using only organic ingredients*

☛ *Chocholá, Yucatán*
+52 554 161 4262
http://chableresort. com

MOROCCO

ROYAL MANSOUR

● *Hammam rituals,* rhassoul *masks and argan oil massages in regal surrounds*
● *Moroccan and French fine dining* ● *An exquisite five-star medina*

Entering Royal Mansour is like passing through the gates of paradise. Marrakesh's palatial medina-within-a-medina is architecturally sublime and an ode to Moroccan craftsmanship. And its extraordinary spa is no exception. The pure-white wrought-iron atrium is designed like a giant, three-tiered bird's cage, with delicate patterns, eight-point stars and keyhole arches, fountains and the scent of flowers perfuming the air. It's so intricate it elicits gasps of wonder, and that's before you even get to the treatments.

In cool contrast to the round-the-clock buzz and dusty heat of the red city, the calm of the spa, with its orangery-style pavilion pool, is like a tonic for the soul. Therapists lead you through to steamy, mosaic-clad hammams, mosaic-tiled and lit by filigree lanterns, where a rubdown with a *kessa* mitt and *savon noir* (black olive soap) is followed by honey-scented masks and soapings with orange flower water that leave you silky and glowing. Other treatment stars include purifying *rhassoul* masks using clay from the Atlas Mountains and the ceremonial marocMaroc massage performed using argan oil, velvety monoi butter and rose extract. For the royal treatment, treat yourself to a private spa suite, or simply go for a wander in the gardens, where birds flit among the date palms, bougainvillea, jasmine and orange trees. Paradise indeed.

ON YOUR DOORSTEP
Beyond the medina walls, Royal Mansour is just a short walk from Koutoubia Mosque, built by the sultan of the same name in the 12th century. Its striking minaret, where the raspy call of the muezzin brings the faithful to pray, crowns Marrakesh's skyline.

$ *Light snacks and speciality teas in the Spa Lounge*
🍽 *Creole-inspired pescatarian menu*

☛ **Marrakesh**
+212 52980 8080
www.royalmansour.
com

NETHERLANDS

THERMEN BUSSLOO

● *Massage, medicinal mud, hammam rituals* ● *More than 20 saunas, baths and whirlpools* ● *Heated sunbeds, posh relaxation rooms, Zen gardens*

Hmm, to unwind in the sauna where a mighty Buddha statue watches over you? Or chill in the Himalayan salt crystal grotto that wafts minerals from Nepal? How about the sauna where geysers bubble up à la Iceland's famed Haukadalur valley? Thermen Bussloo lets you spend the day hopping between its 20-plus saunas, soaking pools, hot tubs and relaxation rooms, all set in the pastoral landscape at the edge of Bussloo lake about 60 miles (100km) east of Amsterdam. Sound massage, hot stone massage and medicinal mud treatments are available for those who need extra indulgence. The spa's main claim to fame is *Aufguss*, a ritual during which a sauna master pours essential oils into the steam and circulates the hot, scented air to intensify sweating. Bussloo offers several of the fab, dripping sessions daily.

ON YOUR DOORSTEP
Hoge Veluwe National Park (above) is 15 miles (25km) southeast, with forests, heathlands and sand dunes to explore. The Kröller-Müller art museum sits in the park's midst and features a killer Van Gogh collection and sprawling sculpture garden.

$ *Admission weekday/ weekend €33.50/35.50*
|●| *Organic dishes made from regional fish, cheeses and vegetables*

☞ *Bloemenksweg 38, Voorst, Netherlands*
+31 55 368 26 40
www.thermenbussloo.nl

NORWAY

THIEF SPA

● *Marine treatments and Moroccan hammams with a dash of Scandi cool*
● *The decadent diva of Nordic spa hotels, with a fjord-side location to steal hearts*

The crowning glory of Oslo's sexiest five-star hotel, Thief Spa readily admits to having pinched the best bits of spas from around the world, pepping them up with a little Scandi style and Nordic light. Its intimate, sensual spa is all dark, shadowy corners, flickering candles and clever backlighting that accentuates the granite, gold and glass. Right on the waterfront, where the Norwegian capital meets the fjord, it certainly has the wow factor.

Here you can swim in a seemingly starlit pool and get a proper Moroccan-style rub-down in the hammam with mineral-rich *rhassoul* clay from the Atlas mountains, leaving you super-smooth, several layers of dead skin later. Or jump-start your circulation with the Finnish sauna, as water and essential oils are tossed on to the sizzling stove and the vapours are wafted around. There are Dornbracht sensory showers, where you can choose to be drenched by a waterfall or rain shower, and treatments playing up the marine theme, including algae scrubs and seaweed wraps.

As everyone knows, though, Nordic souls like a little masochism. Only for the very brave (or foolish), a dip in the fjord can be accessed via the beach and jetty. That minute of ice-cold shock will leave your heart racing and skin tingling – and then you'll know you've well and truly arrived.

ON YOUR DOORSTEP
Explore the slick new waterfront development of *Tjuvholmen*, or Thief Island, where the city's most dangerous criminals were once taken to be executed. It now shines with contemporary art and architecture, including the Renzo Piano–designed Astrup Fearnley Museum.

$ *Day ticket from NOK495*
🍽 *Local fish and meat, global with Nordic twist*

....

☛ **Oslo**
+47 24 00 40 00
https://thethief.com

● Spa Treatments ● Luxury

RUSSIA
SANDUNY BATH HOUSE

● *Eight opulent bathhouse rooms to relax in* ● *Feel like a star as you bask in architectural grandeur faithful to Sanduny's 19th-century origins*

Sanduny offers an insight into how the Russian aristocracy must have lived back in the day: very, very well. It was an actor at the court of Catherine II who originally founded the bathhouse in 1808; they were designed to impress and still do. Reclining in the marble colonnaded Top Class Male Bathhouse, modelled on Roman baths, you might well be forgiven for thinking you had slipped back in time a good few centuries. There are three bathhouses for men and two for women, strictly single sex. Groups can hire the eight separate bathhouse rooms privately: each room is ornately decorated in themes ranging from Roman to Russian fairy tales, and is equipped with its own Russian steam room (*banya*). Here, Russian spa tradition dictates, guests can beat themselves (and others) with birch and oak branches to improve circulation.

ON YOUR DOORSTEP
Up the road is the Vysoko-Petrovsky Monastery (above), a 14th-century religious complex that includes the Moscow Literature Museum. Also nearby is Center MARS, one of Moscow's best contemporary art galleries, and iconic city eateries such as farm-to-table restaurant LavkaLavka.

$ *Top Class Bathhouse entry from ₽2800*
|◉| *Russian/Chinese/Uzbek; in halls as ornate as the baths*

☞ **Moscow**
+7 495 782 1808
http://eng.sanduny.ru

SEYCHELLES

Six Senses Zil Pasyon

● *Jungle hikes and stand-up paddleboarding*
● *Yoga with a view of the Indian Ocean and sleep ambassadors*

Situated in a native forest of mango and papaya trees on the 652-acre (260-hectare) private island of Felicité, Zil Pasyon offers all the perks of a private island retreat while also being within easy reach of 10 other islands. This is the first African resort of the Six Senses spa brand and the location feels both secluded and well connected to its neighbours. The 200-strong team of Seychellois and international staff who look after guests do a lot to make the island feel like a small village. And a very unpretentious and friendly village it is, too.

The spa is set among huge granite boulders typical of the Seychelles and overlooks the surrounding aquamarine water. There are five themed treatment villas, a suspended yoga platform with wonderful ocean views and a gasp-inducing saltwater infinity pool.

On arrival, guests are offered a health screening, a body composition analysis followed by a discussion on diet and lifestyle, the results of which inform a bespoke plan for nutrition, sleep and fitness.

Guest experiences include typical massages and 'detox' therapies, plus yoga, stand-up paddleboarding and guided hikes into the island's jungle interior.

The diving and snorkelling in the crystal waters around the island is excellent. Trips are organised with a local PADI dive centre.

ON YOUR DOORSTEP
You can kayak to the marine reserve of Cocos Island and snorkel with turtles, zoom across the water to nearby islands of La Digue and Praslin to eat octopus curry in beachside shacks or explore the old-growth forest in the Vallée de Mai.

$ *€1800 per night B&B, including free morning yoga classes*
I●I *Creole-inspired pescatarian menu*

☛ *Felicité Island*
+248 671000
www.sixsenses.com

SOUTH AFRICA
GROOTBOS PRIVATE NATURE RESERVE

● *Luxury spa treatments from reflexology to massage*
● *Spot whales, dolphins, sharks and penguins on a marine safari*

Head to South Africa's Western Cape for an eco-luxury escape, where you can recharge in the heart of a private nature reserve. Arise each morning to striking views of Walker Bay from a flower-covered hillside perch. Indulge in a feast of locally sourced seafood and organic produce, paired perfectly with local wines and panoramic views from the restaurant terrace. Or request a private picnic in the reserve or at the beach. If you're feeling adventurous, the 'Marine Big 5' await. Head out on a marine safari in Walker Bay and spot great white sharks, southern right whales, bottlenose dolphins, Cape fur seals and African penguins from the comfort of a private boat, or get a closer look on a shark cage dive. Spend some time at the stables with the horses, tour the on-site organic garden, or treat yourself at the spa.

At the core of every activity, every sip and every bite is Grootbos's 'progressive tourism' approach. A stay at this eco-luxury retreat will rejuvenate your mind and body *and* benefit the local environment and community. Grootbos actively protects this pristine piece of wilderness while facilitating eco-training programs, implementing sustainable practices, and creating economic opportunities for local people. To get the true Grootbos experience, enquire about the Progressive Tourism Package – an opportunity to connect with the community, land, cuisine and culture through engaging and uplifting experiences.

ON YOUR DOORSTEP
Situated on the southern coast of the African continent, Grootbos is located in prime whale-watching and wine-sipping territory. Consider a detour to Stellenbosch and Franschhoek on your way from Cape Town to Grootbos.

$ *Approx R12,300 per night including accommodation, activities, meals*
🍽 *Local seafood, wines and organic produce*

....

☛ *Gansbaai*
+27 28 384 8008
www.grootbos.com

SOUTH AFRICA

LEEU ESTATES

● *Ayurvedic treatments using indigenous botanicals* ● *Fine dining on a world-class wine estate*
● *Sumptuous rooms hung with contemporary art*

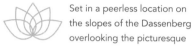

Set in a peerless location on the slopes of the Dassenberg overlooking the picturesque Franschhoek Valley, Leeu Estates is the feather in the Leeu Collection cap. Set amid glorious landscaped gardens, the 19th-century Cape Dutch manor house is filled with an eye-catching contemporary art collection and comprises 17 luxuriously appointed suites with views over the vineyards and mountains.

Indian owner Analjit Singh oversaw the design, which conforms to Vastu Shastra principles, ensuring a sense of calm wellbeing pervades the house and light-filled spa. Set in a secluded location with a 49ft (15m) heated infinity pool, the focus here is on ayurvedic-influenced treatments deploying unusual indigenous botanical oils such as TheraNaka's baobab and neroli oil or the indulgent soothing and hydrating aloe ferox.

When you aren't being nurtured back to health by the team of excellent therapists, you can join Robyn Silberman's ashtanga yoga classes out on the revitalising yoga lawn, or take advantage of specialist tuition from visiting fitness and Pilates experts. There's also a well-equipped gym, although it's more inspiring to borrow a bike for a quick cardio session touring the neighbouring vineyards.

Afterwards, soak in the heated plunge pool overlooking the lily pond before reconvening

for a healthy, multi-course gourmet dinner of salmon with Asian slaw or Karoo lamb *skilpadjie* (liver) with summer peas. Wine pairings from the estate are impeccable, of course.

ON YOUR DOORSTEP
Franschhoek was settled by French Huguenots in 1688, hence the valley's 52 vineyards (above) and 48 top-notch restaurants. Head up to the famous Franschhoek Pass for a view of the valley. Otherwise, Cape Town is a 1½-hour drive west.

$ *90-minute Summer Tree of Life Journey R1500*
▼◉▼ *Taste-tingling fusion food paired with wine from the estate*

☞ ***Franschhoek***
+27 21 492 2222
***https://leeucollection.
com/leeu-estates***

SPAIN
ATZARÓ

● *Pilates, meditation and yoga in a luxurious rural hotel in northeast Ibiza*
● *Signature fusion massages and treatments*

Experience the calming, curative side to Spain's most (in)famous party island with an escape to gorgeously luxe *agroturisme* Atzaró. Queen of Ibiza's blossoming wellness scene, this blissful rural hideaway blends a 300-year-old whitewashed farmhouse with sprawling Mediterranean gardens and bold, rustic-chic design that takes its inspiration from Japan and tribal Africa. It's a dreamy setting for a wellness-focused pause from the world – glam-Ibiza style, of course.

Atzaró hosts an ever-changing selection of multi-day low-season retreats, but also runs a year-round roster of expert-led, small-group classes, some outdoors and all complimentary for guests: meditation, Pilates, yogalates and yoga (hatha, vinyasa, ashtanga).

Soothing gardens of slender palms, lotus ponds, scented citrus trees and fuchsia bougainvillea set the tone for Atzaró's luscious spa. Take a dip in the slim pool (embellished with cabana-like lounges), unwind with a hammam or sauna session, and book in for massages and beauty therapies in wooden huts. Signature 'integration' massages fuse Asian and Western techniques, or try a balancing ayurvedic massage; many treatments are fuelled by organic island-sourced products. La Veranda restaurant serves health-minded, local-produce bites such as avocado gazpacho and garden-fresh salads,

which can be enjoyed poolside at the spa.

Post-spa, outdoor action abounds, from kayaking through translucent seas to half-day hikes to hidden beaches; choose one of Atzaró's guided excursions, or explore independently.

ON YOUR DOORSTEP
The closest village is tiny Sant Llorenç de Balàfia, home to an 18th-century fortress-church. Don't miss Ibiza Town's spectacular Unesco-listed fortified old town, Dalt Vila, settled by the Phoenicians, or the salt-white beaches of the Parc Natural de Ses Salines.

$ 4-day retreat *€506– 710 (including spa)*
!◉! *Seasonal, organic Ibizan ingredients in creative, health-focused combinations*

....

☛ *Ibiza*
+34 971 33 88 38
www.atzaro.com

SPAIN

Vincci Selección La Plantación del Sur

● *Locally distinctive treatments including banana and bamboo-pith facials*
● *Huge space dedicated to wellness with three spa circuits and six pools*

Just back from Tenerife's popular Playa el Duque beach, l a Plantación del Sur is the most luxurious of Vincci's two island hotels, built on a former banana plantation like much of this plush part of Costa Adeje. In homage to this, the hotel is constructed only using natural materials, in Canarian colonial style with cupola-flanked terraces.

A feeling of calm dominates at this getaway, aimed at couples more than families, and the extensive palm-dotted grounds enhance the serenity. The hotel takes advantage of its location to offer plenty of island-inspired pampering, in addition to Thai and ayurvedic therapies and treatments such as lymphatic drainage. Perhaps best is the volcanic cave, where you can receive treatments including a banana facial. Bamboo is a key constituent of wellness here. The pith and sap are used in skin treatments and the canes for massage.

For the more actively inclined, try a workout in the gym, aqua Zumba, Pilates or yoga classes, or tennis. The food on offer at the hotel restaurant is a history lesson in itself: the island's historic place on exploration routes between Europe and the New World mean the menu bridges Spanish classics, such as Iberian pork shoulder, and dishes more associated with the Caribbean, such as *ropa vieja*: a rich meat-and-chickpea stew.

ON YOUR DOORSTEP
As well as numerous big resorts, Tenerife's southwest has access to otherworldly Teide National Park (below), containing Spain's highest mountain, the Mt Teide volcano. Along the coast, try a walk through the La Caleta fishing village to get a feel for Tenerife as the locals live it.

$ *Bamboo-cane massage €89*
🍽 *Southern Europe meets Caribbean: rich on seafood and stews*

☛ **Costa Adeje, Tenerife**
+34 922 717 773
www.vinccihoteles. com

ST LUCIA
Rabot 1745 Spa

● *Mineral-rich cacao treatments* ● *Tree-to-bar experience harvesting cocoa beans, making your own chocolate* ● *Indulgent spa with a view of the Pitons*

Sustainable farming is at the heart of everything Rabot does, and the on-site spa is just one way in which this cocoa plantation harnesses its pods.

Hotel Chocolat – the British chocolatier that owns the estate – came to St Lucia in 2006, revitalising the island's cocoa industry with an ethical farming model supported by a small, high-end hotel and restaurant (Boucan). The indulgent delights of chocolate are everywhere, but Rabot 1745 Spa is also there to remind us of the bean's health benefits. Potions used in the rainforest spa are concocted in small batches on the estate and marry cacao

with other St Lucian ingredients such as fresh banana paste, nutmeg, cinnamon and virgin coconut oil. To see how cacao gets reborn as chocolate, don't miss Boucan's tree-to-bar experience led by a local farmer.

ON YOUR DOORSTEP
Hikers can sweat their way to the top of Gros Piton for fabulous views over golden sands; gentler pursuits include rainforest ziplining and the natural mud baths at Sulphur Springs, St Lucia's dormant volcano.

$ *Cacao Body Exfoliate & Moisturise US$121*
◉ *High-end, cacao-laced healthy cuisine*

☛ *Rabot Estate,*
Soufrière
+1 758 724 6183
www.hotel
chocolat.com

ST LUCIA

VICEROY SUGAR BEACH

● *Coconut polishes and coffee scrubs* ● *Three elegant dining areas with beach and plantation views* ● *Every room or suite sports a jacuzzi or plunge pool*

Set within a former sugar plantation, Viceroy's Sugar Beach address is indeed a sweet assault on the senses. Whether it is a Caribbean-influenced treatment at the resort's Rainforest spa (raw-coconut exfoliations, coconut milk massages beneath the treetops or a coffee scrub), one of a plethora of watersports available (the complex has its own watersports centre with scuba diving, sailing and state-of-the-art water-biking) or relaxing in your ocean-view room or suite with its private plunge pool waiting invitingly, this getaway outdoes others on an island specialising in luxury retreats.

The resort's state-of-the-art gym and fitness centre, with the promise of boot camps up into the surrounding hills, give guests plenty of opportunity to discover that spa hotels do not always entail basking in luxury. But it is the clever and varied treatment menu that best showcases Viceroy Sugar Beach's singular approach to health and wellbeing, with the standout pampering being the 'sulphur seduction experience'. Here, you bathe in St Lucia's sulphuric springs, wallow in sulphuric mud and, after letting it dry, wash off in a waterfall, hopefully allowing any lingering tension to dissipate during a concluding massage.

No doubt about it, though, the star of the show at Sugar Beach is something no amount of human-made pampering can emulate: the

view. Here you have the Caribbean Sea, a scoop of white-sand beach prettily sitting beneath a backdrop of rainforest and soaring mountains.

ON YOUR DOORSTEP

Watersports are big, but this western portion of the island is picturebook St Lucia. Explore the laid-back French colonial town of Soufrière, overshadowed by the formidable dual peaks of the Pitons. Sulphur springs and botanic gardens are also in the vicinity.

$ *Caribbean glow polish with sea salt and raw coconut US$120*
🍽 *Grilled catch of the day; Caribbean fusion*

....

☞ **Val des Pitons, La Baie de Silence, Soufriere**
+1 758 456 8000
www.viceroyhotels andresorts.com/en/ sugarbeach

SWEDEN

Mii Gullo Spa

● *Swedish and head massage with mountain and lake views*
● *Lakeside hot infinity pool at one with the natural surrounds*

Mii Gullo means 'How are you?' in the language of the Sami people (indigenous inhabitants of Europe's far north) – a great question to be asked at the end of a visit to this exclusive spa located in Sweden's oldest mountain hotel, Fjällnäs. No doubt the response will be a string of superlatives as you leave feeling nourished by the clean mountain air, surrounding wilderness and range of high-quality spa treatments.

Hit the slopes for a guided alpine ski tour or trek up to the mountains – any excuse to give your muscles a good beating before sinking into the steaming waters of the outdoor hot tub. The tub sits at eye-level with the rippling lake with its backdrop of looming mountains and gives a feeling of being completely immersed in the natural environment.

There's no need to stay outdoors for the views, though: floor-to-ceiling windows in Mii Gullo's spa provide an indoor nature show while candlelight flickers and ambient music tinkles in the background. For a unique massage therapy, opt for the Fjällnäs Birch Massage where a therapist uses smooth poles of birch to massage the body and stretch out tired muscles. If the idea of that leaves you a bit tense, opt for a gentle head and neck massage – 75 minutes of light massage movements around the skull that will leave your whole body feeling blissed out. Hm... must be time for that hot tub again.

ON YOUR DOORSTEP
Some of Sweden's most beautiful mountain landscapes are available to hikers. Tänndalen is the starting point for extensive trails including the southern Kungsleden (King's Trail) – Sweden's most important hiking route, which from here runs to Storlien.

$ *Birch massage 1295kr*
|⚬| *Gastronomic dishes made from local, seasonal ingredients*

☛ *Tänndalen*
+46 684 230 30
www.fjallnas.se/en/ mii-gullo-spa

SWITZERLAND

B2 Thermalbad & Spa

● More bubbles than a pint of beer in this brewery-turned-spa ● Rooftop infinity pool with front-row views of Zürich's skyline ● Industro-cool boutique digs, with a 33,000-book wine library

Floating above Zürich like the foam on a well-poured beer, the rooftop infinity pool at B2 Thermalbad & Spa is special. Filled with the city's own source of thermal water and with views of the surrounding hills, you'll soon forget you are in the middle of one of Switzerland's largest metropolises. That is until you look down and see the skyline opening like a pop-up book before you. The view is even more alluring after dark when the city begins to twinkle, or when snow is dusting the hills on the city fringes. But rooftop bathing is just one highlight of Switzerland's most architecturally innovative spas.

Lodged in the old Hürlimann Brewery in Zürich's progressive second district and now part of a hip boutique hotel, B2 has stayed true to its roots, with little nods to its former brewing days. The stone cellars have been transformed into a candlelit Roman-Irish bathing grotto, where you can swim and steam in the flickering light of the vaulted chambers. The bathing experience is a 10-step ritual designed to open pores, exfoliate and cleanse the skin. And who wouldn't love the chance to hop into a giant oak beer barrel that's been converted into a whirlpool or be pummelled by the jets of a hydromassage bed? Clever. Wind down afterwards in the cocoon-like warmth of the low-lit relaxation area. Should you wish to ramp up the relaxation, choose from such treatments as herbal stamp massages and soothing milk-and-honey baths in other candlelit spaces.

ON YOUR DOORSTEP
To see how post-industrial Zürich ticks, check out the factories, warehouses and railway viaducts revamped and reborn as hip cafes, galleries and indie shops in Zürich-West (right), the city's ever-evolving fifth district. This is Switzerland with unexpected edge and attitude.

$ *Day entry to thermal baths Sfr36; Irish-Roman spa ritual Sfr60* ●❙ *Healthy snacks, teas and juices at the spa bistro*

☞ *Zürich*
+41 44 205 96 51
www.thermalbad-zuerich.ch

SWITZERLAND

Bürgenstock Hotel & Resort

● *Massive alpine spa with huge panoramic pools*
● *Four luxury hotels including a historic belle époque beauty*

Perched on the forested Bürgenburg ridge, 1476ft (450 metres) above Lake Lucerne, the 148-acre (60-hectare) Bürgenstock Resort is famous for good reason. At its opening in 1873, the belle époque Palace Hotel was an instant success, ferrying guests up to its cloud-busting heights in a trundling funicular that still runs to this day. A second and third hotel were then added, along with restaurants and a vintage spa where Hollywood starlets such as Audrey Hepburn and Sophia Loren flocked to holiday.

Now, after a CHF580-million revamp, it is set to wow the crowds once again with four hotels, 12 restaurants and a spectacular 100,000 sq ft (10,000 sq metre) alpine spa focused on the mind-expanding views. Inside, guests glide from private bath chambers, nap cells and saunas with panoramic views to an Arabian rasul mud chamber and Turkish steam rooms. Outside, the original Hollywood pool remains a protected monument, alongside a breathtaking indoor-outdoor rooftop infinity pool (heated to a blissful 95°F; 35°C) that imbues you with an overwhelming sense of *joie de vivre*.

In the gym, instructors develop bespoke fitness programs, incorporating outdoor hikes, bike rides and even ice-skating. There are also three Davis Cup–standard tennis courts and a nine-hole golf course. Spa treatments use products by Susanne Kaufmann and La Prairie.

Opt for the Diamond Perfection Body Treatment where you'll be scrubbed with diamond powder and swaddled in a caviar cream soufflé for the ultimate film-star indulgence.

ON YOUR DOORSTEP
There are 43 miles (70km) of excellent walking trails on your doorstep, including the half-hour, cliff hugging Felsenweg to the Hammetschwand Lift, Europe's highest outdoor elevator. Back down at lake level, there are boats to Lucerne where you can enjoy refined dining and shopping.

$ *Palace Hotel double room from CHF385 including spa access*
|O| *Mediterranean, Swiss, Asian and 'clean' menus free from animal fats*

☛ *Bürgenstock*
+41 41 612 6000
www.buergenstock.ch

CHOOSING A MASSAGE THERAPY

01

SHIATSU

Shiatsu is an ancient Japanese finger-pressure technique based on traditional Chinese medicine. Practitioners believe that by applying pressure to traditional acupuncture points, they are able to fix imbalances in the body's energy flow, aid relaxation and stimulate lymphatic flow.

02

DEEP TISSUE

Not one for those who like a soft touch, deep-tissue massage involves a highly trained therapist using strong finger pressure and slow friction to affect the sub-layer of muscle tissue as far down to the bone as possible. It can help relieve muscle aches and tension.

03

SWEDISH

One of the most common types of massage, Swedish massage is what most people are referring to when they think of a classic massage. It involves a series of five basic movements: long gliding strokes (*effleurage*), muscle kneading (*petrissage*), friction using fingers or knuckles, rhythmic tapping (*tapotement*) and vibration.

04

HOT STONE

As the name suggests, this type of massage uses smooth hot stones to weigh down the body and act as a kind of rollerball tool for the therapist to work on the muscles. It's generally quite a relaxing massage but can also be invigorating.

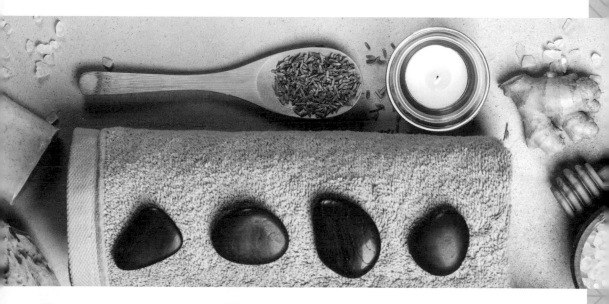

REFLEXOLOGY

Based on an ancient Chinese therapy, reflexology involves applying finger pressure to specific zones on the feet, or hands, that are said to correspond to different organs in the body. Practitioners believe this helps stimulate the internal system to relieve areas of congestion.

THAI

Influenced by traditional medical systems in India, Southeast Asia and China, Thai massage is a rigorous technique where a therapist manipulates the body into stretches applying rhythmic pressures on the body and loosening the joints. It's typically practised on a firm mat on the floor and no oils are used.

REIKI

Not so much a massage but a spiritual therapy of 'energy healing', reiki originated in Japan and involves a practitioner placing their hands above a client's body in positions relating to vital organs and nerve plexes. Reiki practitioners believe this serves as the channel for *qi* (life force) to activate healing energy within receptive points.

SWITZERLAND

SPA TOWN OF LEUKERBAD

● *Cap off a day of skiing with a volcanic mud massage*
● *Enjoy the falling snow from a huge, heated outdoor pool*

 The picturesque alpine spa town of Leukerbad, in the canton of Valais, has several hotel and spa complexes that make use of its mineral-rich thermal waters. Visitors have been drawn here since Roman times; one more recent guest was James Baldwin who wrote about his stay in his 1955 collection of essays, *Notes of a Native Son*.

One of the more chic spas, Walliser Alpentherme offers expansive pools (both indoor and outdoor – perfect for stargazing) and spa treatments that incorporate alpine herbs, hay and flowers. Of particular note is the 'sauna village,' a collection of small lodge-style saunas recreated in typical Valais-style buildings. There's a 'farmhouse' offering a 118°F (48°C) steam bath and a 'stone mill' spilling into a cold-water pool. There's also a sauna-side cafe for nibbles and drinks between sweat sessions. In the Roman-Irish bath, guests pass through 11 stations offering different sauna, steam and soaking treatments at varied temperatures, before concluding the two-hour experience with a massage.

Another option is the Leukerbad Therme with 10 thermal pools and a new sauna complex, which includes a brine bath, steam bath, herbal sauna and Finnish-style sauna. Special activities include champagne breakfasts in the pool (with drinks served on floating wooden boards), Aqua Mystica nights in the baths with

light and sound effects, and tastings of wines made from grapes grown in nearby villages. If your goal is to indulge rather than trim down, have it with a side of hearty Swiss raclette.

ON YOUR DOORSTEP
Depending on the season, the mountains surrounding Leukerbad offer mountain biking and hiking in summer or alpine and cross-country skiing in winter. For a bigger challenge, head to nearby Zermatt, where skiers can take on bigger slopes in the shadow of the Matterhorn.

$ *1-day pass Sfr30*
|●| *Fondue and raclette in town; more diet-friendly options in the spas' restaurants*

....

☛ *Leukerbad*
http://alpentherme.ch
+41 27 472 10 00
www.leukerbad-therme.ch
+41 27 472 20 20

SWITZERLAND

THE DOLDER GRAND SPA

● *A pampering oasis in a huge health spa within one of the world's most luxurious hotels*
● *Spiral meditation maze walk towards mirrored cupola room*

By the time you get to its award-winning spa, your senses will be completely overwhelmed by the sheer drama of the approach to the Dolder Grand Hotel. Located high on Adlisberg Hill above Zürich and looking like a fairy-tale castle, the five-star hotel was redesigned by architect Norman Foster and sprawls across an area of nearly 10 acres (4 hectares). The spa here is pure escapism within escapism.

The Dolder actually began life as a health spa in the 1880s – a place for locals to relax and recharge, but how things have evolved! With 18 different treatment rooms, specialist doctors, fitness coaches and trainers at hand, the challenge will be deciding which treatment to experience first.

There are separate women and men's spas, an aqua zone (mixed) with a large swimming pool overlooking landscaped gardens, outdoor whirlpools, steam baths, a 'snow paradise', and five Japanese-style Sunaburo lounges. There are two spa suites complete with walls clad in mother-of-pearl, and a library of 600 books on health and wellbeing. Perhaps you should just meditate for a bit. Focus. Breathe. Well, there's just the thing for that too: try the Meditation of the Senses guided walk through a candlelit spiral maze into a handcarved mirrored cupola room. Yes, really.

ON YOUR DOORSTEP

If you manage to leave the spa, there is the opulent world of the Dolder Grand itself to explore. Art lovers will find over 100 remarkable pieces by Damien Hirst, Joan Miró, Salvador Dalí and others displayed along the hotel's corridors.

$ *1-hour Meditation of the Senses Sfr120*
|O| *Light meals, juices, teas*

☛ **Kurhausstrasse 65, Zürich**
+41 44 456 60 00
www.thedolder grand.com

SUNABURO *mud bathing*

The inspiration for The Dolder Spa's Sunaburo lounges comes from the Japanese tradition of sand bathing. Part of the onsen (natural hot spring bath) experience, Japanese sunaburo involves lying down while someone shovels hot volcanic sand all over you. The pressure of the warm sand is said to relax the muscles even more than water. At The Dolder, fine warm pebbles are used in the Sunaburo lounges rather than sand.

● Spa Treatments ● Luxury

SWITZERLAND
VICTORIA-JUNGFRAU

● *This grand hotel with big views of the Bernese Alps takes you back to a more elegant age*
● *Results-driven Swiss therapies and Zen-like Japanese Sensai treatments*

The snow-capped peak of Jungfrau peers over your shoulder as you enter this stately hotel in Interlaken. And it's not just the views that are astonishing. This spa is one of Switzerland's largest – and best equipped.

Osteopaths, fitness coaches and physiotherapists are among the specialists on hand should you want to give your body a reboot, while some of the massage treatments on offer include showstoppers like the Swiss Alpine stamp massage, trigger point therapy and Sensai treatments using Koishimaru silk and water from a Japanese hot spring. Or you could just wallow in the steam rooms, saunas

and columned, pavilion-style restaurant post-ski or post-hike in the surrounding Bernese Alps.

ON YOUR DOORSTEP
Oh those mountains! The Alps right on Interlaken's doorstep are so darned spectacular they'll make you want to yodel out loud. Take a train up Kleine Scheidegg to hike in the shadow of Eiger's fearsome north face, or higher still to Europe's highest train station, Jungfraujoch at 11,371ft (3466m).

$ *Day spa packages from Sfr185*
🍽 *Spa Bistro veggie wraps, soups and fresh-pressed juices*

....

☛ **Interlaken**
+41 33 828 28 28
www.victoria
-jungfrau.ch

THAILAND

AMATARA

● *Luxurious pampering sessions* ● *Thai version of a Middle Eastern hammam*
● *Tailored packages and your own personal guru*

You'll feel more relaxed just walking through the door of the luxurious Amatara hotel. Located in an unexpected corner of buzzing Phuket, the whole place is the embodiment of five-star indulgence with sea views and expansive grounds.

Visitors can indulge in a short stay and take advantage of the abundant facilities or go a step further and sign up for one of the wellness packages. This not only gives you a stay in a magnificent room or villa, but your own personalised program – including fitness classes and/or yoga (depending on which package you choose), three healthy meals per day, wellness consultations and luxurious spa treatments.

Enjoy delicious healthy and light dishes at the on-site restaurant The Retreat, or there are other eateries on site for more guilty pleasures. Visiting practitioners of mindfulness, yoga, bodywork and other holistic treatments are on hand to offer guidance and motivation so you can charge forwards with healthy lifestyle changes.

Don't leave without trying the Thai Hammam Journey (included in wellness packages) – a three-hour pampering session based on the bathing traditions of Morocco and Turkey, infusing Thai spa therapy in a delicious concoction of the ultimate indulgence.

ON YOUR DOORSTEP
Amatara is tucked away in Phuket's Cape Panwa, a peaceful area unaffected by intensive urbanisation and tourism, with luxury villas lining the beach and fishermen's huts sleepily dotted in between.

$ *Luxury accommodation starts at THB10,000 per night*
🍽 *An enormous variety of Asian and Western fusion dishes*

☞ **Phuket**
+66 7631 8888
www.amataraphuket.com

THAILAND

CHIVA-SOM

● *Ancient Eastern therapies meet Western medicine* ● *Access to every wellness treatment under the sun* ● *Ultra-chic Thai-inspired suites*

If leaving a luxury resort feeling a little more relaxed than usual feels like a win, wait until you visit Chiva-Som. With its 70 treatment rooms and 54 guest rooms, this Thai temple of wellness means business. In fact, over its 20-odd years in business, Chiva-Som has become the gold standard by which all other health spas are measured, having amassed a legion of loyal fans – including Elle Macpherson, and Victoria and David Beckham – along the way.

Set in a tropical garden behind a white-sand beach, Chiva-Som has every breed of wellness seeker covered, whether you're looking to recover from an injury, improve your yoga technique, embark on a fasting regime, or simply relax and unwind. With a medi-spa on site, you can even add a sneaky laser skin treatment to the mix if you so desire.

Retreat programs begin with a health and wellness consultation to ensure your time at Chiva-Som meets your individual needs and goals, with all 13 retreat packages including up to eight fitness and leisure activities daily, all meals, unlimited use of water therapy suites and a daily spa treatment.

Meals served at the resort's two restaurants are 'clean' yet flavour-packed, with wine and champagne available for guests who subscribe to the relaxing benefits of an evening tipple. After a busy day of Thai boxing, aqua aerobics, cooking classes and breathing exercises, who could blame you?

ON YOUR DOORSTEP
Hua Hin has long been a favoured seaside getaway of Bangkok's elite. Sprawling food markets can be found just a short walk from Chiva-Som, while about an hour's drive to the south lies the iconic Phraya Nakhon Cave with its historic golden throne pavilion.

$ *THB75,000 for a standard 3-night retreat twin share*
I●I *Healthy, flavour-packed Thai and international cuisine*

....

☛ **Hua Hin**
+66 32 536 536
www.chivasom.com

THAILAND
THE PENINSULA

● *A range of treatments fit for royalty*
● *Three-tiered swimming pool* ● *Spa housed in a three-storey Thai villa*

Bangkok's riverside beauty The Peninsula, one of Asia's finest hotels, sits on the western side of the Chao Praya away from the chaos of downtown Bangkok – perfect for a bit of rest and respite. Fusing classic Thai style and modern luxury, all guest rooms look out at river views to a backdrop of the Bangkok skyline. There are plenty of distractions here, from the 197ft (60m) three-tiered swimming pool and tennis court to the numerous dining options and fully decked-out fitness centre. But at the heart of the hotel's offerings is the The Spa, housed in an elegant three-storey Thai villa. For total relaxation try the Essential Mind treatment involving vibrational sound therapy using seven singing bowls for the seven different chakra points on the body. Or opt for the Peninsula Royal Thai Massage – the choice of Thai royalty for generations.

ON YOUR DOORSTEP
Just try to hold on to the serenity of the spa as you hit the buzz of Bangkok's streets. Stand in awe of Wat Pho's Reclining Buddha, get caught up in the chaos of Chatuchak Market and feast on famous Thai street food.

$ *The Essential Mind THB5900 90 mins; Peninsula Royal Thai Massage THB3900*
🍽 *Plenty of dining options; Thai cuisine in the Thiptara restaurant with river views*

☛ **Bangkok**
+66 2 020 2888
**http://bangkok.
peninsula.com**

● **Spa Treatments** ● **Food & Drink** ● **Luxury**

TURKS & CAICOS
COMO PARROT CAY

● *Ayurvedic treatments and complementary Pilates classes* ● *Como Shambhala cuisine incorporating raw food* ● *Private Caribbean island just for hotel guests*

Rediscovering your inner peace miraculously becomes much easier when staying at a resort with exclusive use of an entire sand-rimmed Caribbean cay. Expectations are automatically raised when the words 'Turks', 'Caicos' and 'resort' are mentioned together and Como Parrot Cay does not disappoint.

The resort recently benefited from a brand new spa, the Como Shambhala, that has turned a great place to unwind into an exceptional one. Wellness has a distinctive ayurvedic flavour with shirodhara, pizichili and abhyanga treatments available. Pilates and yoga lovers will be wowed by the impressive spaces for these activities. And

then it is bathing time: in the jacuzzi garden, or – if you have bagged one of the resort's beach houses or villas – your own private pool.

ON YOUR DOORSTEP
This being a private cay means gleaming blue ocean is on your doorstep. Whichever island you are frequenting in the archipelago, most action is adjacent to or in the water. The islands sport one of the world's longest coral reefs – perfect for divers.

$ *Como Shambhala bath and massage US$275*
🍽 *High-end Caribbean, Mediterranean and Asian cuisine*

☛ **Parrot Cay, Providenciales +1 649 946 7788 www.comohotels. com/parrotcay**

UNITED KINGDOM

CHEWTON GLEN

● *Hydrotherapy and holistic treatments in high style* ● *Fine dining and cookery school using local produce* ● *Country escape on the New Forest fringes*

Pulling up to Chewton Glen, you can't help but pinch yourself – this ivy-swathed country manor in manicured grounds looks every inch ready for a role in a costume drama. But beyond its old-school flair, this Hampshire hotel sets itself apart with its rustic-chic treehouse suites high in the canopy and its award-winning spa. The spa itself contains one of Europe's largest hydrotherapy pools, as well as a gorgeous tiled pool complete with Grecian columns and views of the gardens. There is also an outdoor whirlpool, crystal steam room and aromatherapy sauna.

Treatments take the holistic approach, be it a chakra-balancing *kundalini* back treatment, reiki sessions, body scrubs and clay wraps. For their take on a non-surgical facelift try the signature 75-minute Osaki Glow facial.

ON YOUR DOORSTEP
It's an easy stroll to the lovely cliff-backed beach at Highcliffe-on-Sea, with views across to the Isle of Wight and the Needles. The ancient woods of the New Forest National Park unfurl just north of Chewton Glen, with miles of trails for exploring.

$ *Spa days (including treatments) £155–310*
🍽 *Produce grown in the kitchen garden or sourced locally*

☞ **New Milton, Hampshire**
+44 (0)1425 275341
www.chewton glen.com

THE TREEHOUSE *treatment*

If you're lucky enough to stay overnight in one of Chewton Glen's nouveau-rustic treehouse suites (complete with wood-burning stoves and private outdoor hot tubs), you can opt for special forest-inspired treatments, such as the New Forest Flow deep-pressure massage and the soothing Tree Top Tranquility Body Ritual, using hot oil from a rose-scented candle.

UNITED KINGDOM

LUCKNAM PARK HOTEL & SPA

● *Serene health spa within the walled gardens of a luxurious country estate* ● *Well-being House offering Pilates, yoga, sunlight therapy and dry floatation*

The epitome of luxurious escapes, Lucknam Park Hotel looms in all its Grade II–listed, Palladian mansion splendour, like some kind of dream film location. The sound of horses hooves on gravel, fires being stoked, fine china cups laid in saucers, as well as the views across the 500-acre (200-hectare) estate will transport you straight into a *Downton Abbey* drama. Dating from 1720, this five-star stately retreat is as indulgent as it is tranquil. It's easy to wander the grounds and lose yourself in quiet moments: release a black-wrought-iron gate and you're suddenly alone with statues in a perfectly manicured, high-walled rose garden.

Treat yourself to a night here, a package, or just visit the day spa, which was relaunched in July 2017 in conjunction with the ESPA skincare line. The Well-being House, a Cotswold stone building adjacent to the spa, offers yoga, Pilates and mindfulness classes as well as the Haslauer Reflective Sunlight Therapy, a treatment designed to give you all the benefits of sunlight but without the harmful ultraviolet rays. It's the only UK hotel and spa to offer the treatment. You'll likely get into a distracted tizz trying to decide what to revel in first at Lucknam Park: a class at the Cookery School, a ride across the estate on a horse from the Equestrian Centre, a dip in the outdoor salt-water plunge pool? Maybe

quieten your mind with an Inner Calm Massage, featuring a bespoke aromatherapy treatment with ESPA oils made locally in Somerset.

ON YOUR DOORSTEP
Lucknam Park is just 6 miles (9.6km) from the historic town of Bath. A visit to its Roman Baths (Britain's only hot spring) is a must. The Cotswolds are also nearby: perfect for exploring chocolate-box limestone villages and hunting for antiques.

$ *Classic rooms from £295 per night, based on two adults sharing on a room-only basis (including use of spa facilities); one-hour inner-calm massage £102*
🍽 *Organic, local produce: casual brasserie or Michelin-starred dining*

....

☛ **Wiltshire**
+44 (0)1225 742777
www.lucknampark.
co.uk

UNITED KINGDOM

St Brides Spa

● *Thalassotherapy pools and marine-themed treatments* ● *Fine dining with Pembrokeshire produce and local seafood* ● *Seafront beauty of a spa hotel*

Many places wax lyrical about having a sea view but St Brides Spa really has got it nailed. From its hilltop perch above Saundersfoot Bay in the Pembrokeshire Coast National Park, the view is darned spectacular – no matter what the fickle Welsh weather throws at it. And there's something surreal – yet undeniably special – about being gently massaged by hydrotherapy jets in the warm saltwater of the open-air infinity pool, while simultaneously being exposed to the elements, listening to the caw of seagulls and letting your eye drift over cliff, beach and hedgerowed hill.

Part of the swish five-star hotel of the same name, the thermal suite is nice and intimate, thanks to numbers being restricted through time slots of 90 minutes. This keeps things quiet and conducive to proper relaxation in the salt infusion room, the herbal rock sauna and aroma steam room. Glass walls perfectly frame the coastscape in the relaxation room, where you can snuggle up in a robe and sip herbal teas.

The therapists here have an intuitive touch, working small miracles on tense muscles and sensitive skin with the seaweed-based VOYA products, rich in minerals. The treatments have a marine theme, too: from the seaweed leaf wraps to algae facials and lava shell back massages. The ultimate quick pick-me-up?

It has to be the head-clearing peppermint, sugar and seaweed glow scrub. Divine.

ON YOUR DOORSTEP

Beyond Saundersfoot, the glorious Pembrokeshire coast is your oyster. Go slow touring here and you'll uncover some of Britain's most beautiful bays, backed by dramatic cliffs and rock formations, or strike out on foot on the 186-mile (300km) coastal path linking them.

$ *90-minute thermal suite session £35, complimentary with two treatments*
🍽 *From light snacks to fine dining*

☛ **Saundersfoot, Pembrokeshire**
+44 (0)1834 812304
https://stbrides spahotel.com

● **Spa Treatments** ● **Luxury**

UNITED KINGDOM
VALE RESORT

● *Lush ayurveda-inspired treatments* ● *'Sleep' and 'Float' zones*
● *A first-class spa resort set in castle grounds near Cardiff*

It's just 11 miles (18km) from the Welsh capital Cardiff to the country calm of Hensol, where the Vale Resort spreads itself with ease across the 650-acre (263-hectare) grounds of a Gothic-revival castle. The spa is the resort's pride and joy, going beyond the usual sauna, whirlpool and steam room (though it has that too), with its lantern-lit, Indian-inspired 'Sleep Zone' and 'Float Zone', the latter a room of soporific waterbeds complete with trickling wall fountain.

Dragging you away from said bed is a state-of-the-art gym, a pool, classes from spinning to Zumba and two championship golf courses.

Too much like hard work? Book treatments from Clarins, ayurveda-inspired Sundari and British-based Temple Spa. The signature 85-minute 'Champagne and Truffles', a hot stone massage followed by a melting mask and truffle-infused facial, is utterly indulgent.

ON YOUR DOORSTEP
Wander the expansive grounds to Hensol Castle, a late 17th-century castellated manor house in flamboyant neo-Gothic style, and Llanerch Vineyard. The latter offers guided tours and wine tastings of its award-winning Welsh Cariad wines, as well as cookery classes.

$ *Spa days (including 90-minute treatment) £99; Champagne & Truffles facial £75*
🍽 *Healthy spa buffet lunches, indulgent afternoon teas*

☞ *Vale of Glamorgan, Wales*
+44 (0)1443 665888
www.valeresort.com

UNITED STATES
AIRE ANCIENT BATHS

● *Massages with botanical oils* ● *Indulgent soaks at a variety of temperatures, from relaxing to tingling*

Aire Ancient Baths combines sensory indulgence (candles, dim light, a restored historic building) and the soothing power of water to relax even the most stressed-out people. Bathers can choose between hot, warm and cold baths, as well as steam, jet and saltwater options, and then conclude with a massage. Visitors can also hit the relaxation area to rest on warm marble stone with a herbal tea.

The baths comprise the Caldarium (102°F; 38°C), the Frigidarium (50°F; 10°C), the Tepidarium (97°F; 36°C), the Balneum (jet bath) and the Laconicum (steam room), or you can choose to reach a state of total physical and mental escape in the Flotarium (saltwater bath).

Don't miss having one of the full body massages featuring a botanical oil and ending with a scalp massage.

ON YOUR DOORSTEP

Located in Tribeca in NYC, you are in the midst of some of the best restaurants and shops in the world. Your goal will be to hold on to the relaxation you have achieved at Aire once you're out on the hectic city streets.

$ *Bath and 60-minute full body massage from US$200*

☞ **New York City**
+1 646 878 6174
beaire.com

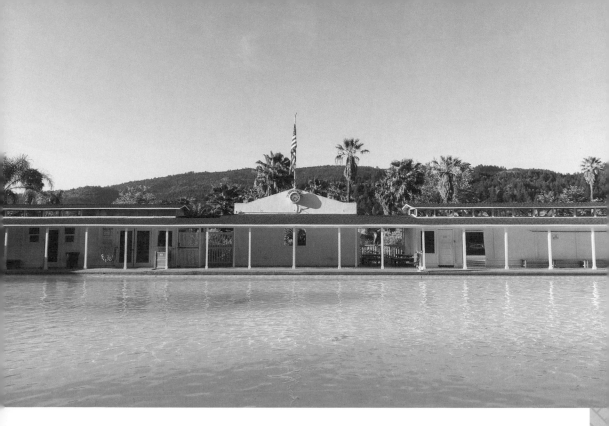

● **Spa Treatments**   ● **Food & Drink**

UNITED STATES
INDIAN SPRINGS

● *Relax into a deep-tissue massage after a mud bath and mineral-water soak*
● *Indulge in a half-dozen Hog Island oysters and Napa Valley sparkling wine*

Calistoga's hot springs have drawn visitors since the Wappo people built sweat lodges over steam vents 8000 years ago. More recent visitors include Leland Stanford, who considered building his namesake university here, before decamping to Palo Alto, 100 miles (160km) south. Now, this resort offers a stylish take on old California. The main pool, built in 1913, is the standout and the place to see, be seen, swim and snap photos for Instagram. Those looking for more privacy and fewer kids will want to continue to the smaller, more intimate Adult Pool. And those looking for the ultimate one-on-one experience will want to book in for a massage at the graceful spa complex, with highly trained therapists offering personalised takes on standard, deep-tissue, and aromatherapy massages, plus mud baths, mineral soaks and various body treatments.

ON YOUR DOORSTEP
Calistoga is the perfect jumping-off point for exploring the winemakers and parks of Napa Valley. Grab a picnic for lunch on the grounds of the nearby Napa Cellars vineyard or get a bird's-eye view of the entire valley from above on a morning hot-air balloon ride.

$ *Room per night from US$220*
|◉| *American classics with Napa roots, think burgers and maple-brined pork chops*

☛ *Calistoga, California*
+1 707 709 8139
www.indiansprings calistoga.com

UNITED STATES

SALAMANDER RESORT

● *Vast spa and wellness centre with infinity pool*
● *Pet-friendly suites with views of Virginia horse country*

Set in the foothills of the Blue Ridge Mountains, this area of Virginia has always been known for its horse farms and is becoming increasingly famous for its wineries, both of which are showcased at Salamander. The resort dedicates 25 of its 340 acres (137 hectares) to equestrian use, and beginners to experienced riders can spend time on the horses.

After a day of hiking, ziplining or riding, you can choose from a variety of spa amenities, including facials, hot stone treatments, massages or swimming in the infinity pool. The 23,000 sq ft (2100 sq metres) wellness centre has both indoor and outdoor workout areas, as well as 14 treatment rooms. Fitness classes range from yoga and Pilates to high-intensity interval training.

ON YOUR DOORSTEP

At Salamander, you are only an hour away from the endless to-do list that is Washington, DC. The top attractions are, of course, the Air and Space Museum, the Lincoln Memorial and the National Gallery of Art.

$ *3-day stay with spa treatments approx US$1899 for two*
🍽 *Wine-country food and drinks from casual to upscale*

☞ **Middleburg, Virginia**
+1 844 303 2723
www.salamander resort.com

HEALING *horses*

"*The silent presence of a horse draws those around into a mindful place and makes us more aware. Our hearts resonate with theirs, and within that resonance we find peace, compassion, mutual respect and strength.*"
Sheryl Jordan, Equestrian Director, Salamander Resort

● **Spa Treatments**   ● **Food & Drink**

UNITED STATES
Ten Thousand Waves

● *Glow with a Japanese organic facial*
● *Savour izakaya-style (Japanese pub) snacks*

Are you in New Mexico or Japan? It's sometimes hard to tell at this impeccably designed spa complex set in a piñon forest. Since it opened in 1981 with a bathhouse and a few private hot tubs, Ten Thousand Waves has grown slowly into a full-service spa and lodge that's still a cornerstone of hip life in Santa Fe. A typical escape here is similar to what you'd find at a Japanese onsen (natural hot spring bath): check in to one of the Zen-meets-Southwest rooms (or go quirkier in the anime-theme studio or Airstream trailer), then spend a couple of days cycling between baths, treatments and meals at the on-site restaurant – in your *yukata* (light summer kimono) and slippers, naturally. Don't miss the house-brand pine-scented lotion, and be sure to get at least one deep shiatsu massage.

ON YOUR DOORSTEP
Head up the nearby mountain for skiing or hiking; Aspen Vista Trail is one of the most famous, for its lush yellow fall colours. And Santa Fe itself, a short drive downhill, is packed with galleries, shops and excellent restaurants.

$ *US$129 for a 1-hour shiatsu massage*
🍽 *Local, organic, Japanese-inspired, including plenty of sake*

☛ **Santa Fe, New Mexico**
+1 505 982 9304
https://tenthousand waves.com

UNITED STATES

THE HOTEL HERSHEY

● *Chocolate immersions and cocoa facials* ● *Chocolate tours and tastings*
● *1930s-built mega-hotel ensconced in verdant Pennsylvanian woodlands*

A hotel that pays homage to the most famous confectionery baron of all time – Milton S Hershey – and his legacy might sound like it would hinder your health more than help it. But the self-proclaimed 'sweetest place on Earth' has a fitness centre, woodsy hiking trails and a golf course nearby to assist in getting back down a belt size after the extravagances of the complex's eating and drinking experiences (chocolate–wine pairings, chocolate tours and a cocoa beanery cafe serving up all manner of wondrous chocolate treats, and all that *before* your main meal!).

The spa raises the levels of Hershey hedonism up a few bars, with a wacky treatment list reading as if it were devised by Oompa Loompas in Willy Wonka's chocolate factory. A cocoa facial? Well, the cacao fruit is apparently an antioxidant. A whipped cocoa bath? Foaming chocolate milk softens the skin. A cocoa bean polish, exfoliated by husks of cacao beans? The sweet temptations stack up like candies in a jar.

If perchance you have come to the Hershey empire with no great love of chocolate, treatments here come in other themes. The Hersheys spent much time in Cuba harvesting Cuban sugar, and Hotel Hershey has cultivated a range of lime-, jasmine- and coffee-based pampering accordingly.

Wash it away with a Vichy shower and a splash in the indoor and outdoor pools.

ON YOUR DOORSTEP
Hotel Hershey is part of a huge estate containing Hersheypark, a chocolate-themed amusement park, and a 23-acre (9-hectare) garden showcasing 5600 types of roses. Outside of chocolate town, Harrisburg and Gettysburg, with their associated American Civil War attractions, are both within an hour's drive.

$ *Chocolate immersion US$205*
🍽 *Iconic American, contemporary Italian and abundant sweet treats*

☛ **Hershey, Pennsylvania**
+1 717 520 5888
www.thehotel hershey.com

Inspired

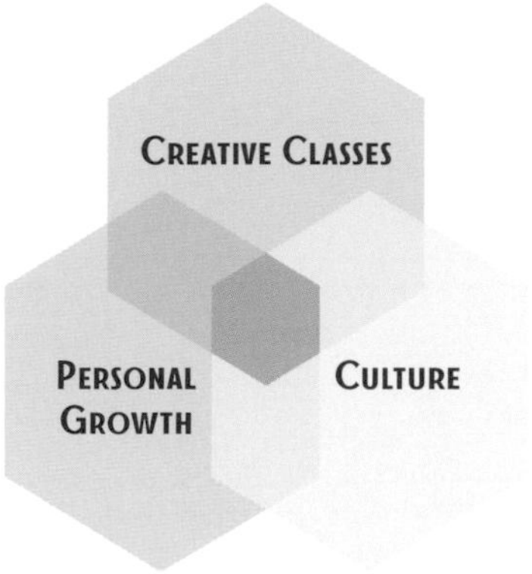

CREATIVE CLASSES

PERSONAL GROWTH

CULTURE

AUSTRALIA

MOUNTAIN SEAS RETREAT

● *A range of creative art programs held in the on-site Arts Centre*
● *Develop life-altering skills for your mind and spirit*

It doesn't get much more inspiring than this. The aptly named Mountain Seas spiritual and artistic retreat sits on the rugged natural beauty of sparsely populated Flinders Island surrounded by 40,000 acres (16,187 hectares) of national parks. In the shadow of Mt Strzelecki and overlooking curiously named Trousers Point Beach, there is no finer place to get your creative juices flowing and to find mindfulness and self-healing.

Mountain Seas runs several programs to suit varied interests, from painting and photography to sculpture and ceramics, with all the tools and equipment provided and workshops held in the Arts Centre on their secluded property. The hosts here invite guests to use the stunning natural environment as inspiration for artistic and spiritual expression.

The retreat offers many yoga classes held in the Yoga Yurt looking out at the views. Soak your aches and pains away afterwards in the outdoor eight-person hot spring spa, or if you still need to burn some energy you can take to the nearby mountains with plenty of hiking trails and wildlife-watching opportunities.

To further your self-healing, the retreat features a Goddess Grove with seven spiritual locations providing a connection to the seven chakras of human existence; the idea being that this can help guests harness the power and energy of their chakras for their general health and wellbeing.

ON YOUR DOORSTEP

Mountain Seas is just 0.6 miles (1km) from the trailhead to Mt Strzelecki and roughly the same distance to Trousers Point Beach from where there is a great 1.1-mile (1.9km) coastal circuit walk. There are bicycles available to explore the area.

$ *2-night minimum stay in a single suite from AU$135 per night*
🍽 *Organic food using produce fom the retreat's garden*

....

☛ *Flinders Island, Tasmania*
+61 3 6359 4553
www.mountainseas. com.au

CHINA

AMANYANGYUN

● *Explore the art of calligraphy and Chinese painting* ● *Live and learn in antique structures that date back over 1000 years* ● *Attend a kūnqǔ opera performance*

Amanyangyun represents an extraordinary feat of architectural and ecological conservation. The story begins 500 miles (800km) south of Shànghǎi in rural Fúzhōu in China's eastern Jiāngxī province, an area famed for its millennia-old camphor forests and historic villages. In 2002, these villages and forests were marked for destruction in order to accommodate a much-needed reservoir. That is until Shànghǎi philanthropist Ma Dadong conceived of an audacious plan to rescue 10,000 trees and 50 Ming and Qing Dynasty structures and relocate them to the outskirts of Shànghǎi.

Fifteen years later, and with the help of the culturally-aware Aman group, Amanyangyun is now one of the most extraordinary wellness retreats in the world. Meaning 'nourishing cloud', *yangyun* is a reference to expanding the 'cloud' of the mind with knowledge. It speaks to the resort's mission to safeguard China's priceless cultural treasures, some of which you can seek out at Nan Shufang, the cultural and spiritual heart of the complex.

A re-creation of the scholars' studios of 17th-century China, the pavilion is a place to learn, contemplate and practise traditional crafts such as calligraphy, music and painting. Kūnqǔ opera is also performed here and guests can take part in tea and incense ceremonies. Outside, the calming scent of the ethereal camphor forest sets the tone for a meditative and introspective experience in which guests learn to immerse themselves in the moment while contemplating thousands of years of history.

ON YOUR DOORSTEP

Amanyangyun's tranquil setting belies its proximity to downtown Shànghǎi. In less than an hour you can find yourself in the historic Bund district where the city's finest cultural, dining and shopping attractions are located. Near the property, you'll also find a golf course and tennis courts.

$ *Calligraphy & Buddhism ¥400; brush painting ¥595*
🍴 *LAZHU specialises in refined Jiāngxī cuisine*

☛ **Minhang District, Shànghǎi**
+86 21 8011 9999
www.aman.com/ resorts/amanyangyun

FRANCE
Couvent Sainte-Marie de la Tourette

● *Stimulating seminars on life's deeper subjects with Franciscan friars*
● *Stay the night in brutalist architect Le Corbusier's distinctly different monastery*

If you are thinking of retreating from the world awhile for some inner reflection, it's worth doing so in style: the style of one of the world's most renowned architects, no less. Constructed in the late 1950s, Le Corbusier's modernist concrete marvel is built on stilts into a hillside near Lyon and offers a rather radical change from typical monastery experiences.

For the duration of your stay, you can share the Franciscan friars' way of life along with pilgrims and architect fanatics. Simple rooms offer those essential monastic requirements, a space for rest and introspection (a bed and a desk) and proximity to nature (a balcony). Silence (let's call it calm, because some guests will occasionally whisper) is observed in the monastery. You can attend weekly courses on spiritual and mind-broadening subjects for an additional fee.

ON YOUR DOORSTEP
Lyon (above) is a 15.5-mile (25km) drive away, with its celebrated restaurants and nightlife providing the antithesis of the Sainte-Marie de la Tourette experience. The point of the convent is that there is precious little around to distract or detract from that contemplation.

$ *Overnight stay with breakfast €32; spiritual contemplation free*
🍴 *Simple French cooking; dinner bookable 2 weeks in advance*

☛ *L'Arbresele, Eveux*
+33 4 72 19 10 90
www.couvent delatourette.fr

FRANCE

Paris Writers' Retreat

● *Five days of workshopping with the finest literary talent*
● *Some of the world's best museums on your doorstep*

Run by *New York Times* best-selling author and literary agent Wendy Goldman Rohm, this writers' retreat in a beautiful Parisian loft is a fantastic creative experience in a beautiful setting. It's presided over by some of the finest contemporary literary talent and attended by a cosmopolitan crowd of serious wannabe writers, some of whom have crossed continents to learn here.

For five intense days, participants workshop structure, setting, style and narration in genres ranging from memoir to romance and psychological thrillers. The sessions are supportive, insightful and challenging, and are followed by guided meditations. Working lunches in bakeries and bistros haunted by literary giants such as Hemingway and Oscar Wilde add another rich dimension. Writing and debating the finer points of paragraphs seems only natural here, rather than the indulgent hobby of dilettantes.

In the evening, there is time for networking soirées with Parisian intellectuals and authors, or drinks and long walks by the Seine. The high-minded conversation, earnest intellectual endeavour and just being in this city combine in a deeply inspiring way, sparking lots of fresh new ideas.

Heading home to a humdrum writing routine will likely bring you back to earth with a bump, but you'll have made an invaluable set of contacts and an important and active writers' group to carry you through to the final chapter.

ON YOUR DOORSTEP
Other than indulging in some excellent lunches and dinners, the all-day, every-day course is intense and doesn't leave much time for sightseeing, so add on a couple of days to enjoy the museums, cafe culture and shopping of the City of Light.

$ *5-day conference US$1995pp*
|O| *Bakery-bought baguettes and bistro lunches*

☞ **Paris**
+1 646 845 9185
www.pariswriters
retreat.com

GREECE

Skyros Centre

- ● *Writing courses mentored by award-winning tutors and published authors*
- ● *Holistic holidays that offer guests a supportive space in which to explore their creativity*

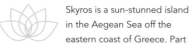

Skyros is a sun-stunned island in the Aegean Sea off the eastern coast of Greece. Part of the wild and woolly Sporades chain, it is remote and little-visited except by in-the-know Athenians who come for the beautiful beaches and alternative vibe, much of which is down to the Skyros Centre, a holistic holiday company that has operated on the island since 1979.

The brainchild of Greek journalist Yannis Andricopoulos and American psychologist Dr Dina Glouberman, Skyros offers mind, body and spirit courses that range from Finding Your Purpose to singing, yoga, creative writing, dance and windsurfing. But Skyros is so much more than a simple wellness retreat. With its unbeatable ingredients of creative camaraderie, meals by the sea, communal life, work groups (because 'work is love made visible'), crazy parties and naked midnight swims, it forges soulful communities that can last a lifetime, which is why people return again and again.

Particularly renowned is Skyros' Writers' Lab, which attracts award-winning guest tutors to the English Villa – or the 'Madhouse', as the centre is locally known. Days here start with early-morning yoga, journalling and chores such as gardening. Then lessons run from 10.30am to 1.30pm and include writing, reading, sharing and critiquing work in a friendly and supportive environment. Communal lunches, afternoon sea swims and further fun, creative classes (massage, pottery or painting) fill up the days all too quickly.

ON YOUR DOORSTEP

It may be tiny, but Skyros is rich in history and attracts a wealthy Athenian crowd, hence the hip shops and the pint-sized museums in Skyros village. There's also a stunning amphitheatre overlooking the sea and an arts festival in June.

$ *2-week Writers Lab from £1295pp*
⦿ *Communal dining on fresh Greek produce*

....

☛ *Skyros*
+44 (0)1983 865 566
www.skyros.com

GUATEMALA
THE STORYTELLER WITHIN

● *Supportive women-only writing circle exploring internal narratives*
● *Daily morning yoga, sound healing, Mayan and Movement ceremonies*

Set in various scenically sited guesthouses on the shores of Lake Atitlán, this women-only writing retreat is an inspiring place to journey inwards and work on readjusting worn-out perspectives that may be holding you back in life.

Hosted by writer and yoga teacher Aimee Hansen, the retreats use writing as a means of self-exploration, teasing out damaging old narratives and awakening more inspiring voices that can help shape a more fruitful, creative and positive life. At each retreat, Aimee is joined by guest facilitators who lead morning yoga sessions and integral evening ceremonies, based on various shamanic traditions, which aim to help guests reconnect with themselves and their energies.

Certainly, the setting, in the lush forest overlooking Lake Atitlán and its impressive volcanoes, is both inspiring and rejuvenating. Reflecting on the area's natural beauty, wild swimming in the lake and meditating along gentle walking trails has an incredibly restorative effect. It also seems to help participants open themselves up to the rare experience of genuine vulnerability and heart-opening sharing that the retreat facilitates.

Many women find the experience of sharing, laughing, crying and bonding with the group liberating and transformative. Despite initial nerves, the ability to speak one's truth to a group of sympathetic and open-minded listeners affords the confidence to unload oppressive emotional baggage and leave the retreat feeling lighter, stronger and more joyful.

ON YOUR DOORSTEP
The retreat is located in a rural setting on the shores of Lake Atitlán in the Guatemalan Highlands. Excursions are arranged to local villages where Mayan culture still prevails, and there are options for hiking, swimming and kayaking during free afternoons.

$ *All-inclusive, 8-night retreat US$1795pp based on double room* 🍽 *Guatemalan-inspired vegetarian meals*

☞ *Casa de Joyce, San Marcos La Laguna*
+502 3094 2087
www.thestory tellerwithin.com

Meditation is a powerful tool in training the brain and nervous system, and learning to be present in the moment. It can help alleviate stress, improve concentration, reduce negative emotions and pain, and increase immune function. Find a quiet spot, become present in your surroundings and try any one of these techniques that feels right for you.

TECHNIQUES FOR M

01

MANTRA MEDITATION

Mantra meditation involves repeating a mantra in your head silently to help calm your thoughts. It can be one of the Sanskrit mantras, such as the purifying *Om mani padme hum*, or you can simply repeat a personal mantra.

02

MANDALA COLOURING MEDITATION

Mandala loosely means 'circle' in Sanskrit and this technique involves colouring geometric shapes as a way of relaxing, enhancing your creativity, promoting sleep and reducing depression.

NDFUL MEDITATION

03

BREATHING MEDITATION

This can be quite a powerful form of meditation. Close your eyes and bring your attention to your breath. Notice as you breathe in and out, let your mind wander but notice when it does and then come back to focusing on your breath.

04

WALKING MEDITATION

One for people who prefer some movement with their meditation. Slowly walk, focusing on each movement as you go. Raise your leg with purpose and be mindful of your actions with each step – how does it change? How does it feel?

05

CHANTING MEDITATION

Similar to mantra meditation, chanting meditation involves saying your mantra out loud over and over. This produces certain vibrations, which help calm the mind and focus your thinking.

ITALY

SIRENLAND WRITERS' CONFERENCE

● *One-on-one writing workshops* ● *Early-evening readings and talks*
● *Sightseeing in Pompeii and boat trips to Capri*

This serious writing retreat (application required) is held in what is surely one of the most beautiful hotels in the world: Positano's cliff-hugging Le Sirenuse. Mornings are spent workshopping manuscripts with impressive faculty members Dani Shapiro (author and professor of creative writing), Jim Shepard (journalist and script writer) and Hannah Tinti (author and editor of *One Story* magazine) while afternoons are dedicated to sightseeing, yoga or spa treatments in the luxurious spa designed by Gae Aulenti.

The signature Le Sirenuse massage using aromatic citrus oil from the region's famous lemons is the perfect antidote to performance nerves conjured by open-mic nights, group readings and discussions. Cocktail evenings and gourmet Campanian dinners, designed by Le Sirenuse owner Antonio Sersale, lift this literary retreat above the fray and ensure memories and friendships linger long afterwards.

ON YOUR DOORSTEP
Afternoons can be spent exploring Amalfi villages or day-tripping to Sorrento, Pompeii and Capri (which can be reached by hydrofoil from Sorrento). The hotel also runs trips, including visits to a local limoncello factory and boat trips to secluded swimming coves.

$ *Le Sirenuse Signature Massage €160*
🍽 *Michelin-starred Mediterranean fare*

☛ **Positano**
+39 089 875066
http://sirenland.net

JAPAN

HOSHINOYA

● *Try your hand at the ancient art of ikebana (flower arrangement)*
● *Early-morning temple meditation to a soundtrack of Buddhist monks chanting*

Temple-filled Arashiyama is one of Kyoto's most popular sightseeing areas and is located at the base of the mountains on the west side of the city. Tucked in among the cypress, maple and cherry-blossom trees is Hoshinoya – one of the city's best ryokan (traditional inn).

This elegant, modern take on a classic Japanese inn is perched on a hillside on the south bank of the Hozu-gawa, with views over the gushing water and mountain surrounds. It's hidden away from the tourist hordes in a secluded spot. To reach Hoshinoya a private wooden boat picks guests up from the dock in the centre of Arashiyama for the scenic 10-minute ride to the hotel.

Hoshinoya is made for checking out of everyday life for a while and experiencing Japanese culture – there are no TVs, rooms feature picture windows for taking in the view instead, and there are a number of cultural activities. The contemplative practice of *kado* – also known as *ikebana* – is the Japanese art of flower arrangement, and Hoshinoya offers lessons by a *kado* master. If you're looking for something more spiritual, join an early-morning Zen meditation practice at a nearby temple.

It's not just about nurturing your mind and creative side here; in-room massages will ensure your physical being is also looked after. Work out the kinks with a 'finger pressure' Shiatsu massage or a traditional Anma massage, which is a dry technique without any oils and given through clothing.

ON YOUR DOORSTEP
Stroll along a winding path through the Bamboo Grove, a forest of swaying thick-stalked bamboo with the light filtering through to produce an ethereal effect. Don't miss Tenryū-ji temple and its beautiful garden, and take in the mountain views at the exquisite Ōkōchi Sansō.

$ *Room per person including meals from ¥81,000*
🍽 *Seasonal kaiseki cuisine with a Western twist*

☞ *Arashiyama, Kyoto*
+81 758 71 0001
www.hoshinoya kyoto.jp

● **Personal Growth** ● **Culture**

MEXICO
AZULIK

● *Swim in cenotes, meet a shamen and dine on cuisine inspired by Mayan heritage*
● *Yoga, sound healing and a range of packages aimed at promoting positive energy*

Azulik is a collection of seemingly primitive wooden structures clinging to the sea shore that takes the idea of barefoot luxury to the extreme. Central to the retreat is a giant yoga dome built using ancient Mayan geometry; daily yoga is complemented by a range of different sessions, from sound healing and reflexology to a pipe ceremony. Mayan culture dominates and the retreat's spa and packages specialise in treatments based on ancestral rituals that date back thousands of years.

Nature is Azulik's other guiding principle; clothing is optional and retreat packages/ villas are designed to help guests connect with their senses, based around the four elements of fire (energy), air (spirit), earth (body) and water (emotions). Achieve full immersion in the retreat's Mayan roots by booking the traditional ceremony *zumpulche*.

ON YOUR DOORSTEP

Azulik is on Mexico's Maya Riviera – a coastline of white beaches lapped by the Caribbean Sea. Offshore there's a teeming reef for underwater explorers; on land are some of Mexico's most important Mayan temple ruins, Chichén Itzá and Tulum (left).

$ *Mayan* zumpulche *ceremony M$2400*
🍴 *Farm-to-table or Mayan–Mexican fine dining*

☞ *Tulum, Yucatán Peninsula*
+54 115 984 1575
www.azulik.com

SOUTH KOREA
Magok-sa Templestay

● *Temple life, including lantern making, hiking and a traditional tea ceremony*
● *Buddhist meditation, Korean language chants and Zen-inducing temple activities*

Find joy and inner quiet while learning about the rich cultural history of South Korea by staying overnight at this 7th-century Buddhist temple. Magok-sa provides a sublime retreat, tucked into the serene mountains of Chungcheongnam-do and full of graceful, curved eaves in ageing wooden halls. A stay here starts with learning the etiquette of temple life: greeting monks, nuns and other temple-stayers, and learning how to prostrate, or bow (*baekpalbae*). During evening ceremonies (*yebul*), you practise bowing and learn Korean-language chants for mindfulness. A customary monastic dinner of locally grown vegetables and rice is taken at long communal tables in the temple's canteen.

During the stay, you're given a comfy cotton uniform to wear; showers are communal and accommodation comprises are simple floor mats in shared rooms, all designed to enhance the feeling of removal from the outside world.

In the evening, a traditional tea ceremony (*da-seon*) encourages you to concentrate by engaging all five senses. Morning is signalled early by a sounding gong and day two brings activities for further mental quietude: a pre-dawn hike, early prostrations and seated meditation (*cham-seon*) next to a trickling stream. You finish your stay with a choice of cultural activities – lotus flower lantern-making, assembling strings of beads or wood-block printing. By the end, you should feel refreshed and removed from the strains of modern life and more at one with your inner self.

ON YOUR DOORSTEP
The nearby city of Gongju was the capital of the Baekje Kingdom in the 5th and 6th centuries and is home to the tomb of the kingdom's 25th king, Muryeong, along with a museum explaining the area's history.

$ *1-night, 2-day program* ₩*70,000*
🍽 *Korean vegetarian dishes made from locally grown ingredients*

....

☛ **Sagok-myeon, Gongju**
+82 10 9516 6226
www.magok.org

Da-seon (tea ceremony)

The traditional tea ceremony has been practised in Korea for a millennium, since Buddhist monks introduced tea plants to the peninsula. A tea ceremony involves elaborate vessel placement, pouring, cup holding, sniffing and tasting, which if practised correctly, are meant to evoke peacefulness, virtue, respectfulness and serenity. Korea uses matcha (powdered green tea), which is thought to be packed with nutrients and antioxidants that boost metabolism and calm the mind.

SPAIN

SANTHOSH RETREATS

● *Dance, yoga and pilates classes with leading tutors*
● *Guidance in wellness and life-coaching with founder Samiya Noordeen*

The brainchild of dance-loving London barrister, Samiya Noordeen, Santhosh Retreats offer an exuberant and uplifting path to personal growth and more polished dancing skills. The four-day retreats are held at Samiya's 800-year-old finca on the quiet northern coast of Ibiza, where expansive views of the sea and 33 fragrant acres (13 hectares) of pine forest provide an immediate antidote to most stress-filled modern lives.

Here, under the expert tutelage of a troupe of Latin American dancing stars, guests are encouraged to leave their inhibitions behind and throw themselves into energetic dance classes that occupy up to five hours every day. Aside from group dance classes, attendees build their own bespoke itineraries with add-on classes of yoga, Pilates, hiking and one-to-one life-coaching with Samiya herself.

Like everything else, meals are communal feasts of bright, fresh salads and healthy platters of grilled fish, marinated chicken and bowls of fresh green vegetables. Some of Ibiza's most celebrated chefs cook here, so food is a highlight and is supplemented by homemade energy bars, protein balls and fruit-infused water.

Evenings are elegant affairs with guests treated to impromptu after-dinner performances from tutors or simply swept up in the dancing fray. Beneath the stars, jiving around the casa's terrace with a sultry salsa wafting on the breeze, it's a revelation to discover a more carefree version of yourself – and one you'll want to hang on to when you get home.

ON YOUR DOORSTEP

Casa La Vista has direct access to the sea. There are plenty of seaside hikes from the house and it's a 0.6-mile (1km) walk to the sandy beach at Cala Xarraca. The nearest town is the small yacht resort of Portinax.

$ *4-night retreat, including daily dancing, yoga, accommodation and meals £1750*
|◎| *Super-fresh salads and fusion food*

☛ **Ibiza**
+44 (0)7557 529 500
www.santhosh retreats.com

UNITED KINGDOM

BRAMBLES ART RETREAT

● *Painting classes in inspirational locations*
● *A nurturing retreat where you can explore your creativity*

Originally held only in their 17th-century cottage near the picturesque moors of Dartmoor, Peter Davies and Janet Brady now lead art retreats to inspirational locations around the world, including Japan, Morocco, Tuscany and the Isle of Skye. Working in oil, watercolour, pencil and mixed media, the versatile duo tailor each retreat to suit guests' abilities and tastes. There's plenty of one-on-one tuition, encouragement and demonstrations, the aim being to grow participants' creative muscles.

Learning to really see things, compose a scene and mix the precise shade of Titian pink in a Venetian sunset has a therapeutic effect. Like any meditative practice, it requires you to slow right down, immerse yourself in the moment and see the world with fresh and attentive eyes. Coming away with much-improved skills is also a huge confidence boost.

ON YOUR DOORSTEP
Dartmoor National Park (above) is just 10 miles (16km) from the tiny Devon hamlet of Sprytown, the retreat's UK base. There's a rambling garden to explore and much of the course is spent out on location at highlight destinations such as the Lost Gardens of Heligan.

$ *5-day Devon retreat £785*
|●| *Tasty country cooking*

☛ *Devon*
+44 (0)1566 784359
http://bramblesart retreat.com

UNITED KINGDOM

TILTON HOUSE

● *Creative and reading retreats set in the South Downs National Park*
● *Choose from a program of activities inspired by the Bloomsbury Set*

'We're Tilton, not the Hilton,' quips host Shaun Treloar, emphasising the relaxed environment designed to allow guests the freedom to express themselves and not feel intimidated. It's clearly working. Such is the popularity of Tilton House that you need to book 18 months in advance for a retreat. Hardly surprising, given the cultural and creative pull here, yet, surprisingly, not many guests are aware of its connection to the Bloomsbury Set: a collection of English intellectuals and artists who found fame during the first half of the 20th century. Tilton House was the former country home of economist Maynard Keynes, a key member of the Bloomsbury Set, and he and his Russian wife Lydia Lopokova regularly hosted Picasso, Virginia Woolf and TS Eliot here, as well as partying with them at nearby Charleston Farmhouse.

Shaun's partner Polly Moore has taken the inspiration these creatives gathered from the environment to build restorative retreats and treatments, and in 2017 she launched the Department of Wellbeing, a business dedicated to the art of living well. At Tilton House, the palpable literary history and quirky bedroom design (travel back in time to your grandmother's house) will get any writer's creative muse flowing. Book ahead for the Bloomsbury Retreat for complete immersion in how the Bloomsbury Set lived: have a treatment in the hut inspired by Virginia Woolf's room, take guided walks across the Downs, read letters by the fire and enjoy food inspired by *The Bloomsbury Cookbook.*

ON YOUR DOORSTEP

The South Downs National Park is your stunning next-door neighbour: expand your mind with a meditative hike along the Seven Sisters chalk cliffs, thrill your senses with wild swimming at Birling Gap, or take in a first-class performance at nearby Glyndebourne, the country house famed for its opera festival.

$ *3-night Bloomsbury Retreat from £495 per person in twin room with shared bathroom*
🍽 *Mostly organic, seasonal, vegetarian, prepared by local chefs*

☞ *Firle, East Sussex*
+44 (0)1323 811570
www.tiltonhouse. co.uk

THE DEPARTMENT
of Wellbeing

"Our Department of Wellbeing is a movement passionate about exploring the big themes in life, by putting wellbeing at the centre of its core values. Through talks, events and retreats, it brings together thinkers, practitioners and technologies to start conversations about how we feel, why we make the choices we do and how we can experience, consume and create life, in a more connected way."
Polly Moore & Shaun Treloar, Founders, Tilton House

UNITED KINGDOM

THE HURST, THE JOHN OSBORNE ARVON CENTRE

● *Writing retreats in the former 19th-century home of playwright John Osborne*
● *Immersion in creative processes leading to the possibility of personal transformation*

If there's such a thing as an idyllic writers' retreat, then this is it: no wi-fi (goodbye procrastination), windows overlooking the enchanting forest-covered Shropshire Hills (stoke that muse), nothing but the sound of a bubbling stream or the wind rustling through giant redwood trees as a soundtrack to your imagination. Once you've clapped eyes on the fairy-tale facade of this 19th-century building, former home of playwright John Osborne, you'll recognise this as the haven from real life that you need to focus, become inspired, and channel your work into new directions perhaps, all with the guidance of expert tutors.

There are myriad retreats to choose from: writing with yoga; comic and graphic novel writing; screenwriting; young adult fiction; life writing; political non-fiction; and poetry, to name a few. The Hurst is the third of the Arvon locales (opened by Dame Maggie Smith in 2003)

—writing retreats are also held at Lumb Bank in West Yorkshire, former home of Ted Hughes; and Totleigh Barton, a 16th-century manor in Devon.

The Hurst has 16 bedrooms with en suite bathrooms, with wheelchair access to every room. Best of all, you don't have to be a published writer or intend to publish your work to benefit from the creative immersion; the five-day Starting to Write course is perfect for beginners, with support and encouragement from tutors and exploration of technique to help discover your unique voice.

ON YOUR DOORSTEP

You're in the Shropshire Hills, a designated Area of Natural Beauty and therefore a beacon for hikers. Stroll the heather and ancient woodlands of The Shropshire Way – a whopping 297 miles (478km) of day walks; look for the distinctive orange waymarks to follow this long-distance path.

$ *£800 for a single room with en suite for a 5-day course*
⦿l *Seasonal, local; breakfast and lunch provided, dinner cooked in teams*

....

☛ **Shropshire**
+44 (0)1588 640658
www.arvon.org/
centres/the-hurst

THE TRANSFORMATIVE POWER OF WRITING

"Arvon believes in the power of creative writing to transform people's lives. Retreats are led by acclaimed writers in historic houses, which are located in beautiful English landscapes. Anyone, regardless of writing experience, can step away from the demands of 21st-century life, immerse themselves in the creative process and release their imaginative potential. Retreats are inspiring, nurturing and restorative."
Natasha Carlish, Centre Director, The Hurst,
The John Osborne Arvon Centre

UNITED STATES
GHOST RANCH

● *Explore a new hobby or hone your skills in art, music, yoga and more*
● *Get to know Georgia O'Keeffe through the painter's beloved landscape*

Abiquiú is best known as the longtime home of painter Georgia O'Keeffe, and in addition to her house in the village, she owned a small cabin on the 21,000 acres (8500 hectares) of Ghost Ranch. From here she had a prime view of flat-topped Pedernal Peak – about which she once said, 'God told me if I painted it enough, I could have it.' Many ranch visitors today are following in O'Keeffe's footsteps, but the Presbyterian Church–owned retreat centre has an amazingly broad course catalogue, with a strong core of creative classes and yoga, as well as get-togethers for bluegrass musicians, eco-activists, spiritual seekers and even budding scientists (important dinosaur-bone discoveries have been made on the ranch land, and many of the findings are on display in the on-site paleontology museum).

Accommodation at Ghost Ranch ranges from campsites and bare-bones bunks and shared bathrooms – think grown-up summer camp – to more luxurious rooms with air-con and fluffy beds. Multiple workshops are often taking place at the same time, but everyone convenes in the large communal, cafeteria-style dining room, which leads to interesting discussions and cross-pollination of ideas. And if you're ever overwhelmed by the activity at the ranch's core, there is plenty of awesome – and truly inspiring – wilderness to explore on your

own. After, say, a six-day outdoor landscape painting course, you too can come away feeling like you own a bit of Pedernal Peak.

ON YOUR DOORSTEP
Georgia O'Keeffe's adobe house, a vision of Southwestern modernism, is just down the road (scheduled visits only), and the wide Chama River is a beautiful spot for an easy rafting trip. Santa Fe is about an hour's drive south.

$ *6-day painting workshop (price depends on lodging chosen) US$660–$1475*
|◉| *Familiar meat and potatoes, with some veg options*

☛ *Abiquiú,*
New Mexico
+1 505 685 1000
www.ghostranch.org

UNITED STATES
OMEGA INSTITUTE

● *Painting and other art classes, as well as creative and social workshops*
● *Leadership practice and networking, qigong, reiki and wellness treatments*

Founded in 1977, the Omega Institute for Holistic Studies was conceived as a university for lifelong learning, honouring the social movement towards unity, balance and wholeness. Since then, Omega has grown to include a Women's Leadership Conference, a Center for Sustainable Living and a wide variety of personal-growth retreats and conferences, taught by well-known people in the movement, such as Deepak Chopra, Marianne Williamson, Bobby McFerrin, Elizabeth Gilbert, Iyanla Vanzant and Paul Hawken. Workshops might include topics such as how to overcome your fear of public speaking, growing your own food, living sustainably, and awakening the creative in yourself.

You can also visit Omega simply for yoga, meditation, rest and relaxation. There are daily classes in yin yoga, reiki, qigong (a movement system based on energy) and stress reduction through mindfulness. It's easy enough to drop in on a day visit from NYC, but there's a huge variety of accommodation for those wishing to stay a while. The most popular option for visitors is the R&R Getaway, allowing you to design your own wellness escape while taking advantage of all that Omega offers.

When it's time to head outdoors, there are walking trails and kayaking on the lake, or if you still need more R&R, you can visit the Omega Wellness Center, which offers acupuncture, massage and other healing arts.

ON YOUR DOORSTEP
Omega is located in Rhinebeck – in the heart of the Hudson Valley – a rural, historic town featuring many restaurants, parks, a performing arts centre and the Old Rhinebeck Aerodrome museum of antique aircraft, which offers biplane rides as well as air shows on weekends.

$ *R&R Getaway from US$25 per day Mon–Fri, US$38 per day Sat & Sun. Open seasonally from May through October*
🍽 *Local, mostly organic, whole food meals*

☛ **Rhinebeck, New York**
+1 845 266 4444
www.eomega.org

INDEX

CREDITS

ACKNOWLEDGEMENTS

Published in November 2018
by Lonely Planet Global Limited
CRN 554153
www.lonelyplanet.com
ISBN 978 17870 1697 2
US-only ISBN 978 17886 8249 7
© Lonely Planet 2018
Printed in China
10 9 8 7 6 5 4 3 2 1

Managing Director, Publishing Piers Pickard
Associate Publisher Robin Barton
Commissioning Editors Dora Ball, Kate Morgan
Editing and Picture Research Kate Morgan
Assistant Editor Christina Webb
Proofing Lucy Doncaster
Art Direction Daniel Di Paolo
Design & Illustration Tina García
Layout Lauren Egan
Print Production Nigel Longuet
Thanks to Neill Coen, Flora Macqueen, Simon Hoskins, Yolanda Zappaterra

STAY IN TOUCH lonelyplanet.com/contact

Written by Kerry Christiani, Caro Cooper, Jayne D'Arcy, Megan Eaves, Sunny Fitzgerald, James Gabriel Martin, Bridget Gleeson, Paula Hardy, Trent Holden, Jessica Humphries, Fiona Killackey, Kate Morgan, Anja Mutic, Isabella Noble, Karyn Noble, Zora O'Neill, Lorna Parkes, Brandon Presser, Donna Raskin, Kevin Raub, Sarah Reid, Simon Richmond, Joshua Samuel Brown, Jo Stewart, Joni Sweet, Fiona Tapp, Diane Vadino, Tasmin Waby, Luke Waterson, Karla Zimmerman

AUSTRALIA
The Malt Store, Level 3, 551 Swanston St,
Carlton, Victoria 3053 T: 03 8379 8000

USA
124 Linden St, Oakland, CA 94607
T: 510 250 6400

IRELAND
Digital Depot, Roe Lane (off Thomas St), Digital Hub,
Dublin 8, D08 TCV4

UNITED KINGDOM
240 Blackfriars Rd, London SE1 8NW
T: 020 3771 5100

Paper in this book is certified against the Forest Stewardship Council™ standards. FSC™ promotes environmentally responsible, socially beneficial and economically viable management of the world's forests.